ARISTEAS TO PHILOCRATES

ARISTEAS to PHILOCRATES

(Letter of Aristeas)

Edited and Translated
by
MOSES HADAS

Wipf & Stock
PUBLISHERS
Eugene, Oregon

Wipf and Stock Publishers
199 W 8th Ave, Suite 3
Eugene, OR 97401

Aristeas to Philocrates
(Letter of Aristeas)
By Hadas, Moses
Copyright©1951 by Hadas, Moses
ISBN 13: 978-1-55635-506-6
ISBN 10: 1-55635-506-8
Publication date 5/30/2007
Previously published by Harper & Brothers, 1951

৵ CONTENTS ৶

Preface	vii
Introduction	1
I. Summary of Contents	1
II. Purported authorship and date	3
III. Objections to purported authorship and date	5
IV. Internal evidence for dating	9
1. The political situation	9
2. The coastal cities	10
3. Idumaea	10
4. The High Priest "adjudged"	10
5. Commoners as kings	11
6. "Hasmonaean" names	11
7. Pharos uninhabited?	11
8. The citadel	12
9. The Temple	13
10. The curtain	14
11. The informers	15
12. Allegorical interpretation of Scripture	15
13. Linguistic usage	17
V. External evidence	18
1. Josephus	18
2. Philo	21
3. Aristobulus	26
4. The Prologue of Ben Sirah	27
5. The decree of Philadelphus: *P. Rainer 24,552*	28
6. III Maccabees	32

CONTENTS

7. Ezra-Nehemiah	38
8. Aristeas on kingship and the Pali *Milindapanha*	40
9. Hecataeus (in Diodorus Siculus) on the ideals of Egyptian kings	43
10. The Zenon papyri	45
11. The *ekphrasis* and Callixinus of Rhodes	47
12. The Utopian element	48
13. The High Priest's discourse and Cynic homilies	50
14. Aristeas and the romancers	51
15. Aristeas and Alexandrian scholarship	52
16. Rabbinic and Patristic writers on Aristeas	53
VI. 130 BCE as a hypothetical date	54
VII. Aristeas as a Greek book	54
VIII. Aristeas on Judaism and the Jews	59
IX. Aristeas on the Septuagint	66
X. The Septuagint legend after Aristeas	73
XI. Modern study of Aristeas: Bibliography	84
XII. Text	90
Text, Translation, Commentary and Critical Notes	91
Index	229

PREFACE

For generous permission to reproduce H. St. J. Thackeray's Greek text of *Aristeas* from H. B. Swete's *Introduction to the Old Testament in Greek* (Cambridge, 1905) grateful acknowledgement is made to the Cambridge University Press. The manuscript of the present work has been read by Professor Solomon Zeitlin, the Editor in Chief of the series (who has appended the notes signed S. Z.), by President Abraham A. Neuman, and by Dr. Joshua Bloch, Professor Robert Gordis, and Professor Ralph Marcus, of the Editorial Board. To these gentlemen, and to Professor V. Tcherikover of the Hebrew University in Jerusalem, who generously supplied a draft of his learned paper on Aristeas, the undersigned expresses his thanks.

Moses Hadas

Columbia University

ARISTEAS TO PHILOCRATES

INTRODUCTION

Taken at its face value the document bearing the heading "Aristeas to Philocrates" (the word "Letter" now commonly used in the title is a modern addition) is an account, with more or less relevant digressions, of the translation of the Hebrew Pentateuch into Greek under the sponsorship of Ptolemy II Philadelphus (reigned 285–247 BCE), written by a contemporary pagan Greek who was himself an official in Ptolemy's court. Before attempting to determine the veracity of these implied claims and the credibility of the account as a whole it will be convenient to survey the contents of the book briefly.

I

SUMMARY OF CONTENTS

An introductory address to his brother Philocrates, who is praised for his love of learning, sets forth the writer's intention to present the story of his embassy to the High Priest Eleazar as a contribution to scholarship and religion (1–8). When the translation of the Hebrew Law was proposed by the king's librarian, Demetrius of Phalerum (9–11), the author seized the opportunity to broach a related matter, to wit the emancipation of the Jews who had been brought into Egypt as slaves by the king's father, as also of the Jews in Egypt who had been enslaved previously (12–16). Moved by divine compulsion, the king issues a decree of total emancipation, providing for compensation to the holders of Jewish slaves (17–27). This business dispatched, the author presents copies of Demetrius' memorandum concerning the translation (28–33), of Ptolemy's letter requesting Eleazar to send him seventy-two competent translators (34–40), and of Eleazar's reply, with the names of the translators subjoined (41–50). The king's offerings to the Temple—a golden table, large mixing bowls of gold and of silver, golden flagons—are described in detail (51–82). Next follows a description of Jerusalem as the emissaries found it, with more or less full treatment of the Temple's doorway, curtain, and altar (83–87), its water supply (88–91), the sacrificial ministrations of the priests (92–95), the High Priest's vestments (96–99), the citadel and its guards (100–104), the city and its streets (105–106) with a comparison of large and small cities (107–111), the produce of the country, its harbors, rivers, and mountains (112–118), and the mines of Arabia (119–120). The character and attainments of the translators are praised and Eleazar's reluctance to part with them described (121–127). Eleazar delivers a defense of the Law, emphasizing God's uniqueness as Creator and Ruler and the vanity of pagan beliefs, and deriving theological principles by allegorical interpretation of commandments concerning forbidden foods (128–171). Upon their arrival in Alexandria the translators are immediately received by the king with high honor (172–181). At a series of seven royal banquets, at which his visitors' dietary usages are strictly observed, the king puts philosophic questions to his visitors, and is delighted by their responses (182–300). Then the translators are taken to the island of Pharos in the harbor of Alexandria for their labors. At the end of each day they compare the versions they had severally made, and the consensus is written down by Demetrius. The entire work occupies seventy-two days (301–307). The translation is read to the Jewish people, who applaud it and ordain that no alterations should be made in it (308–311). The work is then read to the king, who is so impressed that he wonders at the book's not having been mentioned in earlier Greek literature. Demetrius replies that earlier authors had been divinely deterred from making mention of it (312–316). The king orders the book to be carefully preserved, and sends the translators home with rich gifts (313–320). The writer closes with renewed compliments to Philocrates (321–322).

II

Purported Authorship and Date

From this summary we observe that our book touches upon a variety of topics—an important stretch of Egyptian-Jewish history, details of the structure and ritual of the Temple at Jerusalem, an appreciation of craftsmanship in gold and silver under Ptolemy Philadelphus, a justification of the Jewish Law from the lips of the High Priest, "philosophic" responses of Jewish sages to a series of secular questions, and, most important, an account of the origin of the Septuagint. All of this matter is of high interest and much of it is known from no other source, but to evaluate its reliability we must determine, as closely as we may, whether the author is as competent as he claims to deal with these subjects, whether or not he intended his work to be read as sober history, and what his broader purpose may have been.

Except in the superscription, which as we shall see is not trustworthy, our document nowhere states explicitly that its author is Aristeas, but such an inference is clearly intended. The "I" who petitions the king for the emancipation is demonstrably Aristeas, for at 19 the king says, "It is but a small matter indeed that Aristeas asks of us." The description of the Temple is given in the first person, and from 43 we know that Aristeas was one of the king's two emissaries. Hence the writer who declares (1) that he will give account of "our deputation" is clearly Aristeas. Nor did the ancients who knew the document ascribe it to another hand; the "Aristaeus" whom Josephus mentions in connection with his paraphrase of it (*Antiquities* 12.99) is clearly merely a variant spelling, for which, in Josephus' day at least, the pronunciation would be identical, though the variant might possibly be due to an unknown link in the chain of transmission.

The document implies that Aristeas was an influential courtier of Ptolemy Philadelphus (40, 43) whom he served on diplomatic missions, especially in connection with spiritual matters, and that he was on terms of friendship with other courtiers (1, 12, 15, 16, 40), though he never explicitly declares that he is a pagan, as he is made to do in Josephus (*Ant.* 12.23), and he writes Philocrates that he obtained his information concerning Judaism from Egyptian priests (6). The Jews are always "they," and even in the description of the Temple, enthusiastic as it is, an effort is made to preserve the tone of the outsider. His concern for the liberation of the Jewish slaves appears to be motivated by purely humanitarian considerations, though his prayer (which, significantly, Josephus omits) that the king's heart be moved would suggest a more intimate concern. His interest in Temple and Law, similarly, is represented as mainly scholarly, aesthetic, or ethical, but still objective. His own name and his brother's are Greek, and not of the theophoric sort which many Hellenized Jews adopted. His scholarly objectivity is further emphasized by his predilection for writing down his observations—at 322 he promises Philocrates additional material—and the literary form of his writing is itself calculated to imply that the author is an interested spectator rather than a pleader *pro domo sua*. The character our author assumes he maintains, on the whole, consistently. At a superficial glance the account is such as might well have been written by its purported author and at the date implied.

If, as we shall presently see, the author is not what he purports to be, the choice of his pseudonym is of some interest. In the late second or first century BCE an Aristeas wrote a book *Concerning the Jews*, of which a fragment is preserved in Eusebius (*Praeparatio Evangelica* 9.25), and it may be that our author assumed this name, intending the remark about the earlier writing he had sent to Philocrates (6) to allude to the genuine Aristeas' book. The style of the fragment in Eusebius is flat, however, and follows Scripture closely, and hence is in every respect different from our Aristeas.

As for the date of composition, the document clearly implies that it was written shortly after the translation of the Pentateuch was made, and that the personages mentioned, King

INTRODUCTION 5

Ptolemy Philadelphus, Demetrius of Phalerum, the High Priest Eleazar, were still alive. From the praise bestowed upon the king's righteous rule by the visiting elders (279 ff.) it would appear that enough time had elapsed from his accession (285 BCE) for him to have acquired a reputation. Arsinoe II, who is mentioned as his wife (41), became queen not later than 273 and perhaps as early as 277. Except, then, for apparent errors and anachronisms, whose natural explanation is remoteness from the event, we might deduce that the book was written about 270 BCE.

III

OBJECTIONS TO PURPORTED AUTHORSHIP AND DATE

But the author of this story cannot have been the man he represents himself[1] to be, and if his personality, however plausibly and consistently represented, is fictitious, the same would apply to the presumed date. His knowledge of and devotion to the traditions of Judaism are incredible in a pagan. He is especially concerned for the study of Judaism and its promulgation (3, 5); his interest in the furniture, construction, and ritual of the Temple (51 ff.) goes far beyond the limits of scholarly or aesthetic curiosity; the High Priest is for him the supreme authority (3, 86 ff., 130 ff.); and he is filled with admiration for the High Priest's allegorical interpretation of Scripture and for the translators' responses to the king's queries. The religious doctrines and usages of Judaism occupy not only a central but an exclusive position in his regard. He avoids uttering the name of God, and even the epithet "Lord" which was commonly used in Alexandrian Jewish writings, and employs a

[1] All later scholars have accepted, and in some cases supplemented, the irrefutable demonstration of Humphrey Hody, *Contra historiam LXX interpretum Aristeae nomine inscriptam* in *De bibliorum textibus originalibus* (Oxford, 1705). The famous Bentley called Aristeas "a clumsie Cheat" (*Letters of Phalaris*, ed. Bohn, p. 79.).

circumlocution to designate the name of God inscribed on the High Priest's diadem (98), instead of citing the words of Scripture as he otherwise does in the description of the High Priest's vestments. He does not hesitate to represent Eleazar as speaking scornfully of idolatry and of the reputedly wise Greek sages (137). He shows his impatience of Greek and Egyptian polytheism, and speaks slightingly of the books of the romancers (322). The conclusion is inescapable that our author is a Jew, albeit thoroughly Hellenized in all but religion. His thorough Hellenization combined with his concern to justify Judaism to both the Jews themselves and their pagan environment would place him in the company of the Alexandrian Jewish writers. Only an Alexandrian, indeed, could have such accurate knowledge of the usages of the Ptolemaic court and chancellery. Even if the descriptions of Jerusalem and the Temple, particularly such a detail as the fluttering of the curtain in the Temple, bear the authority of an eyewitness account, as some scholars maintain,[2] it is perfectly credible that a Jew so loyal should have gone on a pilgrimage to Jerusalem, as we know that the author of II Maccabees, for example, did. But, as we shall see (14), our author may well have been following earlier writers in these details. In any case it is virtually impossible that our book can have been written by the man who is purported to have written it.

Arguments against its having been written at its purported date are even more cogent, for twice the author betrays the hand of the conscious archaizer, and at least thrice he is guilty of historical anachronisms. One indubitable case of archaizing, charming in its naiveté, occurs at 28: "these kings used to administer all their business through decrees and with great precaution; nothing was done negligently or casually." Not only is the past tense incongruous in the context, but Philadelphus had actually had only one predecessor, Ptolemy Soter; the tone, furthermore, is that of a wistful *laudator temporis acti*. The de-

---

[2] *E.g.*, Père Vincent, "Jérusalem d'après la Lettre d'Aristée," *Revue Biblique Internationale* N.S. 5 (1908), 520 ff.

scription of the arrangements for the entertainment of the elders at 182 similarly implies a plurality of kings and employs a past tense—with the revealing note, "and it may still be seen to this day."

There is a manifest inaccuracy, inconceivable in a courtier of Ptolemy Philadelphus, in regard to the position of Demetrius of Phalerum. It was Ptolemy I Soter who was Demetrius' patron when he was driven from Athens in 307 by Demetrius Poliorcetes. In the question of Soter's succession Demetrius supported Soter's eldest son, Ptolemy Ceraunus, but Soter himself designated Ptolemy Philadelphus as his successor, and immediately upon his accession Ptolemy Philadelphus banished Demetrius, who died in exile.[3] With regard to Demetrius of Phalerum our author has confused the roles of the first and second Ptolemies. Nor was Demetrius ever chief of the Alexandrian library, though it is not unlikely (since he was himself a Peripatetic scholar and writer) that Demetrius supported the plans for the library and may even have suggested the translation of the Jewish books. At least he is a plausible figure for the role, and we shall presently see another reason (51) why Demetrius may have been associated with this particular enterprise.

A similar confusion is involved in introducing the philosopher Menedemus of Eretria to Philadelphus' court (201). Menedemus died about 287, though he had been at the court of Ptolemy Soter as ambassador from Eretria.[4] Again, on welcoming the elders Ptolemy remarks that the day is the anniversary of his naval victory over Antigonus (180). The allusion must be either to the sea battle at Cos about 260 BCE, where the Egyptians suffered a resounding defeat, or to a later battle at Andros, of which neither the issue nor the protagonists are known, though they were a Ptolemy and an Antigonus.[5] In either case (unless

[3] Pauly-Wissowa *s.v.* Demetrius 85, 4 (1901), 2822; the entire article (2817-2841) is extremely useful.

[4] See W. W. Tarn, *Antigonus Gonatas* (Oxford, 1913), 22 f., and *cf.* commentary on 201 below.

[5] E. Bevan, *History of Egypt under the Ptolemaic Dynasty* (London, 1927), 68, and *cf.* Marcus' note on *Ant.* 12.93.

there is an error in our manuscript tradition),[6] not only is there anachronism, for Demetrius was long dead, but the interval after the battle must have been sufficiently long to make the confusion on the part of a reasonably careful writer possible. Demetrius' reported allusions to Theopompus (378–300 BCE; paragraph 314) and to Theodectes (375–334 BCE; paragraph 316) also seem strained from the viewpoint of chronology, though for the mention of these names also we shall presently notice a reason (60). At 296 ff. the author himself protests that incredible as his account may seem it is supported by records and public archives and wholly accurate; it may strike the unprejudiced reader that he protests too much.

There are unmistakable indications, moreover, that the Greek translation of the Torah had long been in existence when Aristeas was written, though the description of the process of translation at 302 ff. and the solemn ratification of the version by the leaders of the Jewish community suggests that the translation was newly made. Not only are the actual words of the LXX used in the description of the table and of the high priestly vestments, but the king himself orders that the prescriptions of Scripture be followed in the construction of the table. The author not only knows the phraseology of the LXX but apparently expects his readers to recognize it. When the memorandum of Demetrius of Phalerum speaks of the faultiness of the existing texts, his expressions seem much more appropriate to the text of a translation than of the original. These details and their implications for the history of the LXX will be enlarged upon below (70). From the point of view of dating Aristeas what emerges is that a considerable interval must have elapsed between the translation of the Greek Bible and the composition of Aristeas. If the implication that the composition is contem-

---

[6] E. Bickermann, "Zur Datierung des Pseudo-Aristeas," *Zeitschrift für die neutestamentliche Wissenschaft* 29 (1930), 280–296, suggests that *Antigonus* supplanted an original *Aristobulus*.

INTRODUCTION 9

porary with the translation of the Bible is false, then the purported authorship of Aristeas must be a fiction.

If the purported authorship is a fiction we are left with the possible range of three centuries, between the *termini* afforded by Ptolemy Philadelphus, who is a central figure in the book, and Josephus, who gives a close paraphrase of it at the beginning of the twelfth book of his *Antiquities*. A proper evaluation of the book would require that we reduce these limits as narrowly as possible. Our means for doing this are an examination of the testimony supplied by other writers of antiquity and a scrutiny of the book itself for evidence to point to a specific conjuncture of time. We shall look first at indications of date which have been discovered in the book itself.

IV

INTERNAL EVIDENCE FOR DATING

1. THE POLITICAL SITUATION

Throughout the book the political situation envisaged is one in which Egypt is a sovereign kingdom under the rule of the Ptolemies, with Judaea enjoying autonomy under the rule of its High Priest. Not only is there no hint of Rome (which destroyed Egyptian sovereignty in 30 BCE) but there is none of the Seleucids, who conquered Judaea in 198 BCE. If we accept the literal implications of the political situation we should have to date the book before 198 BCE, and many competent scholars have so dated it.[7] Those who discount this evidence suggest (1) that the telltale "these kings used to" at 28 implies not only a remoter period of the same dynasty but actually the end of the dynasty; and (2) that Palestine enjoyed autonomy under

[7] *E.g.*, Schürer, Tramontano, Cahana; see 87 below for bibliographical listing of their works.

Herod also, and after Herod's death the High Priests regained much of the power they had lost (*Ant.* 20.10, *Against Apion* 2.23).

2. THE COASTAL CITIES

At 115 Ascalon, Joppa, Gaza, and Ptolemais are listed as coastal cities which were available to the Jews. Of these Ascalon and Ptolemais were never conquered by the Jews, Joppa was taken by Simon in 142 and Gaza by Alexander Jannaeus in 96—which would then supply an upper limit for dating.[8] To this it has been objected[9] that Aristeas does not state that the Jews *possessed* these cities but only that they used them, which they were free to do under the Romans. As for Gaza, Alexander Jannaeus not only took it but destroyed it, and it was rebuilt only under Pompey.

3. IDUMAEA

In 107 Idumaea is spoken of as being adjacent to (but not included in) Israelite territory. Idumaea was annexed to the Hasmonaean realm in 127, and hence it has been argued that the date of Aristeas must be antecedent to 127.[10] But it seems more likely, as we shall see, that the description of Palestine is in fact a farrago of Bible and ideal state, and Idumaea here stands for Old Testament Edom.

4. THE HIGH PRIEST "ADJUDGED"

The expression "adjudged" applied to the High Priest at 98, it has been argued, implies election, which would fit the Herodian and Roman periods better than the Hasmonaean, when the high priesthood was hereditary.[11] But this argument seems to press the word "adjudged" unjustifiably.

---

[8] W., xxv.
[9] Willrich, *Urkundenfälschungen* 88.
[10] Bickermann, *Zur Datierung* 285.
[11] Willrich, *Urkundenfälschungen* 89.

INTRODUCTION 11

5. COMMONERS AS KINGS

An allusion to Herod has been seen also in the emphasis on the cruelty of commoners who ascend the throne (288);[12] but the idea is a commonplace with a long history, and cannot be pressed. The statement has also been taken to refer to Ptolemy Auletes (81–52 BCE), who was not a legitimate successor of the Lagids.[13]

6. "HASMONAEAN" NAMES

From the relatively frequent occurrence of names borne by the Hasmonaeans (Judah, Simon, Jonathan) in the list of translators (47 ff.), it has been argued[14] that the book was composed at a period when the Hasmonaean heroes had become legendary and their names common, in legend as in fact. But the names are Biblical and must have been in common use both before and after the Hasmonaean era, so that no argument for either early or late dating can be based on their use.

7. PHAROS UNINHABITED?

The island of Pharos, where the translation was said to have been made (301 ff.), was not inhabited after 47 BCE, the date of Julius Caesar's Alexandrine War, and this has been taken to point to a date anterior to 47.[15] But the argument is two-edged, for the very solitude might have made it a desirable locale for the task. Philo, indeed, speaks (*On Moses* 2.36) of its being "the most suitable place in the district, where they might find peace and tranquillity and the soul could commune with the laws with none to disturb its privacy," whereas the city "within the walls was full of every kind of living creatures, and consequently the prevalence of diseases and deaths and the impure conduct of the healthy inhabitants made them suspicious of it" (*ibid.* 34).

---

[12] Février, 23 (see note 30).
[13] P. Riessler, *Altjüdische Schrifttum ausserhalb der Bibel* (1928), 1277, would date Aristeas to Auletes' reign on the strength of this identification.
[14] W., xxvii.
[15] W., on the basis of Strabo 17.6.

8. THE CITADEL

A central point for dating, if it could be established beyond doubt, is the identity of the citadel described at 100-104. The question at issue is whether (a) the pre-Hasmonaean citadel built north of the Temple (Neh. 2.8) and pulled down under the Seleucids in 168 BCE (I Mac. 1.33; Josephus, *Ant.* 12.252) is meant, or whether it is (b) the citadel built by the Hasmonaeans (*Ant.* 15.403) and again by Herod, who named it Antonia (*Ant.* 18.91, *Jewish War* 5.238 ff.).

Josephus' description of the Antonia (*Jewish War* 5.238-245) is relevant, both for its agreements and its divergencies:[16]

The tower of Antonia lay at the angle where two porticoes, the western and the northern, of the first court of the temple met; it was built upon a rock 50 cubits high and on all sides precipitous. It was the work of King Herod and a crowning exhibition of the innate grandeur of his genius. For, to begin with, the rock was covered from its base upwards with smooth flagstones, both for ornament and in order that anyone attempting to ascend or descend it might slip off. Next, in front of the actual edifice, there was a wall three cubits high; and behind this the tower of Antonia rose majestic to an altitude of 40 cubits. The interior resembled a palace in its spaciousness and appointments, being divided into apartments of every description and for every purpose, including cloisters, baths and broad courtyards for the accommodation of troops; so that from its possession of all conveniences it seemed a town, from its magnificence a palace. The general appearance of the whole was that of a tower with other towers at each of the four corners; three of these turrets were 50 cubits high, while that at the south-east angle rose to 70 cubits, and so commanded a view of the whole area of the temple. At the point where it impinged upon the porticoes of the temple, there were stairs leading down to both of them, by which the guards descended; for a Roman cohort was permanently

[16] Translation of H. St. J. Thackeray in Loeb Classical Library.

quartered there, and at the festivals took up positions in arms around the porticoes to watch the people and repress any insurrectionary movement.

The earlier citadel certainly commanded the Temple and adjoined it, and there can be no question that it is to a citadel adjoining the Temple and commanding a near view of it (the ritual could be observed from the citadel: 103) that Aristeas refers. Some have thought that the Maccabean and succeeding citadels were built on the site of the ancient structure, so that no conclusions concerning the date could be deduced from the site, but the best modern opinion is that the Seleucid citadel was located on the southern spur of the eastern hill, and Herod's Antonia was an enlargement of the same structure.[17] So far, then, on the basis of the citadel's being built to adjoin the Temple, a pre-Maccabean date would be indicated for Aristeas. But objections may be raised. Aristeas' citadel had towers (100); so did the Antonia (*Jewish War* 5.242). It was built of huge blocks; the Antonia was so strongly built that the Roman rams had difficulty in piercing it (*Jewish War* 6.26), and was probably of the same material as Herod's Temple, which was built of large blocks (*Jewish War* 5.241). Its object of guarding against sudden revolution (101) is said by Josephus (5.244, where the same word is employed) to have been the object of the Antonia. Its complement of 500 men (104) corresponds to the single cohort of the Roman garrison (*Jewish War* 5.244). And finally, Josephus (5.242) insists that a tower of the Antonia afforded a view of all the Temple.

9. THE TEMPLE

What is said of the Temple itself would seem more appropriate to Herod's Temple than to its predecessor.[18] "No expense was spared" (85) recalls the lavish expenditure on Herod's

[17] Schürer, 1.198 n. 37; Vincent in *Revue Biblique* 42 (1933), 83–113; Tramontano, 86 ff.; Marcus on *Ant.* 12.252.
[18] Février, 18 f.

14   ARISTEAS TO PHILOCRATES

Temple (*Ant.* 11.15.3). It had a lofty situation, like Herod's (*Ant.* 15.11.3), which, according to tradition, the older Temple did not have. The reference to the doorway (85) is strikingly like Josephus' (*Ant.* 15.11.3; *cf. Jewish War* 5.210) to the entry to Herod's Temple. Tacitus (*History* 5.12) admires the magnificence of the structure, and it is altogether likely that a Jew of Egypt who saw it shortly after its completion would be greatly impressed by it. But one fresh from the magnificent buildings of Philadelphus in Alexandria could hardly be so impressed by a humble structure already centuries old. The balance of evidence, from the point of view of topographical allusions, would seem to indicate (but not to the point of demonstration) a background of the period of Herod. But no argument based on topography can be conclusive, and it would seem most reasonable, as it is certainly easiest, to suppose that the author is constructing an imaginary picture based upon various and perhaps discrepant sources.

10. THE CURTAIN

An ingenious argument has been drawn from the use of the word *katapetasma* at 86 for the Temple curtain.[19] The regular classical word for a curtain is *parapetasma*, which indicates (as was in fact the case in pagan temples) that the curtains were drawn upward from below, or perhaps inward from the side; the *katapetasma* was different in that it was drawn downward from above. When Pausanias (5.12.4) speaks of the curtain "with Assyrian weaving and Phoenician purple" which Antiochus presented to the temple of Zeus at Olympia, he remarks on its peculiarity in being let down to the ground by cords instead of drawn upward to the roof. It has been plausibly conjectured that this was the very curtain which Antiochus plundered from Jerusalem in 170.[20] Aristeas' description of the curtain in par-

---

[19] Clermont-Ganneau as cited in Tramontano, 86.
[20] I Mac. 1.22.

ticular seems that of an eyewitness, and in any case he would surely have known it if the curtain had been carried away. This circumstance has been taken to indicate a date anterior to 170. But though *katapetasma* does not occur in secular literature (except in a fourth-century BCE inscription, for a table cover) until Heliodorus and sixth-century papyri, it is the regular LXX and New Testament word for the Temple curtain, and hence the normal word for Aristeas to have used, whatever his date.

11. THE INFORMERS

Those who are inclined to late dating attach capital importance to the reference to harsh measures taken against informers by the king (167). They see here an allusion to Roman *delatores*, who were put to death by Tiberius in 33 CE (Tacitus, *Annals* 6.19)[21]. But the Greek word (*emphanistae*) occurs in the Ptolemaic period, and the context does not make the statement so remarkable as to require a far-fetched explanation.

12. ALLEGORICAL INTERPRETATION OF SCRIPTURE

A weightier argument for dating, since the author would probably be unconscious of the anachronism, would be a reflection of certain religious attitudes characteristic of a later rather than of an earlier period. The doctrine of the divine origin of the Law, the abhorrence of pagan abuses on the one hand and the effort at philosophic conciliation on the other, might be illustrated from any date between Ptolemy Philadelphus and Josephus, who are the widest possible limits for dating. The one factor which may be significant is a tendency to allegorical interpretation of the prescriptions of the Law, especially in the High Priest's discourse (128 ff.) and the explanation of the washing of hands (306–7), which is without close parallel in Hellenistic literature before Philo. These passages are omit-

---

[21] H. Graetz, "Die Abfassungszeit des Pseudo-Aristeas," *Monatsschrift für Gesch. u. Wissenschaft des Judentums* (1876), 289–308, 337–349.

ted in Josephus' paraphrase without explanation, and some scholars have found them so incongruous with the work as a whole as to assign them to a post-Philonic interpolator.[22] But here again the fact that Philo is our earliest representative of a manner of interpretation need by no means imply that it was not practised before Philo. Scholars like Professor Wolfson, who attribute the highest measure of originality to Philo, are not for that reason inclined to date Aristeas below Philo.[23]

In the view here taken, that Aristeas' affinities in modes of thought as well as in literary expression are rather with Greek than with Jewish antecedents, Aristeas' priority to Philo in allegory is not only intelligible but to be expected. As Ginzberg has pointed out,[24] Palestinian and Alexandrian allegorical interpretation are disparate things. In the Palestinian method a verse of Scripture was cited, and then allegorically applied to persons or events in Jewish history. The Alexandrians carried their allegory into a generalized philosophical truth. The dependence of the Alexandrians on Palestine, so far as allegory is

[22] Février regards the use of a technique so like Philo's as proof that 128–171 is from the hand of an interpolator. He notes specific similarities (63 ff.) as follows: (a) For each writer the cloven hoof symbolizes discernment and chewing the cud memory; in both the Mosaic regulation is interpreted as showing the intimate connection between discernment and memory (Aristeas 150 ff.; Philo, *Special Laws* 4.106 ff.). (b) Both oppose the view that happiness is centered in material good (141; *Quod. det. pot.* 4–7). (c) In *De fuga et inv.* 95 Philo speaking of God's creative, governmental, and other powers (*dunameis*) mentions as the fourth "His legislative power by which He forbids (*apagoreuei*) what may not be done." In *Joseph* 29 he makes the distinction between prohibition and positive injunction clearer: "And the word of nature enjoins what one ought to do and forbids (*apagoreutikōs*) what one ought not to do." The same contrast is stated in Aristeas 131: "And he expounded them point by point, not only by prohibitions (*apagoreutikōs*) but by commandments." (d) The use of *dunameōs* in 143 is Philonic. (e) In 129 the existence of matter before creation is implied, as in Philo's *On the Creation*. For this reason Février thinks *oikonomoumena* is used at 143, because it implies organization rather than *creatio ex nihilo*. Février agrees that certain differences preclude borrowing one from the other, but thinks that the author of the "interpolation" was a contemporary or pupil of Philo.

[23] H. A. Wolfson, *Philo* (Harvard, 1947), Index *s.v.* Aristeas.

[24] L. Ginzberg, *Jewish Encyclopedia* 1.403 ff.

concerned, is doutbful; their dependence on Greek antecedents is clear and unmistakable. As early as the sixth century BCE, Theagenes of Rhegium applied the allegorical method to Homer, and as moral sensibilities outstripped Homeric mores the method came to be more and more applied. The exploits of Homeric heroes came to be regarded as allegorical interpretations of natural forces or of moral and mental qualities. In the Hellenistic age and among the Stoics in particular the method became a regular procedure and was widely practised. In view of the Greek character of our book and its author's reliance on Hellenistic modes of thought (see section 8 below), it would be odd if he did *not* use allegory on traditions whose literal meanings seemed outmoded or impolitic. He uses the method sparingly, after all, only in respect to dietary regulations. Philo derived from the same Greek sources from which Aristeas had derived, and he may retain the distinction of having developed it to such great scope and with such system without claiming credit for its invention.

13. LINGUISTIC USAGE

There remains the evidence of linguistic usage, where even a conscious archaizer must inadvertently reveal himself. Such inadvertencies are most apt to betray themselves in salutations and closing formulae of letters, and changes in Ptolemaic usage in this respect enable us to date letters within fairly narrow limits. On this basis Professor Bickermann, who is expert in such matters, has established 145 BCE as the upper limit for Aristeas, though he would put its date some half-century later.[25] Careful study of other linguistic criteria has been interpreted as confirming 100 BCE as the probable date of composition for Aristeas,[26] and in view of the equivocal nature of our other

[25] "Zur Datierung des Pseudo-Aristeas," *Zeitschrift für die neutestamentliche Wissenschaft* 29 (1930), 280–296.

[26] This is the conclusion of a detailed study, based on careful study of literary and papyrological materials, by H. G. Meecham: *The Letter of Aristeas* (Manchester, 1935), 311 f.

evidence that date has been provisionally accepted by many recent scholars.[27] In the opinion of the present writer the actual date must be pushed back towards the upper limit suggested by Bickermann,[28] and hence it must be noticed here that nothing in the linguistic evidence compels a dating below the middle of the second century BCE.

V

EXTERNAL EVIDENCE

But some rays of light are thrown upon our problem by ancient literary records other than Aristeas, and we now proceed to examine the evidence of other ancient literature, religious and secular.

1. JOSEPHUS

The earliest author who unquestionably had before him a text of Aristeas largely identical with our own is Josephus, who, in *Ant.* 12.12–118, presents a paraphrase which follows the text of Aristeas, where it does follow it, sentence by sentence. The sentences, it is true, are recast, in keeping with a different style, but the actual words of Aristeas are used to the extent that Josephus is an important help for establishing the text of Aristeas.[29] Josephus follows Aristeas at 9–46, 51–81, 172–187, 292–305, 308–321. His larger omissions are (a) 1–8, introduction; (b) 47–50, list of translators; (c) 82–171, journey to Jerusalem, Eleazar's farewell to the translators, and his defense of the Law; (d) 188–291, the table talk of the translators; (e) 306–7 on ritual washing of hands before praying; (f) 322, conclusion. The omission of *a* and *f* is quite natural. For *b* Josephus specifically says (12.57): "I have not thought it necessary

[27] *E.g.*, W. W. Tarn and Paul Kahle (see 41 and 69 below).
[28] See section 6 below, where 130 BCE is proposed.
[29] The usefulness of Josephus in this respect is discussed in Thackeray's introduction to his text in Swete.

INTRODUCTION 19

to report the names of the seventy elders who were sent by Eleazar and brought the Law, their names being set down at the end of the letter." For *d* again he refers the reader to the original text (100): "so that anyone who wishes to find out the details of the questions discussed at the banquet can learn them by reading the book which Aristaeus composed on this account." The fact that Josephus is scrupulous in indicating these two major omissions makes the long omission of *c* on the journey to Jerusalem and the discourse of Eleazar (and incidentally *e*) more remarkable; Aristeas' transition from 82 to 83, furthermore, is quite awkward. Instead of *c* Josephus joins the material of 82 with that of 172 with the statement (12.85): "These then were the dedicatory offerings sent to Jerusalem by Ptolemy. Now Eleazar, the High Priest, after dedicating them to God and honoring the bearers, gave them gifts to take to the king and sent them back to the king." Since this sentence is not in his original and since he elsewhere makes explicit admission of his omissions, we might deduce either that the material in 83–171 was not in Josephus' text of Aristeas, or that he deliberately omitted it and supplied his own transitional sentence.

The view that this material was not in Josephus' text has been maintained by a number of scholars[30] on the ground that it does not harmonize with the remainder of the book. The description of Jerusalem and the Temple in 83–120 sounds like a report of pious pilgrims, not of ambassadors of a powerful king bringing priceless gifts and the news of the emancipation of the Jews in Egypt; in 103 they actually have difficulty in being admitted to the citadel as sightseers! At 128 ff. the High Priest's disposition follows the allegorical method we know only from Philo, and is severely critical of paganism and especially of theriolatry and incest, which the Egyptians or their king

[30] The fullest statement of the arguments for the theory of interpolation is that in J. G. Février, *La Date, la Composition, et les Sources de la Lettre d'Aristée à Philocrate* (Bibliotheque de l'Ecole des Hautes Etudes, 242; Paris, 1925). Février's arguments have been dealt with in some detail in the paragraphs on allegorical interpretation and on the topography of Jerusalem (16, 13).

practised. The argument is further reinforced by presumed topographical and historical background assumptions which would point to a period of Roman domination of Palestine. On the other hand it is difficult to see what the motives of an interpolator would be. "Aristeas" is itself a pseudonym, and there could therefore be no temptation to give interpolated material credit under the shield of a great name. Moreover, as we shall see below, the literary conventions which are applicable to this book admitted of imaginative treatment and the use of pre-existent materials, and there is therefore no need to invoke an interpolator to explain inconsistencies. The object of our book, in general terms (this question too will be considered more fully below: 60), is to raise the credit of the Jewish community and its doctrines, in its own sight and perhaps in the sight of the non-Jewish community, and nothing which does not contravene this object need necessarily be eliminated or questioned.

But Josephus' alterations of Aristeas' account do have an interest, as showing how Josephus' objects diverged from Aristeas', and hence in clarifying Aristeas' intentions.[31] Some are merely mechanical and supply what look like unintentional omissions in our text of Aristeas: Aristeas leaves the number of goblets in Ptolemy's gift unspecified, Josephus says there were thirty; Aristeas gives only two dimensions of the table, Josephus adds the third. Some involve numbers, in which the ancients were notoriously lax: where Aristeas says (10): "more than 200,000" books, Josephus says "about 200,000"; where Aristeas says (19) "more than 100,000 slaves," Josephus says "more than 110,000"; where Aristeas mentions 20 drachmas as the price of a slave (20), Josephus says 120; and there are other divergences in numbers at 33 and 82. The increase in the price of slaves is apparently due to Josephus' awareness that 20 drachmas was much too low, and involves other alterations of figures in the same connection (see note on 20). Aristeas says the translators were entertained for seven days, Josephus twelve. Where

[31] See G. Stählin, "Josephus und der Aristeasbrief," *Theologische Studien und Kritiken* 102 (1930), 323–331.

Josephus gives the name of the priest who offered prayer (184) as Elisha, instead of Aristeas' Eleazar, it is our MSS of Aristeas that are probably at fault, and modern texts print Elisha.

The more significant divergences are in the direction of making the account inoffensive to non-Jews and more credible to them. Ptolemy does *not* bow down before the Law seven times (177), his courtiers do *not* wait on table for the translators (186), he does *not* decree that informers take possession of those who fail to release Jewish slaves. Ptolemy I's treatment of Jewish captives is made to seem less harsh in Josephus than in Aristeas (12–14). The allusion to anti-Semitism in Alexandria (37) is omitted. Similarly matter of primary interest to the Jews themselves is omitted: Eleazar's apology for the dietary laws (128 ff.), Aristeas' prayer for the captives (17), the significance of the washing of the hands (306–7), the technique of the translators (302). And where Aristeas only implies (16) that he is not a Jew, in Josephus (17) he states categorically that he is a pagan. The conclusion to be drawn is that whereas both Aristeas and Josephus were writing propaganda, Aristeas was addressing himself primarily to the Jewish community and Josephus to the gentile world. Josephus wished to show his readers that Jews were highly regarded by great kings in the (at his day) remote past. His other allusions to Aristeas point in the same direction (*Against Apion* 2.45, *Ant.* 1.10) and he cherishes the approbation of the "pagan" Aristeas as he does that of the "pagan" Hecataeus. Aristeas does not exclude pagan readers (any more than Josephus excludes Jewish), but it is clear that insofar as his book deals with the Septuagint he is endeavoring to establish authority for it among Jews, and in the work as a whole one view of the proper attitude of Jews to their neighbors is set forth, probably in opposition to rival views.

2. PHILO

Philo's account of the genesis of the Septuagint (*On Moses* 2.25–44) does not mention Aristeas by name, and though it reproduces certain features of Aristeas, there are also marked divergences. It is altogether possible that Philo used an independent tradition, perhaps indeed the same tradition which Aristeas himself used. The passage in question must be of interest to the reader of Aristeas and is short enough to be reproduced in its entirety:[32]

> That the sanctity of our legislation has been a source of wonder not only to the Jews but also to all other nations, is clear both from the facts already mentioned and those which I proceed to state. In ancient times the laws were written in the Chaldean tongue, and remained in that form for many years, without any change of language, so long as they had not yet revealed their beauty to the rest of mankind. But, in course of time, the daily, unbroken regularity of practice exercised by those who observed them brought them to the knowledge of others, and their fame began to spread on every side. For things excellent, even if they are beclouded for a short time through envy, shine out again under the benign operation of nature when their time comes. Then it was that some people, thinking it a shame that the laws should be found in one half only of the human race, the barbarians, and denied altogether to the Greeks, took steps to have them translated.
>
> In view of the importance and public utility of the task, it was referred not to private persons or magistrates who were very numerous, but to kings, and amongst them to the king of highest repute. Ptolemy, surnamed Philadelphus, was the third in succession to Alexander, the conqueror of Egypt. In all the qualities which make a good ruler, he excelled not only his contemporaries, but all who have arisen in the past; and even till today, after so many generations, his praises are sung for the many evidences and monuments of his greatness of mind which he left behind him in different cities and countries, so that, even now, acts of more than ordinary munif-

---

[32] Translation of F. H. Colson in the Loeb *Philo*, vol. 6; see Colson's Appendix II, 605 f.

icence or buildings on a specially great scale are proverbially called Philadelphian after him. To put it shortly, as the house of the Ptolemies was highly distinguished, compared with other dynasties, so was Philadelphus among the Ptolemies. The creditable achievements of this one man almost outnumbered those of all the others put together, and, as the head takes the highest place in the living body, so he may be said to head the kings. This great man, having conceived an ardent affection for our laws, determined to have the Chaldean translated into Greek, and at once dispatched envoys to the High Priest and king of Judaea, both offices being held by the same person, explaining his wishes and urging him to choose by merit persons to make a full rendering of the Law into Greek. The High Priest was naturally pleased, and, thinking that God's guiding care must have led the king to busy himself in such an undertaking, sought out such Hebrews as he had of the highest reputation, who had received an education in Greek as well as their native lore, and joyfully sent them to Ptolemy.

When they arrived, they were offered hospitality, and, having been sumptuously entertained, requited their entertainer with a feast of words full of wit and weight. For he tested the wisdom of each by propounding for discussion new instead of the ordinary questions, which problems they solved with happy and well-pointed answers in the form of apophthegms, as the occasion did not allow of lengthy speaking. After standing this test, they at once began to fulfill the duties of their high errand. Reflecting how great an undertaking it was to make a full version of the laws given by the Voice of God, where they could not add or take away or transfer anything, but must keep the original form and shape, they proceeded to look for the most open and unoccupied spot in the neighbourhood outside the city. For, within the walls, it was full of every kind of living creatures, and consequently the prevalence of diseases and deaths, and the impure conduct of the healthy inhabitants, made them suspicious of it. In front of Alexandria lies the island of Pharos, stretching with its narrow strip of land towards the city, and enclosed by a sea not deep but mostly consisting of shoals, so that the loud din and booming of the surging waves grows faint through the long distance before it reaches the land. Judging this to be the most suitable place in the district, where they might find peace and tranquillity and the soul could commune with the laws with none to disturb its privacy, they fixed their abode there; and, taking the sacred books, stretched them out towards heaven with the hands that held them, asking of God that they might not fail in their purpose. And He assented to their prayers, to the end that the greater part, or even the whole, of the human race might be profited and led to a better life by continuing to observe such wise and truly admirable ordinances. Sitting here in seclusion with none present save the elements of nature, earth, water, air, heaven, the genesis of which was to be the first theme of their sacred revelation, for the laws begin with the story of the world's creation, they became as it were possessed, and, under inspiration, wrote, not each several scribe something different, but the same word for word, as though dictated to each by an invisible prompter. Yet who does not know that every language, and Greek especially, abounds in terms, and that the same thought can be put in many shapes by changing single words and whole phrases and suiting the expression to the occasion? This was not the case, we are told, with this law of ours, but the Greek words used corresponded literally with the Chaldean, exactly suited to the things they indicated. For, just as in geometry and logic, so it seems to me, the sense indicated does not admit of variety in the expression which remains unchanged in its original form, so these writers, as it clearly appears, arrived at a wording which corresponded with the matter, and alone, or better than any other, would bring out clearly what was meant. The clearest proof of this is that, if Chaldeans have learned Greek, or Greeks Chaldean, and read both versions, the Chaldean and the translation, they regard them with awe and reverence as sisters, or rather one and the same, both in matter and words, and speak of the authors not as translators but as prophets and priests of the mysteries, whose sincerity and singleness of thought has enabled them to go hand in hand with the purest of spirits, the spirit of Moses. Therefore, even to the present day, there is held every year a feast and general assembly in the island of Pharos, whither not only Jews but multitudes of others cross the water, both to do honour to the place in which the light of that version first shone out, and also to thank God for the good gift so old yet ever young. But, after the prayers and thanksgivings, some fixing tents on the seaside and other reclining on the sandy beach in the open air, feast with their relations and friends, counting that shore for the time a more magnificent lodging than the fine mansions in the royal precincts. Thus the laws are shewn to be desirable and precious in the eyes of all, ordinary citizens and rulers alike, and that too though our nation has not prospered for many a year.

Philo omits the story of the liberation of the Egyptian Jews, the matter relating to the visit to Jerusalem, the role of Demetrius of Phalerum. The most important difference is in the technique of the translation, for Aristeas (302) represents the translators as comparing their work as they write it and producing an agreed upon but not an inspired version, whereas in Philo each of the translators independently arrived at identical phraseology by divine inspiration. The feasting is also more elaborate in Aristeas, and he says nothing of an annual festival. Evidence of Philo's ignorance of Aristeas has been seen in his failure to cite the authority of Aristeas' High Priest for his allegorical method of interpretation, especially where he is dealing with laws (*On Special Laws* 4.104) which Eleazar discusses at 128 ff. But none of the arguments is conclusive, and Philo's foreshortening and differences in emphasis are in keeping with his own purposes and interests. The balance of probability seems to be rather on the side of Philo's having read our Aristeas.[33]

3. ARISTOBULUS

One of the main pillars which has been used to support an early dating of Aristeas is a passage of the Jewish philosopher Aristobulus, quoted in Eusebius, *Praeparatio Evangelica* 13.12.2. The passage reads as follows:[34]

> It is evident that Plato was a follower of our code of laws, evident too that he diligently studied all their details. For before the time of Demetrius of Phalerum, before the dominion of Alexander and of the Persians, a translation had been made by others of the narrative of the leading forth of the Hebrews, our fellow countrymen, out of Egypt, and of the divine manifestation in all which befell them, and of the occupation of the promised land, with a detailed statement of the entire Law. It is thus abundantly clear that the aforesaid philosopher has derived many things therefrom; for he was a man of great learning, like Pythagoras, who also borrowed many of our doctrines and incorporated them in his decrees. But the complete translation of the Law and all its contents was made under the king surnamed Philadelphus, thy ancestor, who displayed the greatest zeal, while Demetrius of Phalerum busied himself with the necessary arrangements.

The basis of the argument is Aristobulus' association of the name of Demetrius of Phalerum with the translation, for, it is

---

[33] L. Cohn, *Neue Jahrbücher für die klassische Altertumswissenschaft* 1 (1898), 521 doubts that Philo read Aristeas; B. Motzo, "Aristea," *Atti della R. Accad. di Scienze di Torino* 50 (1915), 202–226, 547–570 makes a subtle study of the points of contact in Aristeas' and Philo's versions of the story, and concludes that Philo must have known Aristeas. Motzo's conclusions are accepted and confirmed by Tramontano, 170 ff.

[34] Translation of H. St. J. Thackeray, in his *Letter of Aristeas* (London, 1918), 95 f.

reasoned, if the association is unhistorical it must have derived from the originator of the error, to wit, Aristeas. And since Aristobulus is dated, on the authority of Clement of Alexandria (*Stromateis* 1.22.150) and Eusebius (*Chronicle* 151), to the reign of Ptolemy Philopator (170-150) it would follow that Aristeas was earlier. But there are flaws in the argument, for (a) it is possible that Aristeas drew from Aristobulus[35] or both from a common tradition, and (b) Aristobulus' date may actually be much lower, for both Clement and Eusebius are gullible in such matters and all their testimony proves is that at the beginning of the second century CE a work on the Jewish Law addressed to Philometor was current under the name of Aristobulus. There is more impressive testimony in the identification of Aristobulus as the "teacher of King Ptolemy" at *II Maccabees* 1.10, but scholars are inclined to regard that verse as spurious. Negative evidence would suggest a later date for Aristobulus. (a) It is striking that Josephus, to whom the statement that Platonism derives from Judaism would be very welcome in *Against Apion*, fails to mention him; (b) his manner of exegesis seems very like Philo's; and (c) his ascription of spurious verses to Orpheus, Linus, Homer, and others seems strange in a Peripatetic scholar supposed to be a contemporary and perhaps colleague of the great critic Aristarchus. Aristobulus is therefore of no great help in fixing a date for Aristeas.

4. THE PROLOGUE OF BEN SIRAH

It is plain from Aristeas itself that at the time of its composition a Greek version of the Law and perhaps of other books of the Bible was already in existence, and it has been plausibly suggested that the formal authorization which Aristeas evidently seeks to bestow upon a Greek translation of the Bible

---

[35] So Gercke, *s.v.* Aristobulus 15 in Pauly-Wissowa (1896), 918-920. But Motzo (see note 33, above) refutes this and other criticism and agrees essentially with Schürer that Aristobulus supports an early dating for Aristeas; here too Motzo is followed by Tramontano, 166 ff.

refers not to the pre-existent version, which dates from the third century BCE, but to an official revision undertaken at the instance of the constituted authorities of the Alexandrian community.[36] Such a theory would receive weighty corroboration from expressions of dissatisfaction with the existing translation deriving from responsible sources. We do in fact have such an expression of dissatisfaction in the familiar Prologue of Ben Sirah:

> For things originally spoken in Hebrew have not the same force in them when they are translated into another tongue: and not only these, but the Law itself, and the prophecies, and the rest of the books, have no small difference, when they are spoken in their original language.

The criticism is of course applicable to our own LXX (as it would be to virtually any translation, from any language), but may be regarded as striking if applied to a version which is declared unsurpassable and in which changes are forbidden under imprecation. The date of Ben Sirah's *Prologue*, as its author himself tells us, is 132 BCE, and if he indeed reflects dissatisfaction with the existing version of the Bible which impelled the Alexandrian authorities to provide an authorized revision, that date would stand as a *terminus post quem* for Aristeas.

5. THE DECREE OF PHILADELPHUS: P. RAINER 24,552

At 22-25 Aristeas reproduces what purports to be the actual words of the decree by which Ptolemy Philadelphus emancipated the enslaved Jews of Egypt:

> All persons who took the field with our father against the regions of Syria and Phoenicia and in the invasion of the country of the Jews came into possession of Jewish slaves and

---

[36] See 66 for evidences of the pre-existent translation, and 69 for the theory that Aristeas refers to a revision of LXX.

have brought them over to our city and country or have sold them to others—and likewise if any such were in the country previously or introduced subsequently—those holding them shall release them straightway, receiving forthwith compensation of twenty drachmas for each slave, the soldiers with the payment of their stipend, and others from the royal bank. For it is our belief that these persons were made prisoner contrary to the will of our father and to propriety, and that it was to military recklessness that the despoliation of their country and the removal of the Jews themselves to Egypt was due. The booty which accrued to the soldiers on the field of battle was sufficient; hence the further oppression of the people was wholly inequitable. Therefore, since it is our professed purpose to award justice to all men, and more particularly to those who are unreasonably tyrannized, and since we strive in every respect to deal fairly with all men in accordance with justice and piety, we have decreed that so many Jewish persons as are held in bondage in whatever manner anywhere in the kingdom their owners shall release upon receipt of the stipulated sum. No one shall be in any way negligent in the discharge of this obligation. Lists shall be submitted to the officials placed in charge of this matter within three days from the posting up of this decree, and the persons involved shall be produced at once. For we have determined that it is advantageous both for ourselves and for the realm for this business to be accomplished. Any who wish may give information concerning recalcitrants, on condition that the informer acquire ownership of the culprit; the property of the defaulters shall be confiscated to the royal purse.

Aristeas then adds:

The decree as submitted to be read over to the king contained all the rest with the exception of the clause "if any such were in the country previously or introduced subsequently," and the king himself, indulging his munificence and magnanimity, made the addition.

A decree dealing with registration of slaves is found on a papyrus of the Rainer collection, Inv. 24,552;[37] its first editor, H. Liebesny, attributes it to Ptolemy Philadelphus, and calls attention to its similarity to our document. Commenting upon this publication, the celebrated papyrologist U. Wilcken pronounced the Aristeas decree a genuine official document;[38] he had previously pointed out the keen knowledge of Ptolemaic administrative procedure displayed in its composition.[39] Professor W. L. Westermann has called attention to compelling objections to the hypothesis that ours is a genuine decree, but has demonstrated that the Aristeas decree is actually a reworking of the decree of Ptolemy Philadelphus preserved in P. Rainer 24,552, on the basis of close parallelism in language.[40] The possible objection that documents dealing with kindred legal questions would necessarily use the same essentially technical vocabulary Professor Westermann meets with three acute observations which are relevant to our purposes also. (a) Both documents use "Syria and Phoenicia"; "Syria and Phoenicia" or "Syria" alone were the official designations for the Ptolemaic possessions in the area in the third century BC. Elsewhere in his book Pseudo-Aristeas uses "Coele Syria," a term which came into use in the second century and became the customary designation. The fact that Aristeas here uses an expression other than the one habitual with him argues for direct borrowing. (b) The original decree does not and could not have included provision for slaves brought in previously or subsequently. In regard to this Professor Westermann writes (22): "It was probably the absence of this provision in the model used by Pseudo-Aristeas in shaping his decree which suggested to the author the idea that it should be inserted at the special instance of King Ptolemy himself after the *prostagma* has been drafted

[37] Published in *Aegyptus* 16 (1936), 257–291.
[38] *Archiv für Papyrusforschung* 12 (1937), 221 ff.
[39] In G. Plaumann's publication of *P. Gradewitz 1, Sitzungsber. Heidelb. Akad.*, ph.-hist. Kl. 5 (1914).
[40] "Enslaved Persons Who Are Free," *American Journal of Philology* 59 (1938), 1–30.

INTRODUCTION 31

and presented to him. Artistically this addition is turned into a clever literary device for enhancing that 'munificence and greatness of soul' which prompted Philadelphus to accede to the original proposal of Aristeas regarding the Jewish slaves and, in this particular, even to widen its scope." (c) In the original decree, where there is good reason for such terminology, the persons concerned are designated by the somewhat equivocal word σώματα rather than by the more definite expressions δοῦλοι or ἀνδράποδα. The latter expressions, but without the same legal reason, are also avoided in Aristeas, which speaks only of τῶν Ἰουδαικῶν σωμάτων ἐν οἰκετίαις.

If the genuine decree was in fact Aristeas' model, certain deviations from the model are palpably his own fabrication, and since, as we shall see, these additions are echoed in III Maccabees they are relevant to our purposes here. (a) In Aristeas the king motivates his measure (in a sentence which, as Professor Westermann points out, interrupts the flow of the decree) by considerations of abstract justice and the duty of a humane ruler. The apologetic tone is out of place in the pronouncement of an absolute king, and if motivation were required its place would be in a preamble rather than in the body of the decree.[41] But Aristeas is profoundly interested in questions of the theory and practice of kingship, devoting about a third of his whole book (187–292) to a series of banquets where the subject of discussion is the proper conduct of kings and where the king's obligation to show himself just and humane is stressed. The motivation is then not only an alien element in the decree, but strictly in keeping with Aristeas' own interests and purposes.

(b) The Aristeas decree provides that slaves must be declared and their persons produced before officials appointed "within three days from the day when the decree is issued." Professor Westermann notes that this is a physical impossibility; the original decree granted twenty days for the registration of the

[41] In making this point Westermann, *op. cit.* 28, cites "the preamble to the *prostagma* of the king in P. Teb. III, 1, 700, 11.22–36, which contained the reasons for the enactment."

persons involved, and another document dealing with the registration of slaves in Egypt provides two months for Alexandria and six for the countryside.[42] "The three-day period in Pseudo-Aristeas," Professor Westermann writes, "was probably suggested by consideration of the reputed speed which characterized the entire procedure of the translation of the Septuagint. The discussion, formulation, and ratification of the *prostagma* occupied, from beginning to end, only seven days. The translation of the Old Testament books [in point of fact only the Pentateuch was involved] was completed in seventy-two days."

(c) Finally, the provision that informers would be given possession of the persons against whom they informed is unexampled in the entire range of Greek and Hellenistic legislation and highly improbable in the present case.[43] At Aristeas 167, indeed, Philadelphus is praised for his extremely harsh treatment of informers, as being in keeping with his enlightened regime. The inconsistent touch is added in the decree apparently to demonstrate Philadelphus' intense interest in the welfare of the Jews.

The use of the genuine decree, however its language is altered, enhances our respect for Aristeas. It is also of no small weight as an argument for early dating. The decree may, of course, have found its way into some literary work, which the Alexandrian Jewish community in particular may have cherished and preserved. But it is simpler to imagine that the interval between the promulgation of the actual decree and its use by our author was relatively short, and together with the circumstances to be noted under 7, 8, and 9 below constitutes an argument of some weight for an earlier Ptolemaic dating.

6. III MACCABEES

A certain affinity between Aristeas and III Maccabees is to be expected, for both books derive from a single environment—the

---

[42] *Op. cit.*, 24 f. The second document is P. Gradewitz 1, republished by Westermann in his *Upon Slavery in Ptolemaic Egypt* (New York, 1929), 33 f.

[43] Westermann, *Op. cit.* 25 f.

Jewish community of Alexandria, both have a major purpose in common—that of setting forth the relations of the Jews to their non-Jewish rulers in as favorable a light as possible, and, most important, both are Greek books, written, as we shall see, according to Greek canons of form; they are not, like other books on the periphery of Scripture with which they have been associated, translations from Hebrew or Aramaic, nor do they follow the forms of such works. Among the non-canonical books III Maccabees does in fact show the closest resemblance to Aristeas in language and style, and similarities between the two books have frequently been noticed.[44] Perhaps the most tangible point of contact is a parallel in III Maccabees to Aristeas' reproduction of the decree of Philadelphus cited above. III Maccabees, whose fictive date is the reign of Ptolemy IV Philopator, contains two purported royal orders, in the shape of circular letters to officials rather than formal *prostagmata*, which similarly deal with a king's measures concerning the Jews. The first (3.11–29) is an order enjoining the arrest of all Jews for the purpose of inflicting a terrible and ignominious death upon them. After justifying his proposed measure by the stubborn wickedness of the Jews, as shown specifically by their refusal to admit him to their Temple (obviously a contrived link with the matter of the first two chapters),[45] protesting his own general philanthropy, and invoking the prudential consideration (echoing Pharaoh at Ex. 1.10), "lest when some sudden tumult is raised against us hereafter we should have these impious people behind our backs as traitors and barbarous foes," Philopator continues (25–29):[46]

We have ordained that as soon as this letter reaches you, you shall immediately dispatch to us, with harsh and violent

[44] See M. Hadas, "Aristeas and III Maccabees," *Harvard Theological Review* 42 (1949), 175–184.

[45] The connections of the disparate sections with one another and their historical validity are examined in J. Cohen, *Judaica et Aegyptiaca: De Maccabaeorum Libro III Quaestiones Historicae* (Groningen, 1941)

[46] Translation of M. Hadas, to appear in his edition of *III Maccabees* in the present series.

treatment, those that reside among you, along with their women and children, fettered in every way with iron chains, to meet inexorable and ignominious death, as befits malevolent enemies. When these have been punished as a body, we anticipate that our government will be perfectly established for all future times in a sound and excellent state. Whosoever shall shelter any Jew, from old age to infancy, even babes at breast, shall be bastinadoed to death with most horrible torments, along with all his household. Whoso will may give information, on condition of receiving the property of him that incurs punishment and two thousand drachmas from the royal treasury, and he shall also be rewarded with freedom. Every place where a Jew may be detected receiving any shelter at all shall be made anathema and burned with fire; it shall be rendered altogether useless for every mortal creature for all time.

At 7.1–9 this harsh order is rescinded by another letter of Philopator. He exclaims that he had been persuaded to his original cruel measure by wicked friends, and continues (6–9):

But we upbraided them severely for this conduct, in keeping with the kindliness we have for all men, and barely granted them their lives. And because we knew for certain that the God in heaven protects the Jews, being their ally always as a father to his children, and because we took into account the good will, like a friend's, which they had for us and our forebears, we have justly absolved them of all blame, on whatsoever account. And we have ordained for all of them to return, each to his own, and that no one should injure them at all in any place nor reproach them for what had befallen them without reason. Know well that if we devise any evil against them or harm them in any way we shall have not man but the Most High God who is master of all power as our adversary to exact vengeance for what is done, in every way and at every time, ineluctably. Farewell.

At 2.27-30, finally, we have what purports to be an edict in the form of an inscription, which also has to do with the status of the Jews:

> He designed to inflict a stigma upon the Jewish nation publicly, and erected a pillar on the tower at the palace and inscribed upon it: That none of those who did not sacrifice should be allowed to enter their temples; that all the Jews should be reduced to the popular census and slave condition; that those who spoke against it should be carried off by force and put to death; that those who were registered should be branded by fire on their persons with an ivy leaf, the emblem of Dionysus, and that they should be brought back to their former limited status. In order not to appear an enemy to them all he subjoined that If any of them prefer to join those who are initiated in the mysteries, they shall have equal rights with the citizens of Alexandria.

The turgid rhetoric, exaggeration, and accentuated Jewish separatism in the first two passages correspond closely to the style and outlook of III Maccabees as a whole and stamp them as fabrications of the author. Yet that author knew something of proper Ptolemaic chancellery forms. On the basis of their formulae of salutation and farewell Bickermann was able to propose a date for the composition of the book,[47] and the form and content of the third passage (2.27-30) indicate that it is based on an actual document. It accords with what is known of the policy of Philopator, who used the cult of Dionysus as a means of unifying sections of his population and was the first to employ native Egyptians in his phalanx. Moreover it fits badly with the rest of the book, for the registration envisaged is for status, not for annihilation.

The similarities between these "documents" and the Aristeas decree are too vague to admit of anything like demonstration that the one author was directly influenced by the other; nevertheless the similarities, I believe, are too pronounced to be

[47] Ca. 100 BCE, in Pauly Wissowa 14.797-800; 25 BCE is in fact a more likely date: see 38 below.

explained by the fact that both authors are familiar with Ptolemaic chancellery usage and both are dealing with a question of Jewish status. We can argue best not from the genuine decree which was Aristeas' model but from the alterations which, as we saw, Aristeas probably introduced into his model; and it happens that these alterations are apparently in the mind of the author of III Maccabees, no less when he is opposing than when he is adopting them. (a) In Aristeas Philadelphus is represented as justifying his measure (contrary to normal official usage) on the grounds of enlightened principles of kingship. In III Maccabees Philopator protests his general clemency, but makes his decisive motivation for releasing the Jews fear of God, who is always their ally. (b) Aristeas' decree provides that his measure be carried out with highly improbable if not impossible speed. III Maccabees, whose rhetoric intensifies everything, calls for action "as soon as this epistle reaches you" instead of Aristeas' shrift of three days. (c) The provision in Aristeas that informers be given possession of the persons of recalcitrants was, as we saw, as unlikely as it was unprecedented. III Maccabees' provision for rewarding informers *against* the Jews seems to be a clear echo of the added touch in Aristeas.

These points, tenuous in themselves, gain in plausibility when one considers the general motives of III Maccabees *vis à vis* Aristeas. Sterling Tracy was undoubtedly right in supposing that the two works consciously advocate opposing views with regard to a proper *modus vivendi* for the Jewish community in relation to its neighbors and rulers.[48] In the High Priest's apologia for the Law at 128 ff. (see notes *ad loc.* and section 8 below) Aristeas is at pains to show that ritual observances are not an end in themselves, but, on the basis of allegorical interpretation, means to an ethical way of life, of which enlightened gentiles must needs approve. The omnipotence of God and His providence extend over gentiles as well as Jews, and not merely

[48] Sterling Tracy, "III Maccabees and Pseudo-Aristeas," *Yale Classical Studies* I (1928), 239–252.

to protect the Jews from pagan persecution; and the merits of this ethical theology are recognized and approved by the pagan "philosophers." Aristeas seeks to show that it is possible for Jews to participate in the social and intellectual life of the larger community without compromising basic Jewish values; such an attitude is seen to result in the respect and admiration of the secular authorities and the "philosophers" and in general harmony. III Maccabees, on the other hand, premises a basic hostility on the part of secular officials, insists upon full compliance with the requirements of religion, and abhors any compromise in the direction of assimilation. The denouement shows not a restored harmony but a turning of the tables, by God's intervention, which gives the Jews the upper hand. Surely the books represent rival views within the Jewish community, perhaps contemporary, more likely evoked by different conjunctures in history.

It is perhaps natural to regard Aristeas' view as the more enlightened, and when Tracy wrote it was natural to assume that the normal course of thought was from the less to the more enlightened. This may explain his assumption that Aristeas is an answer to and a correction of III Maccabees. Recent years have again impressed upon us that external pressures may shift the direction from the more enlightened to the less enlightened, and this would seem to be the case in the two works before us. In the earlier Ptolemaic period relations between Jews and the authorities had not yet been subjected to extreme strain, and a Hellenized Jew might well believe that even completer harmony could be envisaged. In III Maccabees this hope seems frustrated, and in the atmosphere of hostility and suspicion which had grown up the only recourse seemed to be a retreat to narrower observance of religious duties as a means for securing divine protection.

On the basis of III Maccabees' hypothetical use of Aristeas' version of the decree of Philadelphus we may safely say that Aristeas is the earlier book. There are cogent reasons for dating

III Maccabees to *ca.* 25 BCE,[49] but it is impossible to say, on the basis of III Maccabees' use of Aristeas, at what point between 270 and 25 BCE Aristeas was written. In the case of Aristeas itself, use of the genuine decree of Philadelphus would suggest a short interval, but Aristeas may well have become something of a classic in the Jewish community of Alexandria, and even if III Maccabees was intended as a direct reply to it we need not assume that the response followed immediately upon the challenge. A "liberal" and a "conservative" party whose history extends over a long period need not produce their best-known pamphlets simultaneously.

7. EZRA-NEHEMIAH

Insofar as Aristeas is an account of a new promulgation of the Law it is reminiscent of the story told in Ezra and Nehemiah, and indeed Février[50] believes that Aristeas used these books, freely, to be sure, and perhaps in part unconsciously, as a model. The points of resemblance become distinct in a tabulation:

(a) Nehemiah petitions the king on behalf of the distressed inhabitants of Jerusalem, and prays "to the God of heaven" (Neh. 1, 2). The Jews in Babylon are authorized to return to Jerusalem under the conduct of Ezra (Ezra 7.13).

Aristeas intercedes with the king on behalf of the enslaved Jews in Egypt, and prays to God to ensure their release (15 ff.).

(b) Ezra thanks God for granting him favor with the king and his counsellors (Ezra 7.28).

Aristeas secures the cooperation of the king's officers, Sosibius and Andreas, to support his petition (12).

(c) Ezra and Nehemiah journey to Jerusalem, one with royal authority and the other on an official mission and with military

---

[49] To be set forth at large in my introduction to that book. The principal argument is the special use of *laographia*, for which see V. Tcherikover, *The Jews in Egypt in the Hellenistic-Roman Age in the Light of the Papyri* (Hebrew, with English summary; Jerusalem, 1945), 91 ff.

[50] Février, 31 ff.

escort. Ezra appears to have been charged with some duty in relation to the Law (Ezra 7.14). Each carries a royal letter.

Aristeas is commissioned to visit Jerusalem to obtain an authentic text of the Law and competent translators (38 f., 46). He carries a letter from Ptolemy to Eleazar.

(d) Ezra departs to Jerusalem with royal presents destined for the Temple, and with further provision "unto an hundred talents of silver" etc. (Ezra 7.15, 21–22).

Aristeas takes royal gifts for the Temple, including a hundred talents of silver for sacrifices etc. (40).

(e) In the decree of Darius the Jews are encouraged to offer God sacrifices and prayers on behalf of the king and his sons (Ezra 6.10).

Eleazar, the High Priest, states that he has offered sacrifices for the king, his consort, children, and friends (45).

(f) Nehemiah assembles the people for a solemn reading of the Law, which thus receives a sort of popular authorization (Neh. 8.2–3, 6).

Demetrius assembles the Jews of Alexandria, and reads the completed translation, which is then solemnly ratified by the whole assembly (308 ff.).

(g) Ezra 6 and 7 contain official communications, as the letters of Ptolemy and Eleazar are contained in Aristeas.

(h) At Ezra 6.17 and 8.16 embassies of *twelve* representatives are mentioned. There is reason to think that the number of seventy-two (rather than seventy) translators is Aristeas' own invention,[51] and the explanation for his divagation may well be that he chose the multiple of twelve nearest to seventy.

There are, of course, significant differences in the stories. In one case the motive for the promulgation of the Law is religious reform; in the other, at least ostensibly, to supply a gap in the collections of a royal library. The intercessor is in one case a Jew, and in the other a presumed gentile, whose concern for the

---

[51] See 42 and 71 below; Février does not make this point.

40 ARISTEAS TO PHILOCRATES

liberation of the Jews is only incidental to the story. Such alterations, it may be argued, are to be expected in a writer like Aristeas, who makes no pretense of writing exact history and who would thus freely adapt details to suit his own framework. On the other hand, such items as the dispatch of royal gifts, the citation of official documents, prayers and sacrifices for the welfare of kings, and the like, would naturally find place independently. If Aristeas were to be read as history, the similarities to Ezra-Nehemiah would nevertheless be disturbing, and a defense of Aristeas' historicity would entail a denial of the possibility of influence. But if Aristeas is read as the edifying romance it is, then there can be no objection to supposing that its author was influenced by memories of Ezra-Nehemiah. Indeed the hypothesis of such reminiscences supplies a missing piece in the pattern; as a whole and in detail Aristeas is, as we shall see (54), a Greek book, composed according to Greek "rhetorical" rules, and this Jewish source may well be a pattern for the subject matter. It is *a priori* likely that a writer so well acquainted with Scripture as Aristeas would know Ezra-Nehemiah, and if he knew it that he would be influenced by it. For purposes of dating the assumption of the use of Ezra-Nehemiah is of little help, for these books were early translated into Greek.

8. ARISTEAS ON KINGSHIP AND THE PALI MILINDAPANHA

Testimony in the same direction, less demonstrable in character but plausible nevertheless is afforded by another section of our book which bears a relationship to works outside the Jewish tradition. The largest single section of Aristeas, about a third of the whole (187–292), is the account of the seven banquets which Philadelphus offered the company of translators, at which he received from each a response to some "philosophical" question. The questions deal specifically with the theory and practice of kingship and the king himself summarizes the proceedings by thanking the men for "the doctrine which you have grounded for me with reference to kingship" (294). Each response, it is true, concludes with a reference to God, but these

INTRODUCTION 41

devout expressions seem to have been added specifically to make the responses appropriate to the Jewish sages; "these men," we read in 235, "were far in advance of the philosophers, for they made their starting-point from God." Aside from these tags there is little in the questions and answers that has to do with the Jewish people or religion. On the contrary, the words for "benevolence," "mildness," "humaneness" (*euergesia, epieikeia, philanthropia*) which recur frequently in this section[52] are a special characteristic of Hellenistic philosophical writings.[53] The change in political organization introduced in the Greek world by Alexander and his successors evoked a mass of writings on the theory of kingship, *Peri Basileias*, philosophers of all schools endeavoring to supply a rationale and a code for the institution.[54] This section of Aristeas clearly has affinities with the treatises *On Kingship*, and W. W. Tarn has suggested with great plausibility that the Pali *Milindapanha*, which has similar affinities, is directly related to our book.[55] Tarn posits a "Questions of Ptolemy Philadelphus" written by a Jew in the reign of Ptolemy III,[56] with no propaganda purpose other than showing that a great king regarded Jews highly. These questions

[52] The *Index Verborum* in Wendland's ed. shows some 20 examples of the use of these words alone.

[53] Cf. Max Mühl, *Die antike Menschheitsidee in ihrer geschichtlichen Entwicklung* (Leipzig, 1928).

[54] See especially E. R. Goodenough, "The Political Philosophy of Hellenistic Kingship," *Yale Classical Studies* 1 (1928), 53–102. One of the earliest and most highly esteemed of these treatises was Theophrastus, *Peri Basileias*, of which there is a fragment in P. Oxyrhynchus 1611; cf. Kunst, *Berliner Klassikertexte* VII.

[55] "The Milindapanha and Pseudo-Aristeas," an appendix to his *The Greeks in Bactria and India* (Cambridge, 1938), 414–436. The Milindapanha or Questions of Milinda (Menander, *fl. ca.* 200 BCE) is translated by Rhys Davids in vols. 35 and 36 of the *Sacred Books of the East* (1890, 1894).

[56] The dating depends on Aristeas 252, which prescribes that the king must administer petitions. After the beginning of the second century special officials were appointed for petitions, and none reached the king. The date (according to Tarn) must fall when Ptolemy II was still a great memory, and before the troubles between Ptolemy IV and the Jews, hence the reign of Ptolemy III (247–222).

were employed by the Pali writer as a basis for Buddhist propaganda, as they were by the author of Aristeas for a broade Jewish propaganda. Tarn further suggests that the eleventh questions in the last two sets were added on by Aristeas to conform to his own invention of seventy-two (six from each of the twelve tribes) instead of the seventy sages we should expect from the title of Septuagint and from the number of Moses' elders (Ex. 24.1, 9). The literary and philosophic tradition of presenting maxims for enlightened rulers continued, to be sure, throughout antiquity. The tradition is reflected, for example, in such a work as Plutarch's *Apophthegms of Rulers and Commanders*, in Dio Chrysostom's *Orations on Kingship*, and in the orations presented by "philosophers" of the fourth and following centuries (*e.g.*, Libanius or Themistius) to the Emperors at Constantinople. But the tradition was at its strongest and freshest early in the Hellenistic period when the problem of kingship was new and pressing, and since this section of Aristeas is really not integral to his book but appears rather to reflect a current interest it may be legitimate to deduce from it a rather early date for the book as a whole—well before the period of Roman domination of Egypt. It is to be remembered that Josephus' text included this material, for though his paraphrase omits it, he refers readers who may be curious about it to the book itself.

The discussion of philosophic problems at table is, of course, a familiar literary form, and we have examples from the *Symposia* of Plato and Xenophon down to the *Doctors at Dinner* of Athenaeus. Changes in form between Plato and Athenaeus are of some but no great help in dating. The original practice was to have the discussion last no longer than one day, but Cicero, for example in his *Tusculan Disputations*, carries his over several days, as does Aristeas, and must have had Hellenistic models for his practice. In the early *Symposia* the discussion is a real conversation, with conclusions emerging from the give and take of the interlocutors, but Plutarch's *Symposiacs* are, like Aristeas,

INTRODUCTION 43

a catechism, with a king putting questions and the sages replying, and Plutarch too must have had predecessors in this form.

9. HECATAEUS (IN DIODORUS SICULUS) ON THE IDEALS OF THE EGYPTIAN KINGS

The advice given the king by the sages consists largely of ethical commonplaces for which it is impossible to point to a specific origin with any assurance. But we do have an idealized picture of the conduct of Egyptian kings which shows certain rather striking parallels with the phraseology of some of our Questions, and it is of some significance that this picture derives, in all probability, from that of Hecataeus who seems to have a foremost place in Aristeas' mind. After his account of the early history of Egypt down to the death of Amasis (1.1–68), Diodorus Siculus proceeds to speak of the way of life of Egyptian kings. It is obvious that the account is based on an idealized "philosophical" view, appropriate to the Ptolemies rather than to their Persian or Egyptian predecessors, and it is generally agreed among scholars that Diodorus' immediate source is Hecataeus of Abdera. The portions of Diodorus' extract which are significant for our purpose are the following (beginning with 1.70):[57]

> In the first place, then, the life which the kings of the Egyptians lived was not like that of other men who enjoy autocratic power and do in all matters exactly as they please without being held to account, but all their acts were regulated by prescriptions set forth in laws, not only their administrative acts, but also those that had to do with the way in which they spent their time from day to day, and with the food which they ate. In the matter of their servants, for instance, not one was a slave, such as had been acquired by purchase or born in the home, but all were sons of the most distinguished priests, over twenty years old and the best

[57] Translation of C. H. Oldfather in Loeb Classical Library.

educated of their fellow-countrymen, in order that the king, by virtue of his having the noblest men to care for his person and to attend him throughout both day and night, might follow no low practices; for no ruler advances far along the road of evil unless he has those about him who will minister to his passions. . . . When the victims had been brought to the altar it was the custom for the High Priest to stand near the king, with the common people of Egypt gathered around, and pray in a loud voice that health and all the other good things of life be given the king if he maintains justice towards his subjects. And an open confession had also to be made of each and every virtue of the king, the priest saying that towards the gods he was piously disposed and towards men most kindly; for he was self-controlled and just and magnanimous, truthful, and generous with his possessions, and, in a word, superior to every desire, and that he punished crimes less severely than they deserved and rendered to his benefactors a gratitude exceeding the benefaction. And after reciting much more in a similar vein he concluded his prayer with a curse concerning things done in error, exempting the king from all blame therefor and asking that both the evil consequences and the punishment should fall upon those who served him and had taught him evil things. All this he would do, partly to lead the king to fear the gods and live a life pleasing to them, and partly to accustom him to a proper manner of conduct, not by sharp admonitions, but through praises that were agreeable and most conducive to virtue. After this . . . the sacred scribe read before the assemblage from out of the sacred books some of the edifying counsels and deeds of their most distinguished men, in order that he who held the supreme leadership should first contemplate in his mind the most excellent general principles and then turn to the prescribed administration of the several functions. . . . More remarkable still was the fact that kings were not allowed to render any legal decision or transact any business at random or to punish anyone through malice or in anger or for any

INTRODUCTION 45

other unjust reason, but only in accordance with the established laws relative to each offence. . . . And since the kings followed so righteous a course in dealing with their subjects, the people manifested a good will towards their rulers which surpassed even the affection they had for their own kinsmen; for not only the order of the priests but, in short, all the inhabitants of Egypt were less concerned for their wives and children and their other cherished possessions than for the safety of their kings.

Specific similarities in Aristeas which have been pointed out[58] are 188, commending the king for giving punishments milder than are deserved; 189, maintaining just dealings with all men; 206, being without deceit; 226, being free-handed; having the qualities of self-control (278) and gentleness (188); and others less tangible. Whatever be the validity of these specific parallels it is evident that the paramount concern shown in the Diodorus-Hecataeus passage for truth and absolute justice, and even more, for the approval of the king's subjects, represents an ideal rather than an actuality, either of the absolute Egyptian or only slightly less absolute Ptolemaic kings, and a Hellenistic rather than Egyptian ideal. It is the same ideal which is envisaged in the Questions, and it is not unreasonable to conjecture the same general, if not particular, source for both. We know that Aristeas leaned heavily on Hecataeus (see on 31), and Hecataeus is almost certainly Diodorus' source. Again, inferences on dating are hazardous, but on the basis of the name of Hecataeus and the likely period of the greatest interest in such matters, probability points to an early Ptolemaic date.

10. THE ZENON PAPYRI

The presence of Jews in Egypt and their activities there are well attested from the sixth century BCE and onwards,[59] and

---

[58] Some are noticed in Wendland, 52; they are expanded and enlarged upon in Février 43 ff., and summarized in Meecham, *Oldest Version* 308.
[59] See commentary on 12 ff. for details and documentation.

the large accretion to their numbers under the first Ptolemy, as described in 12-14, is mentioned also in Josephus.[60] But for the presence and activity of the Jews of Egypt in the reign of Ptolemy Philadelphus in particular, recent years have added a mass of epigraphical and papyrological evidence. Alexandria has yielded numbers of Jewish grave inscriptions which are attributed to the middle of the third century,[61] and a more intimate light is thrown on the commercial and other relations between Palestine and Egypt by the great mass of papyri, over 1200 in number, from the archives of Zenon, which were discovered at the site of ancient Philadelphia in 1915.[62] Zenon was the business agent of Apollonius, who was Philadelphus' principal financial official, and in particular managed Apollonius' large estate in the Fayyum. A number of papyri in the collection have a specific Jewish interest.[63] In 259 BCE Zenon went on a business trip to Palestine and Transjordan, and certain of his communications of that year are preserved, as are communications received from Palestine in the years following. These reveal a lively trade in wheat, olive oil, and slaves from Palestine to Egypt, and tell us a good deal about the chronology and the administration of Palestine. Of particular interest to the student of Aristeas are *P. Cairo Zenon* 59003 and 59075 which deal with a certain Tobias[64] and contain letters of Tobias to

[60] *Apion* 1.186 ff., 2.35, 42; *Jewish War* 2.487; *Ant.* 12.7.

[61] Breccia, *Bulletin de la Société Archéologique d'Alexandrie* 9 (1907), 67; 25 (1930), 108; *Juifs et Chrétiens de l'Ancienne Alexandrie* (1927), 6; Clermont-Ganneau, *Recueil d'Archéologie Orientale* 8 (1924), 59 ff.

[62] The collection was dispersed and is published in several series: P. Cairo Zenon 1-5; P. Soc. It. 4-6; P. Michigan Zenon; P. Columbia Zenon. *Cf.* M. Rostovtzeff, *A Large Estate in Egypt in the Third Century B.C.* (Madison, 1922).

[63] Particularly P. Cairo Zenon 59003, 59004, 59006, 59015, 59016, 59075, 59093; P.S.I. 406, 554, 594, 616, 632. On the Zenon papyri from Palestine see V. Tcherikover, "Palestine in the Light of the Zenon Papyri," Tarbiz 4, 226 ff. and 354 ff. and 5, 37 ff., and his "History of the Jews of Fayyum in the Hellenistic Age," *Sepher Magnes* (Jerusalem, 1935), 199 ff.

[64] See Josephus *Ant.* 12.154-236 and Marcus' notes and App. E (Loeb *Josephus*, vol. 7).

Apollonius and to Philadelphus.[65] The letter is courteous but the writer assumes an air of autonomy, preserves his own dignity, and deals with the great Egyptian monarch virtually on terms of equality. The writer's tone and assumed prerogatives are closely parallel to those of Eleazar's letter at Aristeas 41 ff. and give the latter a certain verisimilitude. A High Priest at Jerusalem in the reign of Philadelphus might well have received a letter from the Egyptian king couched in the terms of our "copy" (Aristeas 35 ff.), and there is nothing at all preposterous in the tone in which Eleazar is reported to have replied. In the light of the Zenon papyri there is nothing so fanciful in the relations between Palestine and Egypt as depicted in Aristeas as to impel us to assume that that book was written at a long interval after its fictive date, and the detailed information supplied by the papyri make this negative evidence more impressive than ordinary *argumenta ex silentio*. Either, then, the date of Aristeas is to be pushed backward, or the author had sound traditions of the period to which he attributes his story.

11. THE EKPHRASIS AND CALLIXINUS OF RHODES

Still less tangible but to be considered nevertheless is the relationship of the section describing Philadelphus' gifts to the Temple (51–82) to kindred work. A recognized species of literary production in the Hellenistic age was the *ekphrasis* or formal description, usually of a work of art or of a natural scene, as if it were a work of art.[66] This tradition goes back to Homer, whose description of the shield of Achilles is an *ekphrasis*, but it flourished in the Hellenistic and later ages. The Alexandrian poets and the writers of romance so described not only landscapes and persons but embroideries, paintings, and chased and jewelled vessels of gold and silver. Our completest extant specimens of the manner are Philostratus' descriptions of pictures in

[65] The implications of these (and other) documents are discussed fully in Tramontano 32 f.
[66] See 56, below.

a gallery and Callistratus' of a series of sculptures.[67] In Aristeas (51–82) the description of the workmanship of the golden table and the gold and silver mixing bowls and cups which Ptolemy Philadelphus sent to Jerusalem goes far beyond the simple requirements of the context to represent them as superlatively beautiful and costly. The closest parallel to the description in Aristeas, is, curiously enough, the description of another series of similar vessels made by Ptolemy Philadelphus. This was in the fourth book of a work on Alexandria by Callixinus of Rhodes, cited at length in Athenaeus 5.196 ff. The occasion for the display was the exhibition and banquet organized by Ptolemy Philadelphus at the beginning of his reign. Closest to the Aristeas passage is the description of the goblets and cups of gold encrusted with gems (5.199 BC). It may be significant that Aristeas' description of the bowls and cups is clear, so that a reader might sketch the vessels as described, whereas the description of the table, which rests in part on that of the table of shew-bread in the LXX, is so confused in important details that all commentators despair of picturing its appearance with any precision. Whether or not Aristeas actually had Callixinus' book before him, the tradition of such *ekphrasis* was current, and our passage clearly fits into the tradition. Again, the fact that the *ekphrasis* remained a literary style throughout antiquity (the Philostrati belonged to the third century) prevents us from using this aspect of Aristeas for dating. But the similarity to the description of so obscure and specialist a writer as Callixinus would suggest an earlier rather than a later dating.

12. THE UTOPIAN ELEMENT

Another "insulated" section of Aristeas is the account of the journey to Palestine and the description of the country and its Temple (83–127). Accounts of travels to exotic countries too have a continuous history from the *Odyssey* onward, but came to a special prominence when Alexander's conquests had so

---

[67] These two authors are available in a Loeb volume by A. Fairbanks.

greatly enlarged geographical horizons. Many authors of travel books, like Pytheas of Marseilles, were sober geographers; others, like Antiphanes of Berge, wrote fantastic accounts of incredible places and peoples. Our knowledge of such works is based on the parody of them in Lucian's *True History* and on the residue they have left in Strabo and Diodorus Siculus. But of the great vogue of the travel book as a vehicle for useful or entertaining information or misinformation there can be no question.[68] The form survived in such a fanciful romance as Antonius Diogenes' *Wonders beyond Thule*, of which we have excerpts, and in such a serious ethical work as Philostratus' *Life of Apollonius of Tyana*. Some writings of this class were definitely conceived of as Utopias, picturing ideal political or other institutions in some imaginary island, and by implication criticizing existing institutions.[69] Theopompus' *Meropis Ge* and Euhemerus' *Hiera Anagraphe* were probably of this character; Iambulus' Utopia, of which we have a revealing excerpt in Diodorus Siculus 2.55–60 and a characterization in Lucian, *True History* 1.3, probably reflected Stoic social doctrine. Sphaerus of Borysthenes, the first generation disciple of Zeno who was teacher to Cleomenes and so instigator of the social revolution at Sparta at the end of the third century BCE, is credited with such titles as *On Kingship, On the Spartan Polity, On Lycurgus and Socrates*.[70] The orderly and symmetrical distribution, layout, and management of land which was prescribed in the "Lycurgan" constitution to which the reformers urged a return, they had themselves doubtless contrived in a kind of Utopian *plasma*.[71] Now the description of Palestine in Aristeas frequently suggests a similar sand-table plan in a

[68] See E. Rohde, *Der griechische Roman und seine Vorläufer*² (Leipzig, 1900), 167–193.

[69] See Rohde, 194–241, and R. von Pöhlmann, *Geschichte der sozialen Fragen und des Sozialismus in der antiken Welt*, revised by F. Oertel (Munich, 1925).

[70] Diogenes Laertius 7.177 f. The same passage tells us that Sphaerus visited the court of Ptolemy Philadelphus and conversed with him.

[71] See my "The Social Revolution in Third Century Sparta," *Classical Weekly* 26 (1932), 65–68, 73–76.

lecture room. We get the impression of a symmetrical layout, with the capital on an eminence in the center, the tilth and orchard lands ideally plotted and socially administered, and the whole surrounded by barriers of mountains and a river. "When we reached the region"—which seems more appropriate as an introduction to a *terra incognita*—"we beheld the city situated in the center of all Judaea upon a mountain which rises to a lofty height." An ideally planned agriculture is suggested in 107 ff.; the emphasis on the fertility of the soil and the diversity of its vegetable and mineral products suggests an ideal rather than actuality, and such a statement as "around it flows the river called Jordan" (116) even completer disregard for easily ascertainable reality.

The rhetorical character of the entire section is demonstrated by the comparison of small cities and large, the experience of Judaea and that of Alexandria (108–11). The *synkrisis* or "comparison" was a fixed element in the rhetoricians' *progymnasmata*;[72] the specimens most familiar to readers are the "Comparisons" which are part of Plutarch's *Lives*. Whatever the direct influence of travel books and Utopias upon Aristeas may be, it is sufficient to prevent us from seeking to extort a date from the apparent prerogatives of the High Priest, who is an idealized ruler, or from the fact that the harbor cities apparently belong to Judaea (115) and Idumaea does not (107). Every reader would have recognized that he was dealing with an imaginative work and not a history claiming literal truth.

13. THE HIGH PRIEST'S DISCOURSE AND CYNIC HOMILIES

Another species of Hellenistic writing may be invoked to explain certain difficulties in the discourse of the High Priest Eleazar which follows (128–169). The *chreia* or "homily" was a regular production of Cynic and Stoic preachers which was remarkable for its outspoken frankness. The principal difficulty

---

[72] See 57, below.

in the High Priest's discourse lies in its outspoken condemnation of paganism (134 ff.) and especially of Egyptian theriolatry (138) and apparently incest (142): would a courtier of Ptolemy, elsewhere concerned to minimize religious differences (15-16) make room in his book for such criticism? It may be urged, in explanation, that its didacticism, sententiousness, and paradoxes make this discourse something of a *chreia*, and that the *chreia* always retained a certain license, in keeping with its Cynic origins.[73] Outspoken criticism of Greek ways might appropriately be put into the mouths of astute and distinguished foreigners, like Anacharsis.[74] Orators like Dio Chrysostom could refer to the Cynic Diogenes things they would not dare say before an Emperor in their own person, and if the author of Aristeas is the devout Jew we suppose him, it was a skillful stroke on his part to make the privileged High Priest the bearer of his criticism of paganism.

14. ARISTEAS AND THE ROMANCERS

In his concluding paragraph Aristeas makes a point of speaking disparagingly of the romancers, remarking that Philocrates, because of his more serious interests, would take greater pleasure in his narrative than in the books of the romancers. This indicates that Aristeas was at least aware of romances as a possible rival to his work, and indeed a number of aspects of the form of Aristeas are suggestive of the practice of the romances. When we come to discuss the literary form of Aristeas (56) we shall see that its closest affinity is in fact with that branch of literature. The description of the vessels, the discourse of the High Priest, the account of Judaea and the Temple, the Questions, are all *emblemata*—ornaments embedded in the narra-

---

[73] See Christ-Schmid-tählin, *Geschichte der griechischen Literatur* II, i⁶ (Munich, 1920), 54, and notes. It may be mentioned that Demetrius of Phalerum was known as a writer of *chreiai*.

[74] See Christ-Schmid-Stählin, 483 f., and Schmid in Pauly-Wissowa 1.2017 f.

tive to enrich it. But the narrative itself, so far as it has a plot which "marches," follows a Greek scheme of construction. The first part of the story, which sets forth the inception of the enterprise, is told in a series of documents—the king's edict of emancipation (22–25), the memorandum of Demetrius of Phalerum (29–32), the king's letter to Eleazar (35–40), and Eleazar's reply with its appended list of the names of the translators (41–50). Now it is a fixed element in later Greek fiction that events important for the plot are frequently set forth in letters or other documents; this is notably true of the *Alexander Romance*, which deals, in however distorted a fashion, with historical figures.[75] In the romances the denouement and assurance of the happy ending regularly take place before a multitude of spectators;[76] in Aristeas a minor denouement is the acclaim won by the sages at the close of the questioning, and a major denouement is the official approval of the translation. Both take place before a crowd of admiring spectators. It may be significant that III Maccabees, which shows many other points of contact with Aristeas, exhibits the same features of construction.[77]

15. ARISTEAS AND ALEXANDRIAN SCHOLARSHIP

The special interest we most frequently associate with Alexandrian science is literary scholarship. This involves establishment of correct texts, researches into literary history, investigations of obscure cult usages, such as have left their precipitate in our scholia. The pose of objective scholarship is very noticeable in Aristeas. His addresses to Philocrates at the beginning and end speak of the humane value of learning; he makes the requirements of the Library the occasion of the whole enterprise (there can be no question that the Scriptures were translated

[75] See Rohde, 184 ff.

[76] The use of this technique in Dio Chrysostom 7, "The Euboean Discourse," may here be cited, because of the ethical earnestness of the piece, a quality which the romances do not share.

[77] See M. Hadas, "III Maccabees and the Greek Romance," *Review of Religion* 13 (1949), 155–162.

INTRODUCTION 53

not for the Library but for the Egyptian Jewish community); the memorandum of Demetrius (29–32) speaks of the accuracy of textual recensions; and the author claims that he acquired information concerning Judaism from the learned priests of Egypt (6), which was a traditional procedure for curious Greeks from Herodotus downward, but a palpable absurdity for the author of Aristeas. There is a suggestion that his motives for being concerned about the emancipation of Egyptian Jews were mainly humanitarian, and for his interest in the Temple ritual mainly scholarly. His citation of the High Priest's apologia fits with the scholarly pose. Naturally the pose breaks down on occasion, most noticeably perhaps in his devout prayers when Ptolemy is considering the question of emancipation. From the point of view of dating, this aspect of Aristeas suggests an earlier, or at least Ptolemaic, rather than a later date. The period of flower of Hellenistic literary scholarship falls in the third century,[78] and though work of high scholarly competence continued to be done in later centuries, the general interest in such work declined rapidly after its first bloom.

16. RABBINIC AND PATRISTIC WRITERS ON ARISTEAS

The story of the Greek translation of the Bible underwent interesting vicissitudes and occurs in a number of Patristic writers, but these are all naturally later than Aristeas and plainly derive from his account. Rabbinic legends on the subject in the form in which they are preserved are similarly later than any possible dating for Aristeas. Whether these latter go back to an earlier or independent tradition must remain a matter of conjecture, as in the parallel case of Philo, discussed above (25). What the rabbis and the Fathers say of the Greek translation of the Bible, then, is of little relevance for dating Aristeas but interesting rather for the history of the propagation and development of the legend, a topic which will be treated below (73).

---

[78] See J. E. Sandys, *A History of Classical Scholarship*² (Cambridge, 1908), ch. 8.

VI

130 BCE as a Hypothetical Date

None of the external evidence here cited provides anything like conclusive proof of dating, but their cumulative tendency definitely points in the direction of a Ptolemaic and perhaps even an early Ptolemaic period. It would seem reasonable to follow this direction as far as it is not blocked by other considerations. Since the objections adduced from internal evidence are all equivocal in nature, the only real check is linguistic usage, and there is nothing in Aristeas' linguistic usage which compels a dating below 150 BCE. If, as seems not unlikely, the version referred to in Aristeas is indeed a revision and Ben Sirah's objection refers to the unrevised version,[79] it would seem most reasonable to assign a date shortly after 132 BCE for the composition of Aristeas. On the basis of the evidence of our book itself and of the external and internal history of the Greek-speaking Jews such a date seems least liable to objection.

But in the opinion of the present writer precise dating of such a work as Aristeas is of less consequence than has generally been supposed, because neither the author of the book nor its first readers would have regarded it as other than an imaginative work of literature. We shall now endeavor to determine the category of literature to which Aristeas belongs, whence we may infer the quality of belief which it might claim.

VII

Aristeas as a Greek Book

The preceding pages will have shown certain points of contact of Aristeas with secular writings of the Hellenistic period, and these contacts in turn suggest an approach to the book as a whole somewhat different from the traditional approach. Be-

---

[79] See Section IX, below.

INTRODUCTION 55

cause its principal burden seems to be the account of the genesis of the LXX, Aristeas has been studied chiefly for the light it throws upon Hellenistic Judaism and Christian origins. It has usually been associated with non-canonical writings on the periphery of Scripture, as in the collections of Charles and Kautzsch, and has been subjected to the criticism appropriate to such works. But Aristeas is neither a translation from a Semitic original, nor does it follow the forms of Semitic writings. The prime factor in the criticism of Aristeas is that, to a unique degree in the literature with which it has been associated, it is a Greek book. The author makes obvious pretensions to literary expertness and expects an audience of practised Greek readers. He shows and expects familiarity with such literary figures as Demetrius of Phalerum, Hecataeus, Menedemus, Theopompus, Theodectes, and with the techniques and scope of technical literary scholarship. He uses poetic tags (*e.g.*, 2) and the ideas or actual terminology of Peripatetics, Stoics, Euhemerus, and other Hellenistic philosophies. His scenes are laid with elegance in the greatest cultural metropolis of the Hellenistic world and the most interesting (at least to him and his readers) center of exotic civilization, and the most magnificent royalty of the Hellenistic world is made to play a part. Not only are the structure of the book as a whole and its component parts (as indicated above) "literary" in character, but the style, in vocabulary and syntax as well as allusiveness, is similarly "literary." This appears even to the lay reader at once in the highly formalized and self-conscious proem, and in the conclusion which is its pendant—features that at once proclaim that the author is following an artistic literary tradition. The "literary" nature of the book becomes most obvious to the non-professional reader, perhaps, in the extraordinary variety of expressions used, in introducing each of the seventy-two questions, to paraphrase the single fact that the king thanked the man who had just spoken and proceeded to direct another question to the man next in order. Nor are the expressions of extreme courtesy used throughout the book calculated to convey the impression of a straightforward chronicle. In an age when literary craftsmanship was extremely conscious of itself it is inconceivable that a professed writer should ignore the canon of the schools. If, then, we could determine what Aristeas' affinities in pagan literature are, we should get some light on the author's intentions with respect to its historicity. We should know, specifically, whether he expected his work to be received as literal truth, as wholly imaginary, or as an imaginative treatment of basic truth.

First of all it must be noticed that the document is not a letter, despite the virtual unanimity of modern editors and translators in styling it such.[80] The superscription is simply "Aristeas to Philocrates," and none of the ancients who mention the work speak of it as a letter.[81] Philocrates is addressed in the vocative in the opening sentence, at the close, and at the end of long sections within the book, but this is rather proof that it is not a letter than otherwise.[82] Many essays of Plutarch which have nothing of the epistolary character similarly compliment an addressee, and on the other hand, writings of Seneca which maintain an epistolary character do not follow this form. This, then, is not a letter, where deviations from veracity would simply mark the author as an impostor or plagiarist. The author himself introduces his work as a *diēgēsis* (Latin, *narratio*) of his deputation to the High Priest Eleazar, and it is as a *diēgēsis* that we must consider it.

Now the *diēgēsis* along with the *ekphrasis* and the *chreia* of

[80] The texts and translations of Wendland, Thackeray, Andrews, Meecham, Tramontano, Cahana (see listing at 86 below) all bear the word "Letter" in their titles.

[81] Josephus, *Ant.* 12.100 calls it τὸ 'Αρισταίου βιβλίον, "the book of Aristaeus"; Eusebius, *Praep. Ev.* 9.38, περὶ τῆς ἑρμηνείας τοῦ τῶν "Ιουδαίων νόμου, "on the interpretation of the law of the Jews"; Epiphanius, *De mensuris et ponderibus* 9, σύνταγμα "composition." A XIV century MS (Q) which contains some fragments of *Aristeas* first uses the word "letter" with reference to it—ἐπιστολῆς 'Αριστέως πρὸς Φιλοκράτην ἔκφρασις: see Thackeray in Swete, 542; Meecham, *Oldest Version*, 88, 204; Tramontano, 10.

[82] See Dziatzko s.v. *Brief*, Pauly-Wissowa 3.836–843 (1897).

which we have spoken above, as well as other recognized forms, were elements in the *progymnasmata*, or rhetorical and literary curriculum.[83] Most of what we know of *progymnasmata* derives from the rhetorician Theon,[84] who lived in the second century C.E. but who is surely retailing traditional material. Theon declares (70.25) that the canon must be followed not only by intending rhetors but by writers in various categories.[85] The διήγησις Theon defines (78.15) as λόγος ἐκθετικὸς πραγμάτων γεγονότων ἢ ὡς γεγονότων—"a discourse expository of things which happened or might have happened."[86]

The distinction between a continuous chronological history and a *narratio* is set forth by Cicero, without doubt in accord with ancient principles of criticism, in his invitation to Lucceius to write a treatise on his life (*Ad Familiares* 5.12). Whereas history serves *veritas* and *utilitas*, a *narratio* may supply *delectatio* also.[87] The ancient canon of veracity for such treatises is clearly stated by the grammarian Asclepiades of Myrlea,[88] in Sextus Empiricus, *Adversus Grammaticos* 252. Three categories of truth are set down: ἀληθὴς ἱστορία, ψευδὴς ἱστορία, and ὡς ἀληθὴς ἱστορία, πλάσματα.[89] The first two categories would apply to what is literally true or wholly imaginary; the third (*plasma*) to an imaginative treatment of history which should however

---

[83] On the whole subject see G. Reichel, *Quaestiones Progymnasmaticae* (Leipzig, 1909).

[84] Ed. C. E. Finckh, *Theonis Sophistae Progymnasmata* (Stuttgart, 1834); citations are by page and line of Finckh.

[85] Quintilian 3.8.49, echoing Theon, says that this *exercitatio* is *utilissima*: *poetis quoque aut historiarum futuris scriptoribus plurimum confert*.

[86] The identical definition is given by the Latins: Cicero, *De Inventione* 1.19.27, *narratio est rerum gestarum aut ut gestarum expositio;* Auctor ad Herennium 1.3.4, *narratio est rerum gestarum aut proinde ut gestarum expositio;* Quintilian 4.21.31, *narratio est rei factae aut ut factae utilis ad persuadendum expositio*.

[87] *Cf.* similar remark in Polybius 10.21.

[88] See B. A. Mueller, *De Asclepiade Myrleano* (Leipzig, 1903). Asclepiades himself wrote travel books of the kind mentioned in V, 12 above.

[89] So the Cynic Timon could indicate that he doubted everything by saying that he applied this canon: "So it all seems to me to be a fable, now that I have a correct canon of truth" (Sextus Empiricus, *Adv. Mathematicos* 11.20).

preserve historical verisimilitude and present a higher "poetical" truth.[90] One thinks of Aristotle's dictum that poetry is truer than history (*Poetics* 1451b). A conscious literary artist might then, like the tragic poets, enhance "historical" legend and characters by whatever means might serve a higher poetical truth, and his audience would understand that the treatment might be imaginative but that the moral or ethical burden of the piece was to be accepted seriously. Inconsistencies in a work like Aristeas are not then marks of bad faith or even necessarily of faulty scholarship, but of indifference or at worst negligence.

We have noted above that the largest single section of our book has close affinities with the popular treatises on kingship, that the description of Palestine and the Temple may have been influenced by the popular Utopias, that the inventory of the royal gifts is of the nature of a rhetorical *ekphrasis*, that the discourse of the High Priest is like a Cynic-Stoic *chreia*, the comparison of Jerusalem and Alexandria a regular *synkrisis*, and that the narrative as a whole shows some of the characteristics of the romance. Altogether every considerable section of Aristeas finds a parallel in some·traditional aspect of imaginative writing in the Hellenistic and succeeding periods, and the style of the work as a whole points to a writer of belles-lettres rather than of history.

If the literary character of the book and its secular parallels do not help us fix a decisive date for it, they do show that the problem of dating is largely academic. Aristeas is a *plasma*, and its chief purpose, in the intention of the author and the understanding of the reader, is to produce a general ethical effect rather than to communicate trustworthy historical data. The author is neither the impostor or plagiarist we should have to

[90] *Cf.* R. Reitzenstein, *Hellenistische Wundererzählungen* (Leipzig, 1906), 84 ff. For a thorough treatment of the relations between history and imaginative literature see B. L. Ullman, "History and Tragedy," *Transactions and Proceedings of the American Philological Association* 73 (1942), 25–53.

label him if we thought that he expected his implications as to his own person and date to be believed. Nor are we constrained to resort to a theory of interpolations. All that fixing the limits of date can contribute to our historical evaluation of his account is to determine the limits of the period of which he could have direct knowledge, and, by corollary, to assign a date to the theologic and social views he expresses. His views of Judaism and of the relationship which should subsist between the Jews and their neighbors are perhaps of greater interest, as they are certainly more fully treated, than the matter of the translation of the Greek Bible. The analogy of the structure of other books, indeed, might suggest that the theme of the translation is designed as a "historical" framework to serve as a vehicle for other matter.

VIII

Aristeas on Judaism and the Jews

An unprejudiced reader to whom Aristeas is presented as an account of the genesis of LXX must be puzzled by the relatively slight space allotted to this theme in the book. The writer's declaration of intention in the opening sentence speaks indeed of a deputation, but gives no hint of its purpose. Demetrius of Phalerum's proposal (9-11) seems rather a peg on which to hang the story of the liberation of the Jews of Egypt. Paragraphs 28 to 51 are germane to the question of the translation, as they include Demetrius' memorandum and the letters of Philadelphus and Eleazar; we then have a long digression on the Temple and Jerusalem, after which the author assures us (120) that "in what follows I shall give you an account of the translation." But the merits of the translators are lauded in two sentences, and it is only at 176-177, when Philadelphus welcomes the translators at Alexandria, that we hear that they had brought elegant scrolls of the Law with them. The actual work of translation is dealt with in only two sentences (302-307), and there are a half-dozen others on the reception of the translators. Insofar, indeed, as the book has a single guiding thread of major interest to which digressions however disproportionate are attached, that thread is the story of the LXX. But the disproportion nevertheless suggests that the LXX theme may be regarded as an embellishment for a work of more general interest, for which that theme itself presents the best illustration of the views which the author wished to set forth.

Broadly speaking, Aristeas is obviously in the tradition of "apologetic" Alexandrian Jewish writings whose general aim was to demonstrate the high antiquity and respectability of Judaism, for the purpose of strengthening the self-esteem of the Jews themselves and perhaps heightening their esteem in the eyes of their dominant environment.[91] It was part of this tradition to show that the Jews had possessed a highly developed polity in high antiquity, that Greek sages had learned from Jewish teachers and Jewish writings, that eminent kings and philosophers had acknowledged the merits of Jewish claims. Works that are purely belletristic, such as the tragedy on the Exodus by Ezekielos or the epic of the Elder Philo, merely demonstrate that Jewish tradition affords literary materials comparable to the Greek. Historians, like Demetrius, Eupolemus, or Artapanus, and culminating in Josephus, demonstrated the antiquity of the Jewish polity by narrating its early history directly. Pseudepigrapha, like Phocylides or the *Sibylline Oracles*, and philosophical and exegetical works, culminating in Philo, showed that Jewish legislation is of a high ethical order such as might be approved by Greek thinkers. Aristeas affords

---

[91] In a well-informed article entitled *Roshe Perakim l'Hikur ha-Safrut ha-Yehudit ha-Alexandronit, Sefer Levi* (Jerusalem, 1949), 139–160, A. Tcherikover presents just and timely objections to the cliché repeated by virtually all scholars that the Alexandrian Jewish literature was addressed to non-Jewish readers and was "apologetic" in nature. He shows that they cannot have entered the general book trade, which was concerned solely with the classics, and maintains that their contents, when considered against the respective backgrounds of their several dates, demonstrate that they were addressed to Jews.

illustration of all three elements, and yet has a unique quality of his own. To a greater degree than other writers in the tradition he seems secure in his convictions and his status, less on the defensive, less fearful of his structure's being suddenly shattered, under less constraint to make himself agreeable to the gentiles. In part this difference of attitude is due to his device of making his spokesman a professed pagan and then looking upon Judaism and the Jews from an imagined pagan point of view. But this is not the full explanation, and indeed, his choice of a pagan mask is rather an indication of his general position than its cause.

That position is one of great latitude—indeed of laxity, from the stricter standpoint of such a book as III Maccabees. The toleration, both on the part of the Jews and of the pagans be it noted, is not the toleration of sufferance but of mutual respect. And on both sides the respect is earned, not bestowed as a bounty or extorted by *force majeure* or the sheer weight of tradition. The king's letter to the High Priest reveals more genuine regard than the formal courtesy which a powerful king can afford to show an inferior, and the High Priest's reply demonstrates that he has pondered the matter and determined it upon its merits; he is not merely yielding to the caprice of a more powerful overlord. When he receives the company of translators and entertains them, the king is not lionizing exotic freaks or prudentially showing consideration out of political expediency. The men merit his esteem by reason of their own worth, and they are careful to say that it is his worth as well as his position which elicits their esteem. The peculiarities of their dining habits are neither made conspicuous nor brushed aside. Many nations have like peculiarities, and the royal ménage is fully organized to meet various requirements. There is no need for Jews either to dissemble or to take the opposite course of calling attention to their own usages. Indeed, in the social and official intercourse as depicted in Aristeas there is not even any question of tolerance: men of differing traditions understand one another and, recognizing their differences, live together in harmony.

But it is in the professed apologia for the Law, as uttered by the High Priest (at 128 ff.), that Aristeas' latitudinarianism appears most clearly. The allegorical interpretation of the Law contains no hint that its observance can be dispensed with or need be apologized for; but it is made clear that observance of the ritual is not for its own sake but for the sake of a higher religious view of life which ritual observances symbolize and protect. The theology premised is applicable to all mankind, not to the Jews alone, and God's providence is universal. It is not suggested that God will show special consideration for the Jews simply by virtue of their being Jews, nor is there any hint of proselytization, which would be the logical conclusion of belief in an exclusive providence on the one hand and concern for the welfare of non-Jews on the other. The Jews follow their own traditional usages to attain a religious end; the same end may be attained by others by a different path. If the High Priest speaks scornfully of unenlightened pagans, enlightened pagans would have done the same. When he derides Euhemerism he was not alone in his own day, nor was he alone in speaking against theriolatry and other superstitions. There is no hint of either truculence or cringing, and the impression of the treatise as a whole is of a communion secure in its self-respect and not uneasy in regard to the attitudes of others. The creed is ethical and universalist. It rests upon revelation and entails special responsibilities for the recipients of revelation, but they are not the exclusive objects of providence, and the special observances required of them are meritorious not for their own sake but as ensuring a higher and more consistent observance of ethical rules. The homeland and the Temple and its cult are central, but mainly as the paramount element in Jewish history and as a manifestation of God's continuing interest in that history. The principal element in Judaism remains its spiritual character: by intention or otherwise the Judaism of Aristeas is of a form that could survive loss of national independence and even of the central sanctuary. Though the divine origin of the Law is stressed and the special responsibility of the Jews is related to revelation, yet greater prominence seems to be given Moses as a lawgiver devising legislation under general rather than specific and detailed inspiration. Possibly because of the usage and associations of the Greek word *nomothetes* a greater measure of independent authority—analogous to that of a Solon or a Lycurgus—seems to inhere in Moses than would be implied in rabbinic literature. This too is in keeping with the usages of the Hellenistic tradition. In works on ancient Near-Eastern peoples written in Greek there was a tendency for a single individual hero—Semiramis for the Assyrians, Ninus for the Babylonians, Sesostris for the Egyptians, Manes for the Phrygians—to be made the exemplar and bearer of the disparate national traditions.[92] In the Greek Jewish literature written at Alexandria Moses appears to have served a similar function. He seems to have occupied a chief place in the historians and perhaps more significantly in belletristic works such as those of Ezekielos and the Elder Philo. Perhaps its special association with Moses was a contributory reason for the special concern of the Alexandrian community with the Pentateuch. It may not be too extreme to suggest that whereas in the usual tradition the greatness of Moses is a reflection of the Law with which his name is associated, the Alexandrians may have regarded the Law merely as another illustration of the greatness of the national hero.

Books are not written in a vacuum, and Aristeas' views of Jews and Judaism cannot have been merely his own but must reflect the unique social, intellectual, and spiritual climate of the Egyptian Jews in the second century BCE, when their numbers and prestige had made them a considerable element in the population and before anti-Semitism had raised its head. Aristeas shows us that the Egyptian Jews embraced the dominant culture enthusiastically, and assimilated their own to it to the extent of adopting its social usages, literary forms, and philosophical beliefs insofar as they were not in direct opposition to

---

[92] Admirably pointed out in M. Braun, *History and Romance in Graeco-Oriental Literature* (Oxford, 1938). *Cf.* my "Aeneas and the Tradition of the National Hero," *American Journal of Philology* 69 (1948), 408 ff.

central religious tenets of their own.[93] The High Priest himself is praised as a *kalokagathos* (3), which may fairly be rendered "a Greek gentleman," and the translators are distinguished for their *paideia* (121), which means their Greek culture. The Jews of Alexandria felt at home in their world and saw no reason to apprehend a change in their condition. Apologetics proper and the impulse to proselytization, which is only an exaggerated defense, came a century later, at the end of the Hellenistic and the beginning of the Roman period, when anti-Semitic attacks such as Josephus confronts in *Against Apion* called forth the vigorous responses which culminate in Josephus himself. Aristeas itself is neither apologetic nor evangelic.

It is because the Alexandrian Jews looked forward to an untroubled continuance of their prosperous state that they could separate themselves from close concern with contemporary Palestine. All references to that country in Aristeas envisage a remote and idealized Biblical Palestine and seem purposely to ignore contemporary reality. There were of course no twelve tribes from which translators could be chosen; and similarly the site of the Temple on a mountain top, its orientation and its water supply, the priestly vestments and other details (83 ff.) derive not from contemporary actuality but from idealized biblical allusions.[94] The Jordan is said to flood (117) not on the analogy of the Nile, but because Joshua 3.16 said it did, and in language (in LXX) which Aristeas clearly echoes. It is the Bible which is now the central factor in Jewish survival, and Palestine is of interest as comprising, as it were, a part of the Bible.

We might indeed surmise that the thoroughly "emancipated" Alexandrians would find distasteful or uncomfortable the orthodoxy or nationalism or parochialism or general intensity of their Palestinian brethren, and especially of such as had but recently

[93] For the material that follows, to the end of the section, I am deeply indebted to suggestions in Tcherikover's *Ha-Maza ha-Ideologi shel Iggeret Aristeas*, in *Sefer Dinaburg* (Jerusalem, 1949), 83–101. Tcherikover kindly sent me the working copy of this paper while the present work was in preparation.

[94] See Commentary *ad loc.*

arrived and were not yet integrated in the modern community. Perhaps the dissatisfaction with the Greek version of the Bible expressed by Sirah's grandson, newly arrived in Egypt, is a reflection of the tension between the two groups. In Aristeas itself it is said that the translators "eschewed a crude and uncouth disposition" and "avoided conceit and the assumption of superiority over others" (122). This may well represent the Alexandrian attitude to the highly self-conscious Palestinians.[95]

But if prosperity and tranquillity provided no impulse to apologetics and proselytization, neither did it provide temptation to apostasy. In all that pertained to outward life the best that the environment had to offer was to be embraced wholeheartedly, but assimilation was not to go so far as rejecting the hereditary religion. "Our lawgiver fenced us about with impregnable palisades and with walls of iron, to the end that we should mingle in no way with any of the other nations, remaining pure in body and in spirit, emancipated from vain opinions, revering the one and mighty God above the whole of creation" (139). This seems a strange contradiction indeed to the bland equation of Zeus with God in 18. But to Aristeas and his readers there was no inconsistency. They found it reasonable to suppose that a Judaism divorced from nationalism and so interpreted as to be free of offense to the best current philosophical thought was not only adequate as a religion but did in fact represent the intentions of Moses.

If the teachings of Aristeas are as they are here represented, it becomes all the more evident that the book was addressed not to pagan but to Jewish readers. The attention to Greek forms, including the mask of pseudonymity, was in keeping with the cultivated tastes of the Alexandrian Jewish community, and is in itself a manifestation of the author's doctrine. If we assume a Jewish audience, certain questionable points have their explanation. Surely a pagan reader would

[95] *Cf.* Tcherikover, *op. cit.* in note 93, p. 89; and Menahem Stein, "Baal Iggeret Aristeas k'Sanegor shel ha-Yahadut," in *Zion*, N.S. 1 (1926), 132 ff.

penetrate Aristeas' pagan mask at once, and only be amused by the picture of Ptolemy Philadelphus bowing down seven times before the Law and showing the translators such unexampled reverence. It would be very strange, moreover, that a High Priest explaining Jewish peculiarities to a presumed pagan would omit entirely those practices which struck pagans most forcibly—circumcision, observance of Sabbaths and major festivals, abstinence from pork—and have applied himself rather to an exposition of lesser matters, such as the significance of the cloven-hoofed and ruminant beasts, herbivorous and carnivorous fowl, *zizit* and *mezuzot*. The explanation is simple. The Jews of Alexandria had not yet come to question the major observances (by Philo's day they would question even these), and it was the less striking aspects which invited interpretation, and by a system of allegory in the direction of a universal ethic.

IX

Aristeas on the Septuagint

Despite its numerous digressions the central theme of our book remains the account of the origin of the Greek translation of the Pentateuch. Indeed it is doubtless due to Aristeas that the name *Septuagint*, properly applicable only to the Pentateuch, came to be applied to the entire Greek Bible. But Aristeas clearly implies that the translation was made immediately before he wrote, and his evidence would seem to be vitiated by the fact that the translation had long been in existence before Aristeas wrote. Actual LXX phraseology is used in the description of the table, even where LXX differs from the Hebrew (see on 57), and of the High Priest's vestments, and there are echoes of LXX (and not alone of the Pentateuch) elsewhere. The king himself, before the translation was made, orders that in details where the Law prescribes the plan of the table those prescriptions must be followed (56). Moreover in Demetrius' memorandum to the king it is said, with what appears to be calculated ambiguity (30), that the books had previously been "interpreted" somewhat carelessly. It is hard to see why either the king or his librarian should be concerned with the state of the Hebrew text (where royal "forethought" would in any case not apply); what must be meant is the inadequacy of an earlier translation. Again, the fourth-century writers Theopompus and Theodectes are represented as having familiarity with Scripture (314–316), which they could only have obtained through a Greek translation. Furthermore, the imprecations ordained by Jewish officials against any who should alter the text (310–311) surely imply antecedent differences of opinion concerning its merits and validity. It is hard to imagine such stringent decrees to enforce the authority of a version unless its authority had been questioned. There is also external evidence that the LXX Pentateuch had obtained currency by the latter part of the third century. The historian Demetrius, for example, who wrote under Ptolemy IV Philopator (222–205 BCE), and whom Josephus (*Against Apion* 1.23) confuses with Demetrius of Phalerum, took the LXX Pentateuch as the basis for his chronology of the Bible.

What, then, is the relationship of Aristeas to the Greek Bible? Of the numerous theories which have been advanced two are of special interest. Moses Gaster[96] has maintained that the Pentateuch was translated into Greek neither under Ptolemy Philadelphus nor in Alexandria, but at an earlier period and in Palestine; that it was subsequently brought to Alexandria, where the Jews used it as the basis for the claim that offerings, including the official offerings of the king, should be sent to Jerusalem, in opposition to the Samaritan claim—based upon their version of the Pentateuch—that offerings should be sent to Mount Gerizim; that the matter was adjudicated by Phila-

[96] M. Gaster, *The Samaritans* (London, 1925), 112 ff.

delphus in favor of the Jews; and that in consequence the version known as LXX received canonical status and Philadelphus was celebrated as its patron. Against the generally accepted position that the translation was evoked by the requirements of the Jewish community of Egypt which had forgotten Hebrew, Gaster argues that the Jews brought to Alexandria by Alexander and the first Ptolemy were slaves whose only interest in Greek was to hate it, and that in any case only the Hebrew original could be acceptable for synagogue use. (Both these premises are subject to grave question.) The occurrence of Egyptian-Greek words and phrases in the LXX, Gaster points out, are no valid argument for an Egyptian origin, for such expressions would naturally creep in when the LXX later became the Bible of the Egyptian Jews. In favor of a Palestinian origin he argues from the need for an effective piece of apologetic to stem the flood of Hellenism and to provide an answer to Greek pretensions. It is well known that the LXX exhibits traces of Palestinian exegesis, and S. Lieberman has now demonstrated that the rabbis of Mishna and Talmud, and presumably their predecessors, were familiar with Greek.[97] Only a Palestinian origin, Gaster holds, would invest a version with the requisite authority for acceptance in the diaspora. It was naturally used by the Alexandrian Jews to counter the claims of the Samaritans, and the fact that it was effective in so vital an issue would endow it with high authority and generate such a body of legend as is contained in Aristeas. Gaster's theory is more ingenious than convincing. It is very clear in view of their attitude to the world about them and to Judaism, as set forth above, that the Alexandrian Jews would absolutely require a Greek version of the Bible and actually prefer it to the original whether or not they could read Hebrew. On the one hand the Bible had become their sole bond with Judaism, to which, with proper universalization, they were determined to cling; and on the other hand, they were ill at ease with the loyalties which the use of Hebrew seemed to

[97] S. Lieberman, *Greek in Jewish Palestine* (New York, 1942).

involve. That is why Aristeas emphasizes the crescendo of approval given to the Greek version—first by the selection of accredited translators representing all the tribes and vested with the High Priest's sanction, then by the Jewish community acting in its official capacity, then by the king, then by heaven itself, who is invoked in the imprecation. But if Gaster's theory is not acceptable, the problem of explaining the interval between the production of the Greek version and Aristeas' assertion of its authority becomes more pressing.

The ardor with which the validity of the translation is asserted does indeed seem to reflect a present crisis. Paul Kahle[98] agrees that the LXX is much older than Aristeas, and points out that people "do not make propaganda for something a hundred years old." He concludes, therefore, that what is involved in Aristeas is a *revised* version of the LXX, which is here being given exclusive authority over the unrevised version and perhaps over rival revisions. We have indeed anced inkling of dissatisfaction with the LXX from Ben Sirah, who says in his *Prologue*: "For things originally spoken in Hebrew have not the same force in them when they are translated into another tongue; and not only these, but the Law itself, and the prophecies, and the rest of the books, have no small difference when they are spoken in the original language." This *Prologue* is dated to 132 BCE, and a revision of the existing translations, made at roughly the same period and endowed with official authorization, may be the answer to such dissatisfaction as is expressed by Ben Sirah. It is likely, Gaster to the contrary notwithstanding, that a Greek version was required and made by the Jews of Egypt shortly after their numbers were so greatly increased by Ptolemy I's increments. It is unlikely that the version should receive official authorization from the outset (the Targumim provide analogy). Opinions concerning its

[98] P. Kahle, *The Cairo Geniza* (London, 1947), 112 ff. Kahle was apparently unaware that he had been anticipated in his surmise by B. Motzo (see note 33, above).

merits must have changed in the course of time, and individual alterations were probably introduced. Eventually, to prevent chaos and answer a communal need, sanction was given to the revision which is the basis of our LXX text as the sole authorized version.

Kahle's theory offers a plausible and perhaps correct explanation for a late second-century effort to give the LXX authority, but certain elements in the story of the translation, such as Ptolemy Philadelphus' connection with the enterprise and the number of translators employed in it, remain to be accounted for. These and other impressive details would naturally cluster about the work and form a legend in the course of a century, and the legend may have been fostered and crystallized by teachers and preachers who sought to enhance the prestige of the translation, midrashic hyperbole eventually assuming the character of history. Aristeas certainly had before him a tradition concerning the translation of the Law which had been made in the third century, and this tradition probably involved the number of translators (perhaps seventy rather than seventy-two: see 39, above) and other semi-miraculous details. Possibly the names of Demetrius of Phalerum and Ptolemy Philadelphus were in the tradition. Philadelphus' was a natural name to associate with the story: he was the *Grand Monarque* of the Ptolemies, he was a great patron of literature and concerned with establishing correct texts, and he was friendly to the Jews. But it is quite possible that the introduction of Philadelphus was Aristeas' own invention, suggested by the famous edict of Philadelphus of which Aristeas made use in his account of the emancipation (see 30, above). This is particularly likely to be the case if the main object of Aristeas is rather to produce a general work of propaganda, advocating certain attitudes for Jews and gentiles, with the account of the translation only one element in his work. For a general work of propaganda Philadelphus is clearly the most suitable figure, if only because the emancipation of the Egyptian Jews could be attributed to him, and if he is the central figure in the book as a whole, he must be the central figure in the story of the translation.[99]

Seventy-two as the number of translators, as of the days required for the translation, is more patently legendary embroidery. Seventy was the traditional number for a supreme council, both for the Sanhedrin and for other bodies.[100] The basis of the tradition is doubtless the body of seventy elders which Moses set up. At Ex. 24.11 where the elders are spoken of and where the Hebrew gives "And upon the nobles of the children of Israel He laid not His hand," the LXX gives "And of the chosen ones of Israel not one perished." The verb used is *diaphōnein*, of which the common meaning is "disagreed." Such a homonym is ideal material for midrashic ingenuity. The

[99] [This story that seventy-two elders were sent by Eleazar to Alexandria may or may not be historically true, but that the Pentateuch was translated in the time of Ptolemy Philadelphus seems to be a historical fact. This translation of the Hebrew Bible into Greek was not brought about by Ptolemy but by the Jews themselves. Most of the Jews of the privileged class did not speak nor understand Hebrew, having been reared in an environment of Greek culture, and it was therefore necessary to have the Bible translated into the language they spoke. There was another reason, moreover, that might help to explain the translation of the Holy Scriptures into the vernacular at this time; a reason sinister in its import. At that time, a Greek-Egyptian historian, Manetho by name, wrote a history of Egypt in Greek. In this history he accused the Jews of having been expelled from Egypt in the days of the Pharaohs because of leprosy. The Jews of Alexandria wanted their fellow-citizens to know that they had not been driven out of Egypt because of leprosy, but had gone out of their own free will. They sought also to impress their neighbors with the antiquity of the Jewish race, and the glory of their history. They desired, furthermore, to exalt their past by emulating the great lawgiver and philosopher of their people, Moses. They sought, therefore, to uncover the treasury of the Bible and make its splendors accessible to the Hellenists. The Ptolemaic Court was pleased with the idea that the Jews were translating their sacred Book into Greek, for this fitted in with their general policy of Hellenization. The purpose of this policy was undoubtedly to make the different racial groups independent of their mother countries. The translation of the Hebrew Bible into Greek was favored by the Ptolemies because, in the study of their sacred books, it made the Alexandrian Jews independent of Jerusalem. (S. Z.)]

[100] Josephus chose 70 men to be rulers of Galilee (*Jewish War* 2.570), and the Zealots in Jerusalem set up a tribunal of 70 (*ibid.* 4.336).

context in Exodus is the solemn transmission of the Law, for which the elders represented the people. No better verse could be imagined to prove the unanimity and demonstrate the authority of a new transmission of the Law; and since the representatives of the people numbered seventy in the one case, it is easy to see how they came to number seventy in the other. Perhaps this midrashic turn was employed when the revision which Kahle posits required ratification; more likely it is earlier. Seventy-two (as distinguished from seventy) is perhaps Aristeas' own invention,[101] but the two numbers are frequently confused. Thus at *Ant.* 12.57 Josephus gives the number of translators as seventy, though in the preceding sentence he says there were six from each of twelve tribes. If Moses and Aaron are added to the seventy at Ex. 24.1, 9 and Num. 11.16, we have seventy-two. At Enoch 89.59 the shepherds number seventy, but at 90.1 half of them are thirty-six. At Luke 10.1 "seventy-two" is a variant reading. So in *Massekhet Sopherim* 1.9 readings vary between "seventy" and "seventy-two." That same treatise (1.8) says that the translation was carried out by *five* scholars, and this is highly probable, for our text shows indications that each book of the Pentateuch was translated by a separate hand.[102]

Though the two most striking circumstances which Aristeas relates in connection with the translation are thus shown to be unhistorical, it may not be amiss to point out that as a *diēgēsis* Aristeas is still not to be discredited and that even these two circumstances may possess a certain poetical truth. If the connection of the king and the library as stated in Aristeas is an invented device to give higher prestige to the translation and to show that the literature of the Jews was comparable to other literary treasures preserved and studied in the library, it is a

[101] We have seen that Aristeas may have chosen the multiple of 12 nearest 70 to conform to the 12 emissaries in Ezra 6.17 and 8.16 (above, 39), and that royal questions were traditionally in groups of 10 (above, 42).

[102] This view of Z. Frankel, *Ueber den Einfluss der paläst. Exegese* (1851) has met with wide approval; see 81 below.

INTRODUCTION 73

probable enough tale that the king and his royal librarian showed an interest in the enterprise, certainly after it was completed and perhaps even when it was planned. And if the actual work was performed by a smaller number, they were an authorized body and comparable in function to Moses' seventy. Significantly, the welcome accorded the translation by the Jewish community and the authority given it by the officials of that community are mentioned first and at length, and its presentation to the king comes afterwards. This is a clear enough index of the main object of the translation, which should be obvious enough in any case: the translation was made to meet the needs of the Greek-speaking community of Egyptian Jews, and only secondarily, if at all, for the edification of non-Jewish readers. Aristeas' main purpose, insofar as it relates to the LXX, is equally obvious: it is to give official authority to the Greek version of the Bible, and probably not that made in the third century but a revision nearly contemporary with the date of Aristeas.

X

The Septuagint Legend after Aristeas

The account of the growth of the legend concerning the genesis of the Greek Bible as presented in Aristeas has of necessity been based largely on conjecture. Certain accounts posterior to Aristeas—most notably, as we have seen, Philo's—may have drawn on a pre-existent body of tradition on which Aristeas himself drew; certain elements in the rabbinic tradition, for example, especially where that tradition diverges from Aristeas, may derive from such an independent source. But the literary works in which the tradition finds expression are all posterior to Aristeas (for the doubtful case of Aristobulus see 26, above), and unless there appears to be reason for a contrary opinion, it is natural to assume that they are in some sense dependent on Aristeas. This is more obviously the case with writers of

Greek, chiefly Christian, but it is altogether possible that knowledge of Aristeas penetrated to the rabbis also, of whom we now know that they possessed fuller familiarity with Greek than had previously been credited to them. We turn first to the Greek tradition as being the older. Aristobulus, Philo, and Josephus, the Jewish bearers of the Greek tradition, have been dealt with above (18–27); after them the Greek tradition is naturally carried by Christian writers.[103]

Of these the first in point of time is Justin Martyr (*ca.* 100–165). Speaking of the spread of Scripture among Christians Justin says (*Apology* 1.31):

Now when Ptolemy, the king of the Egyptians, was forming a library and endeavored to make a collection of all men's writings, he heard tell, among the rest, of these prophecies, and sent to Herod who was then king of the Jews with a request that the books of the prophecies might be transmitted to him. And king Herod sent them, written in their native Hebrew tongue of which I have spoken. But, since the Egyptians were unacquainted with the things written therein, he sent yet again and requested him to dispatch men to render them into the Greek language. This was done and the books remained with the Egyptians and are there to this day.

The twofold embassy, first for the books and then for the translators, is a natural expansion of Aristeas, nor is the mention of Herod remarkable, for to a second-century Christian Herod would be the Jewish ruler *par excellence*. (In point of fact the Alexandrian library was no longer in existence in Herod's day.) The reference to "prophecies" is similarly quite natural but marks a definite stage in the growth of the legend: LXX henceforward refers to the entire Bible, and not, as it properly should,

---

[103] The relevant texts are printed in the *Testimonia* of Wendland's ed. (85–166) and for the most part translated in Thackeray's S.P.C.K. version (101 ff.); the tranlsations given below are drawn or adapted from Thackeray. The passages are discussed fully in Tramontano 193 ff., and more briefly in Meecham, *Oldest Version* 125 ff.

to the Pentateuch alone. The statement that "the books remained with the Egyptians and are there to this day" might but need not suggest a source other than Aristeas. Justin is either using a "memory" version of Aristeas supplemented by *cicerone* details, or the whole is from a *cicerone* who used a "memory" version. Another reference in Justin is in his *Dialogue with the Jew Trypho* (68), where, rejecting the version of Aquila, he speaks of "the translation which your seventy elders made in the time of Ptolemy king of Egypt."

The earliest recorded fanciful embellishment of the tale is in Pseudo-Justin, *Exhortation to the Greeks* 13. After giving the traditional preliminaries Pseudo-Justin continues:

> Ptolemy charged the attendant ministers to see that they wanted for nothing, but to keep them from communicating with each other, in order that their agreement might afford a further proof of the accuracy of the translation. When he found that the seventy men had not merely expressed the same ideas but had employed the very same phraseology, and had not so much as in a single word failed to agree with each other . . . he held the books to be divine and laid them up in his library. . . . We ourselves have been in Alexandria and have seen the traces, still preserved, of the cells in the island of Pharos, and have heard this story which we tell you from the inhabitants, who have had it handed down as a tradition of their country. You may learn it from others also, and chiefly from those wise and distinguished men who have written of it, Philo and Josephus, but there are many others besides.

Philo, it will be remembered, not only introduced the notion of inspiration, which is here merely enlarged upon by a natural accretion, but connected the story with the topography of Pharos and with a surviving commemorative celebration. There is nothing in Pseudo-Justin for which we need to posit a literary source other than the two authors he names.

The story, as here embellished, persisted. Irenaeus (175 CE) in his *Against the Heresies* 3.21.2 insists emphatically on the inspired character of the translation, and also cites the isolation of the translators as proof. He does say that the enterprise was initiated by Ptolemy son of Lagus, who made his petition to the "inhabitants of Jerusalem." Clement of Alexandria (150-212) in his *Stromateis* (1.148) evidently follows the Irenaeus tradition, adding an interesting analogy to the revivification of Scripture under Ezra after "it had perished in the captivity under Nebuchadnezzar." Tertullian (b. ca. 160) is the first writer after Josephus to mention (*Apology* 18) "Aristaeus" by name, nor does he include the miraculous accretions of the intervening writers. The only tradition patently derived from a different source is his statement that "to this day the libraries of Ptolemy are shown in the Serapeum with the actual Hebrew documents." A principal channel through which Aristeas was transmitted to posterity is the *Praeparatio Evangelica* (8.1 ff.) of Eusebius (265-340), who presents an unadorned and generally reliable epitome of about a fourth of Aristeas, accurate enough to be of use in textual criticism of that book.[104] Quite sober also is the allusion in St. John Chrysostom (344-407), who says (*Homilies on St. Matthew* 5.2) that the Seventy made their translation "a century or more before the coming of Christ," and that their work deserves greater credence than other translations "by reason of their date, their number, and their agreement."

Far the most extravagant of all the elaborations is that of Epiphanius (*ca.* 315-403), the sheer fantasy of whose account (*On Weights and Measures* 3-11) must be of interest to any reader of Aristeas:

> They were seventy-two in number and were shut up from morn till eve in the Pharian island . . . over against Alexandria, in six and thirty cells, one pair to each cell. At even they would cross over in thirty-six skiffs to the palace of

[104] For the place of Eusebius' paraphrase in the textual criticism of Aristeas, see Thackeray in Swete, 548 ff.

Ptolemy Philadelphus and feast with him. They slept in pairs in thirty-six bed-chambers. Such was the life they led, to the end that they should have no collusion with each other and should produce an unadulterated translation. The thirty-six cells which I mentioned were erected by the aforesaid Ptolemy in the island across the water. He made them in two compartments and shut in the men two and two, as I said; and he shut in with them two ministering attendants to cook and to wait upon them, and they had shorthand writers in addition. He did not so much as make windows in the walls of those cells, but had what are called "skylights" opened in the roofs above their heads. So they lived from morn to eve under lock and key and so they translated. To each pair one book was delivered, that is to say, the book of the Genesis of the world to one pair, the *Exodus* of the children of Israel to a second pair, Leviticus to a third, and so on. Thus were translated the scriptural and canonical books, twenty-seven in all, or twenty-two if the reckoning is made to correspond to the number of letters in the Hebrew alphabet. . . . The method was as already described: the books were distributed periodically to each pair of translators, passing from the first pair to the second, and again from the second to the third in rotation. Thus each book was translated thirty-six times; such is the story which is told. There were also twenty-two of the apocryphal books. When the work was completed, the king took his seat on a lofty throne, and thirty-six readers sat at his feet having the thirty-six reproductions of each book, while one held a copy of the Hebrew volume. Then one reader recited and the rest diligently attended; and there was found no discrepancy. . . . where they added a word they all added it in common, and where they omitted the omission was made by all alike.

There follows, quite disjointedly and probably from another source, material corresponding to the earlier portion of Aristeas: the names of the translators (extant only in the Syriac version, where the list is in some respects better than ours: see on 47 ff.), the requirements of the library, and two letters of Ptolemy to the sages in Jerusalem, very different from the letters in Aristeas.

The legend was marked as the fabrication it is by the sane criticism of St. Jerome (348–420), whose *Preface to the Pentateuch* declares:

> I know not who was the first lying author to construct the seventy cells at Alexandria, in which they were separated and yet all wrote the same words, whereas Aristeas, one of the bodyguard of the said Ptolemy, and long after him Josephus have said nothing of the sort, but write that they were assembled in a single hall and conferred together, not that they prophesied. For it is one thing to be a prophet, another to be an interpreter.

But Jerome's critical sanity did little to prune the growth. In the *City of God* 18.42 St. Augustine (354–430) repeats the fiction of the separate cells and the miraculous consensus of the translators. He adds one noteworthy remark, to wit, that "the custom has now become prevalent of calling their translation the Septuagint." It was in his commentary on this passage that Ludovicus de Vives (1522) first challenged the authenticity of the tale; de Vives was supported by Joseph Scaliger and rebutted by other writers, until Humphrey Hody finally demonstrated that Aristeas was fiction and not history.[105]

Before we turn to glance at the traces of the legend in Jewish tradition it may be of interest to note one instance of its influence in non-theologic channels. Speaking of the constitution of the Homeric texts, the Byzantine grammarian Diomede[106] (ninth century?) reports that after the original text was lost

---

[105] The older critical literature on Aristeas is listed in Schürer 2, 3, 310 ff.

[106] The text of the relevant passage is quoted in the famous *Prolegomena* of F. A. Wolff (1795) 1. cxlvii ff. It is to be noted that Tertullian, in the passage cited above, mentions Peisistratus as a model for Ptolemy Philadelphus.

by fire or earthquake or water, Peisistratus offered rewards to any who would bring in verses of Homer they might possess. Many batches were brought in, a few lines or a few hundred at a time, and Peisistratus duly paid the rewards. He then assembled a panel of *seventy-two* scholars, who were told off to select the authentic verses and arrange them in order. The story, whenever it may have originated, persisted, and seems to have received embellishment. At any rate Tzetzes (twelfth century) violently attacks a rival grammarian named Heliodorus for propagating a similar story and insists that Peisistratus employed only four editors.[107] There can be little question of the origin of the number seventy-two in this connection, or indeed of the inspiration of the whole story.

For none of the Christian writers mentioned need we posit sources other than Aristeas, Philo, and Josephus. Aristeas had supplied the number of the translators and Philo the notion that the translation was divinely inspired, as witness the consensus of the translators. The embellishments involving isolated cells and the like might readily be viewed as a natural growth out of the amalgamation of the two elements. But in rabbinic literature, as we shall see (*a*, below), the tradition of seventy (or seventy-two) isolated cells goes back to tannaitic times, and since the concept is so odd that it is unlikely to have developed independently, chronology and probability alike would suggest that the embellishments first noticed in Pseudo-Justin and reaching their culmination in Epiphanius took their source from a rabbinic tradition. But this rabbinic tradition itself may derive from Aristeas, the basis for the notion of the consensus being a midrashic play on the two meanings of the Greek word *diaphonein* (see above, 71). But one very significant element in a rabbinic source (*c*, below) may point to a tradition independent of Aristeas and earlier than that book. The difficulty in bringing the rabbinic tradition to bear on our problem is the question of dating. A book of quite late date may embody material

[107] The relevant texts of Tzetzes, with discussion, are to be found in F. Ritschl, *Opuscula* (1866), 1.124, 12 ff., 206, 5 ff.

80   ARISTEAS TO PHILOCRATES

transmitted intact from high antiquity, but it is sometimes impossible to tell how high. Arranged roughly according to probable chronology the relevant passages in rabbinic literature are as follows:

(a) *Babylonian Talmud, Megillah 9a*[108]

It happened that King Tolmai [Ptolemy] assembled seventy-two elders and placed them in seventy-two cells, and did not make known to them wherefore he had assembled them. He came in to each of them in turn and said to them, "Write me out the Law of Moses your master." God put counsel into the heart of every one of them, that they were all of one mind, and they wrote out for him the Law. But they altered thirteen passages in it.

(There follows the list of the alterations, actually fourteen in number, chiefly to avoid implications of polytheism or other undesirable misinterpretations.)

The preceding Mishna states that Scripture may be written in any foreign language, and cites the view of R. Simon b. Gamaliel that they might be written only in Greek. The Gemara then proceeds: R. Judah said that the permission as to (writing in) Greek extends only to the book of the Law, and that because of what happened in the case of King Tolmai.

(b) *Palestinian Talmud, Megillah* 1. 71d

This merely lists the alterations cited in *a*, with the introductory sentence: "Thirteen (eighteen) passages were altered by the Sages for King Tolmai; they wrote thus for him."

(c) *Massakhet Soferim* 1. 7-10

This section is a conflation of two passages.

The Law must not be written in Hebrew (*i.e.*, the ancient characters such as appear in Hasmonaean coinage) nor in Aramaic nor in the Median language nor in Greek. A copy

[108] *Cf. Mekilta* on Exodus 12.40; *Midrash R. Exodus* 5; *Midrash Tanchuma Exodus* 22.

INTRODUCTION 81

written in any [foreign] tongue or characters shall not be used for [ritual] reading, but only one written in the Assyrian (*i.e.*, "square") characters.

It happened once that five elders[109] wrote the Law in Greek for King Tolmai; and that day was a hard day for Israel, like the day on which Israel made the [golden] calf,[110] because the Law was not capable of being interpreted according to all its requirements.

The mention of *five* (instead of seventy or seventy-two) translators working for King Ptolemy makes this far the most significant of our variants. The theory first proposed by Z. Frankel[111] and based on internal evidence of the LXX Pentateuch that the version was in fact made by five hands has met with acceptance. Five seems a more reasonable number for a commission of translators than the larger figures. It will be remembered that Philo made no mention of the number of translators. We have then a tradition that the translation was made *for Ptolemy*, but with the larger number of translators specifically rejected and the other circumstances ignored. There can be no dependence of this passage on Aristeas, but it would rather seem that Aristeas himself used the tradition of a

[109] [Most probably the reading "five" is a scribal error. The original reading was *ha-zekenim*, "the elders." Some scribes wrote the *he* as a separate word and thus it came to be read *he zekenim*, "five elders." (S. Z.)]

[110] [The two conflicting opinions expressed in the Talmud regarding the attitude of the sages toward the Septuagint, one of which was favorable and the other derogatory, were due to the chronological historical development of Judaism and Christianity. During the Second Commonwealth the Septuagint was highly regarded by the Jews. In fact, Philo said that the men who translated the Pentateuch into Greek were inspired prophets. The sages of the Talmud also spoke very highly of the Septuagint. The seventy-two men who translated the five books of Moses were regarded by the sages as having divine inspiration. They were called *Zekenim*, a title which was given only to scholars. Only when the Christians made use of the Septuagint for the purpose of furthering Christianity and hence interpolated Christological passages, did a change of attitude towards it come over the rabbis. According to the rabbis of the later period, the day when the Pentateuch was translated into Greek was as bad a day for Israel as the day when the golden calf was melted. (S. Z.)]

[111] *Ueber den Einfluss der paläst. Exegese* (1851).

Ptolemaic translation which he himself or some intermediary embellished.

If the next paragraph in *Soferim* mentioned only the larger number we might accept it as a parallel to or even a source for Aristeas. But that paragraph presents the story in its embellished form, with the translators insulated from one another. Aristeas would certainly have employed that detail if it were available to him, and his failure to do so makes it reasonably certain that the latter part of the *Soferim* passage is post-Aristean in date. Philo had spoken of the miraculous consensus of the individual versions, though he did not emphasize the insulation of the translators. That new turn is a very normal midrashic expansion, and it is much more likely that the Christian writers who used the embellished version derived it from the rabbis than the reverse.[112] The remainder of the *Soferim* passage is identical with that given in the *baraita* and is virtually in the same language as the *Talmud Meg.* passage, including the list of alterations here slightly expanded.

> They do not write [the Law] in gold [letters.] It happened in the case of the copy of the Law of Alexandria that all the names of God were written in gold; and when the matter came before the Sages, they said, "Store it away."

In connection with writing in gold, it will be recalled that at 176 Aristeas says that the *entire* manuscript was so written. The passage above provides the real explanation of the basis of such an exaggeration, and so a foothold (but the only foothold at present visible) for the hypothesis that Aristeas used the Rabbinic tradition here cited. On the other hand, if, as was apparently the case, a scroll with the divine names written in gold existed in Alexandria, there is no reason why Aristeas may not have had knowledge of it directly and without the aid of a tradition, and hence it may have been the fact rather than a literary tradition which he embellished.

[112] The use of Rabbinic materials by Patristic writers has been demonstrated in Ginzberg's classic *Die Agada bei den Kirchenvätern;* see his *Legends of the Jews 5* (Philadelphia, 1925), ix.

INTRODUCTION 83

(d) *Gaonic Addition to the Megillat Taanit*[113]

On the eighth [*v. l.* seventh] of Tebet the Law was written[114] in Greek in the days of King Tolmai and darkness came upon the world for three days.

Examination of the entire tradition of the legend, then, would seem to yield the following results: (1) It is universally agreed that the translation was made under a Ptolemy. (2) The most credible and very probably oldest tradition speaks of only five elders. (3) Philo introduces the element of inspiration, but does not mention the number of translators. Since other of his details seem to stem from the Aristean tradition, he may here have heeded the rabbinic tradition of the smaller number—or merely have omitted the large number as being improbable. (4) The principal embellishment of the legend, to wit, the insulation of the translators, goes back to tannaitic times. (5) This tradition was probably the basis for the further embellishments to be found in Patristic writers.

None of the rabbinic sources mentions the name of Aristeas, and if his book was actually ever known in Palestine it dropped out of the main stream of Jewish tradition along with other Jewish literature written in Greek. Here it is worth noting that its reintroduction to Jewish scholarship in the sixteenth century provided the initial impulse for the modern critical study of Jewish historical records. Azariah de Rossi read a Latin translation of Aristeas in 1570, and published a Hebrew version of it, with comments on the LXX, in his *Meor Enayim* in 1573–1575.

[113] The present passage occurs in an appendix of fasts in Neubauer's edition, *Anecdota Oxoniensia, Semitic Series* 1, 6; *Medieval Jewish Chronicles* 2, (Oxford, 1895).

[114] Perhaps transliteration into Greek rather than translation is meant. M. Gaster, *The Samaritans* (London, 1925), 120 believes this is the case, and maintains that it was the transliteration which was "rightly considered by the Jews as a grievous calamity." In the XVIII century O. G. Tychsen proposed the theory, refurbished by F. X. Wutz in 1925, that LXX was made not from a Hebrew but from a transliterated text. For the present discredited state of this theory see H. M. Orlinsky, "Current Problems and Progress in Septuagint Research," in H. R. Willoughby (ed.), *The Study of the Bible Today and Tomorrow* (Chicago, 1947), 155 ff.

Probably no single work was as revolutionary as Aristeas, therefore, in giving a new and wider scope to Jewish historical scholarship.[115]

XI

MODERN STUDY OF ARISTEAS: BIBLIOGRAPHY

The survival of over twenty MSS of Aristeas,[116] dating from the eleventh to the fifteenth century, testifies to a continuing interest in Aristeas. Like many other Greek works the book was first printed in a Latin translation—by Matthias Palmerius (Rome, 1471)—and it was doubtless this version that de Rossi used. The first Greek text, based upon only two MSS, was brought out by Simon Schard in Basle in 1561, and this remained the standard Greek text until 1870. It was reprinted, for example, in Hody's *De Bibliorum Textibus Originalibus* (1705), Havercamp's *Josephus*, and Gallandi's *Bibliotheca Patrum*.

The genuineness of the story was first challenged by Ludovicus de Vives in his commentary on Augustine's *City of God* 18.4 and later by Joseph Scaliger. Hody's essay *Contra Historiam LXX Interpretum Aristeae Nomine Inscriptam Dissertatio* (1685; enlarged and incorporated in his *De Bibliorum Textibus* of 1705) demonstrated the unhistorical character of Aristeas, though sporadic attempts have been made to rehabilitate him even as a historian. Hody's low opinion is reflected in his preface: "I am not unaware that manuscript copies of Aristeas are preserved in the Royal Library at Paris and elsewhere. But for such a trifling work, which I reject completely as a supposititious foundling, I did not regard it worth while to trouble my friends and to send to distant places."

[115] See I. Abrahams, *Bypaths in Hebraic Bookland* (Philadelphia, 1920), 117; S. Baron, "La méthode historique d'Azaria de Rossi," *Revue des Études Juives* 86 (1928), 151–175 and 87 (1929), 43–78.

[116] MSS are listed, stemmata established, and previous critical work assessed in Thackeray's introduction to his edition.

The credit of Aristeas as communicating useful historical data even if his main story is essentially fictive was first raised by G. Lumbroso,[117] who wrote of Aristeas:

> During the last forty years unexpected illumination from inscriptions and papyri have thrown a new light upon it. Here is a remarkable thing: there is not a court title, an institution, a law, a magistracy, an office, a technical term, a formula, a remarkable turn of language in this letter, there is no piece of evidence of Aristeas concerning the civil history of the epoch, which is not found registered in the papyri or the inscriptions and confirmed by them.

Lumbroso's enthusiasm is somewhat exaggerated, but remains essentially justified, and if Aristeas' evidence for history is unsatisfactory, at least the evidence of the papyri is of great value in interpreting Aristeas.

The year 1870 also saw the first modern treatment of the text of Aristeas. This was the edition of Moritz Schmidt,[118] which was far from satisfactory, however, inasmuch as it made use of only three MSS. A recension of much larger scope was undertaken by L. Mendelssohn but interrupted by the editor's death; only about a fifth of the work reached print.[119] Mendelssohn's work was taken over and enlarged in the admirable edition of Paul Wendland (1900), which is most useful for its *Testimonia*, *Index Verborum*, and other subsidia; the paragraph numbering which all subsequent editors employ was introduced by Wendland. In the same year H. St. J. Thackeray produced an equally scholarly text, based on virtually the same MSS which Wendland used, and published as an appendix to H. B. Swete's *Introduction to the Old Testament in Greek* (Cambridge, 1900). In the revision of this work, published in 1902, Thackeray took full cognizance of Wendland's work.

---

[117] G. Lumbroso, *Recherches sur l'économie politique de l'Égypte sous les Lagids* (Turin, 1870), xiii.
[118] Published in Vol. I of Merx' *Archiv*.
[119] *Aristeae quae fertur ad Philocratem epistulae initium* (Dorpat, 1897).

Thackeray's revised text (which is that used in the present volume) was reproduced by H. G. Meecham in his *Letter of Aristeas* (Manchester, 1935). This is an extremely useful book to the student of Greek. It examines the Greek of Aristeas with full reference to other contemporary specimens of the language, and provides a running commentary of the linguistic aspects of the text. The same author had previously published *The Oldest Version of the Bible: "Aristeas" on its Traditional Origin* (London, 1932). This includes a fresh translation and numerous excellent essays on various aspects of the book. Its chief interest is indicated by the subtitle, *A Study in Early Apologetic*. The fullest commentary on Aristeas' exegetical, linguistic, and textual is Raffaele Tramontano S. J., *La Lettera di Aristea a Filocrate* (Naples, 1931). Tramontano's text does not follow that of any of his predecessors, nor is it an independent recension; the consensus of MSS readings as drawn from the apparatus of his predecessors is printed, with cruces to indicate questionable readings, for which possible emendations are discussed in the commentary. Tramontano also provides a translation. Finally there is a Hebrew edition, with translation, short introduction and notes, but no text by A. Cahana in *Ha-sepharim Ha-Hizonim* (Tel Aviv, 1937).

Modern translations other than those mentioned above are Thackeray's and Andrews' in English, and Wendland's and Riessler's in German. Bibliographical details of these and other works of major usefulness for the study of Aristeas will be listed below. The list given herewith makes no claim to completeness but includes works of whose existence the student should be aware. These books will in turn direct him to further titles.

Texts

P. Wendland, *Aristeae ad Philocratem Epistula* (Leipzig, 1900). Contains apparatus, testimonia, and index verborum.

H. St. J. Thackeray, *The Letter of Aristeas*, Appendix to H. B. Swete, *Introduction to the Old Testament in Greek* (Cambridge, 1902). Contains introduction and apparatus.

H. G. Meecham, *The Letter of Aristeas* (Manchester, 1935). Reproduces Thackeray's text but provides a detailed study of Aristeas' Greek and a running commentary on the language.

R. Tramontano, *La Lettera di Aristea a Filocrate* (Naples, 1931). Contains a full introduction (pp. 208), an Italian translation, and a very ample commentary, exegetical, linguistic, and textual.

Translations

H. St. J. Thackeray, *The Letter of Aristeas* (S.P.C.K., London, 1917). This is a revision of Thackeray's earlier translation which appeared in *Jewish Quarterly Review* 15 (1903), 337–391, and occasionally follows readings not accepted in Thackeray's text. An appendix offers translations of passages, Jewish and Christian, which refer to the story of the translation of the LXX.

H. T. Andrews, *The Letter of Aristeas* in R. H. Charles, *The Apocrypha and Pseudepigrapha of the Old Testament* (Oxford, 1913), 83–122. Contains introduction and notes.

H. G. Meecham, *The Oldest Version of the Bible: Aristeas on its Traditional Origin* (London, 1932). Contains, besides a translation, many useful chapters on historical, literary, and doctrinal problems.

P. Wendland, *Der Brief des Aristeas* in E. Kautzsch, *Apokryphen und Pseudepigraphen des Alten Testaments* (Tübingen, 1900), 2.1–31. Contains brief introduction and notes.

P. Riessler, *Brief des Aristeas* in *Altjüdisches Schrifttum ausserhalb der Bibel* (Berlin, 1928), 193–233. Contains brief notes.

R. Tramontano: See under Texts.

A. Cahana, in *Ha-sepharim Ha-Hizonim* (Tel Aviv, 1937). Contains brief introduction and notes.

Critical Works

E. Bickermann, "Zur Datierung des Pseudo-Aristeas," *Zeitschrift für die neutestamentliche Wissenschaft* 29 (1930), 280–296.

J. G. Février, *La Date, la composition, et les Sources de la Lettre d' Aristee à Philocrate* (Bibliotheque de l'Ecole des Hautes Etudes 242; Paris, 1925).

Z. Frankel, *Vorstudien zu der Septuaginta* (1841).

M. Friedländer, *Geschichte der jüdischen Apologetik* (1903), 84–104.

M. Gaster, *The Samaritans* (London, 1925).

E. R. Goodenough, "The Political Philosophy of Hellenistic Kingship," *Yale Classical Studies* 1 (1928), 53–102.

H. Graetz, "Die Abfassungszeit des Pseudo-Aristeas," *Monatsschrift für Gesch. und Wissenschaft des Judentums* (1876), 289–308, 337–349.

J. Gutmann, "Mozaah u' Magmatah ha-Ikrit shel Iggeret Aristeas," in *Ha-Goren* 10 (1936), 54 ff.

P. Kahle, *The Cairo Geniza* (London, 1947).

K. Kuiper, "De Aristeae ad Philocratem fratrem epistola," *Mnemosyne* 20 (1892), 252–272.

G. Lumbroso, *Recherches sur l'économie politique de l'Egypte sous les Lagids* (Turin, 1870).

S. Tracy, "III Maccabees and Pseudo-Aristeas," *Yale Classical Studies* 1 (1928), 241–251.

R. P. Vincent, "Jérusalem d'après la Lettre d'Aristée," *Revue Biblique Internationale* N.S. 5 (1908), 520 ff., 6 (1909), 555 ff.

P. Wendland, art. "Aristeas," *Jewish Encyclopedia* 2.92 ff.

W. L. Westermann, *Upon Slavery in Ptolemaic Egypt* (New York, 1929); "Enslaved Persons Who Are Free," *American Journal of Philology* 59 (1938), 1–30.

H. Willrich, *Urkundenfälschungen in der hellenistisch-jüdischen Literatur* (Göttingen, 1923); *Judaica* (1900).

H. A. Wolfson, *Philo* (Harvard, 1947).

History and Literature

E. Bevan, *History of Egypt under the Ptolemaic Dynasty* (London, 1927).

Cambridge Ancient History 7 (Cambridge, 1928).

Bacchisio Motzo, "Aristea", *Atti della R. Accademia di Scienze di Torino* 50 (1915), 202–226, 547–570.

E. Schürer, *Geschichte des jüdischen Volkes im Zeitalter Jesu Christi* (Leipzig, 1901–1911).

G. Stählin, "Josephus und der Aristeasbrief," *Theologische Studien und Kritiken* 102 (1930), 323–331.

Menahem Stein, "Baal Iggeret Aristeas k'Sanegor shel ha-Yahadut," *Zion* N.S. 1 (1927), 132 ff.

W. W. Tarn, *The Greeks in Bactria and India* (Cambridge, 1938): Appendix on "The Milindapanha and Pseudo-Aristeas," 414–436.

A. Tcherikover, "Ha-Maza ha-Ideologi shel Iggeret Aristeas," *Sefer Dinaburg* (Jerusalem, 1949), 83–101; "Roshe Perakim l'Hikur ha-Safrut ha-Yehudit ha-Alexandronit," *Sefer Levi* (Jerusalem, 1949), 139–160.

V. (A.) Tcherikover, *The Jews in Egypt in the Hellenistic-Roman Age in the Light of the Papyri* (Hebrew, with English summary; Jerusalem, 1945).

Christ-Schmid-Stählin, *Geschichte der griechischen Literatur*, Part II, 1 and 2 (Munich, 1920–1924).

L. Fuchs, *Die Juden Aegyptens* (Vienna, 1924)

E. Meyer, *Ursprung und Anfänge des Christentums*, 2 (Berlin, 1925).

A. Momigliano, *Prime Linee di Storia della Tradizione Maccabaica* (Rome, 1931).

M. Rostovtzeff, *The Social and Economic History of the Hellenistic World*, 3 vols. (Oxford, 1941).

W. W. Tarn, *Hellenistic Civilisation*^{2} (London, 1930).

V. Tcherikover, *Hayehudim veha-Yevanim* (Jerusalem, 1930).

Ancient Authors

Most of the Greek writers cited in introduction and commentary are available in the Loeb Classical Library series, from which translations are regularly drawn. A special word must be said of Ralph Marcus' vol. 7 of the Loeb *Josephus*, which contains the paraphrase of Aristeas; Marcus' running commentary and relevant appendices with rich bibliographies make this volume a most important tool for the study of Aristeas.

XII

TEXT

The Greek text presented in the pages following is reproduced without change from Thackeray's revised text, which is the most satisfactory in existence. For a full record of the manuscript tradition the student will naturally go to Thackeray's apparatus. All that the notes at the foot of each Greek page of the present edition aim to do is to record significant variants and emendations, giving the sources for the latter, whether or not they are received in the text. The abbreviations are self-explanatory: W-Wendland; T-Thackeray, Mend.-Mendelssohn; the names of other critics are written out. *Euseb.* or *Jos.* mean that the reading in question is supported by the paraphrases of these authors. *MSS* means all, or the preponderant number of good, manuscripts; *MS* means a single manuscript. Identification of the individual manuscripts in question would involve a preliminary detailed discussion of their values; and such a discussion is beyond the resources of the present editor and the scope of the present series. At least the reader can see when he is following a well-attested or a dubious text, and what suggestions have been made for improving passages judged corrupt.

TEXT, TRANSLATION, COMMENTARY AND CRITICAL NOTES

ΑΡΙΣΤΕΑΣ ΦΙΛΟΚΡ

¹Ἀξιολόγου διηγήσεως, ὦ Φιλόκρατες, περὶ τῆς γενηθείσης ἡμῖν ἐντυχίας πρὸς Ἐλεάζαρον τὸν τῶν Ἰουδαίων ἀρχιερέα συνεσταμένης, διὰ τὸ σὲ περὶ πολλοῦ πεποιῆσθαι, παρ' ἕκαστα †ὑπομιμνήσκων†, συνακοῦσαι περὶ ὧν ἀπεστάλημεν καὶ διὰ τί, πεπείραμαι σαφῶς ἐκθέσθαι σοι, κατειληφὼς ἣν ἔχεις φιλομαθῆ διάθεσιν, ²ὅπερ μέγιστόν ἐστιν ἀνθρώπῳ, προσμανθάνειν ἀεί τι καὶ προσλαμβάνειν, ἤτοι κατὰ τὰς ἱστορίας, ἢ καὶ κατ' αὐτὸ τὸ πρᾶγμα πεπειραμένῳ. οὕτω γὰρ κατασκευάζεται ψυχῆς καθαρὰ διάθεσις, ἀναλαβοῦσα τὰ κάλλιστα· καὶ πρὸς τὸ πάντων κυριώτατον νενευκυῖα τὴν εὐσέβειαν ἀπλανεῖ κεχρημένη κανόνι διοικεῖ. ³Τὴν προαίρεσιν ἔχοντες ἡμεῖς πρὸς τὸ περιέργως τὰ θεῖα κατανοεῖν, ἑαυτοὺς ἐπεδώκαμεν εἰς τὸν προειρημένον ἄνδρα πρεσβείαν, καλοκἀγαθίᾳ καὶ δόξῃ προτετιμημένον ὑπό τε

1 ὑπομιμνησκων MSS, ὑπομιμνησκειν Diels, ὑπομιμνησκοντα Mend.   2 αναλαβουσα] W conjectures <εαν> αναλαβουσα. ... διοικη / MSS put full stop after διοικει την προαιρεσιν

1-8. PROEM: A superscription in the form "Aristeas to Philocrates" seems unexampled in Greek literature as the title of a book. Josephus' "Book of Aristaeus" (*Ant.* 12.100; citations of Josephus by paragraph only will refer to *Ant.* 12) is a description rather than a title; the true title may be preserved in Eusebius, *Praep. Ev.* 9.38: "On the translation of the Law of the Jews." Nor are modern editors and translators justified in calling the work a letter: see Introd. 56.

1. ACCOUNT: *Diegesis* used here and in 322 is a technical term for a literary prose *narratio*: see Intro. 56.   PHILOCRATES: Not otherwise known; the name is not uncommon, and occurs in the Zenon papyri. The addressee is named here and at the end, and at the close of long sections within the book (120, 171, 295, 322), each time in the vocative.   ELEAZAR: Josephus, *Ant.* 43, says he succeeded Simon the Just as High Priest, Simon's son Onias being a minor; but the identity of Simon is ambiguous (see Marcus' "The Date of ... Simon the Just," App. B of his Loeb *Josephus* 7.732 ff., which lists the abundant literature on the subject) and Josephus' account of the

ARISTEAS TO PHILOCRATES

1 Inasmuch as the account of our deputation to Eleazar, the High Priest of the Jews, is worth narrating, Philocrates, and because you set a high value, as you constantly remind me, on hearing the motives and purposes of our mission, I have endeavored to set the matter forth clearly. I appreciate your characteristic love of learning, ²for it is indeed man's highest function "ever to add knowledge, ever to acquire it," either through researches or by actual experience of affairs. It is thus that a pure state of soul is fashioned, by seizing upon what is fairest; and in its pursuit of piety, the greatest good of all, it enjoys an unerring gauge for its guidance. ³It was because of my predilection for the careful study of religious matters that I offered myself for the embassy to the man mentioned above, who is highly esteemed both by his countrymen and by others for his worth and renown, and who

succession is dubious. *Cf.* also S. Zeitlin, *The History of the Second Jewish Commonwealth, Prolegomena*, p. 10. The name Eleazar (like Simon) is traditional in this literature for a hero of the spirit: cf. II Mac. 6.18; III Mac. 6.1; IV Mac. 6.5, 7.1. The picture of our Eleazar is consistent: as High Priest he exercises wide civil authority; he writes to the king as an equal (see on 41, 46); the king sends him presents suitable for a sovereign (320); he pronounces an impassioned defense of the Law (128 ff.); and shows fatherly concern for the welfare of the translators (46, 123, 172). THE HIGH PRIEST: *Archiereus*, the common Greek word, is used regularly in the books of Mac. but rarely in the rest of LXX, where the expression is *ho hiereus ho megas*.

2. EVER TO ADD KNOWLEDGE, EVER TO ACQUIRE IT: These words form an iambic line, and are possibly a fusion of Sophocles *frgs.* 779 and 622 (Dindorf) or from some lost tragedy; in any case they indicate the "literary" character of Aristeas. For the sentiment cf. Hillel in *Abot* 1.13.

3. MY: The Greek employs the "editorial" plural, here and elsewhere.
MENTIONED ABOVE: The frequent use of "aforementioned" or an equivalent is characteristic of Aristeas' style; it is common in inscriptions and papyri.
LAW: Only the translation of the Torah is dealt with in Aristeas.

ΑΡΙΣΤΕΑΣ ΦΙΛΟΚΡΑΤΕΙ

τῶν πολιτῶν καὶ τῶν ἄλλων, καὶ κατακεκτημένον μεγίστην ὠφέλειαν τοῖς σὺν ἑαυτῷ καὶ τοῖς κατὰ τοὺς ἄλλους τόπους πολίταις, πρὸς τὴν ἑρμηνείαν τοῦ θείου νόμου, διὰ τὸ γεγράφθαι παρ' αὐτοῖς ἐν διφθέραις ἑβραϊκοῖς γράμμασιν. ⁴ἣν δὴ καὶ ἐποιησάμεθα ἡμεῖς σπουδῇ, λαβόντες καιρὸν πρὸς τὸν βασιλέα περὶ τῶν μετοικισθέντων εἰς Αἴγυπτον ἐκ τῆς Ἰουδαίας ὑπὸ τοῦ πατρὸς τοῦ βασιλέως, πρώτως κεκτημένου τήν τε πόλιν καὶ τὰ κατὰ τὴν Αἴγυπτον παρειλη-
5 φότος. Ἄξιόν ἐστι καὶ ταῦτά σοι δηλῶσαι. ⁵πέπεισμαι γάρ σε μᾶλλον ἔχοντα πρόσκλισιν πρὸς τὴν σεμνότητα καὶ τὴν τῶν ἀνθρώπων διάθεσιν τῶν κατὰ τὴν σεμνὴν νομοθεσίαν διεξαγόντων, περὶ ὧν προαιρούμεθα <δηλοῦν, ἀσμένως σε> ἀκούσεσθαι, προσφάτως παραγεγενημένον ἐκ τῆς νήσου πρὸς ἡμᾶς, καὶ βουλόμενον συνακούειν ὅσα πρὸς ἐπισκευὴν ψυχῆς ὑπάρχει. ⁶καὶ πρότερον δὲ διεπεμψάμην σοι περὶ ὧν ἐνόμιζον ἀξιομνημονεύτων εἶναι τὴν ἀναγραφήν, ἣν μετελάβομεν παρὰ τῶν κατὰ τὴν λογιωτάτην Αἴγυπτον λογιωτάτων ἀρχιερέων περὶ τοῦ γένους τῶν Ἰουδαίων. ⁷φιλομαθῶς γὰρ ἔχοντί σοι περὶ τῶν δυναμένων ὠφελῆσαι διάνοιαν δέον ἐστὶ μεταδιδόναι, μάλιστα μὲν πᾶσι τοῖς ὁμοίοις, πολλῷ δὲ μᾶλλον σοὶ γνησίαν ἔχοντι τὴν αἵρεσιν, οὐ μόνον κατὰ τὸ συγγενὲς ἀδελφῷ καθεστῶτι τὸν τρόπον, ἀλλὰ καὶ τῇ πρὸς τὸ καλὸν ὁρμῇ τὸν αὐτὸν ὄντα ἡμῖν.

---

4 σπουδη] Diels marks a lacuna after this word, for which W suggests α δε διελεχθημεν
5 δηλουν ασμενως σε Schmidt, δηλουντες μεν ως σε MSS
6 λογιωτατην bracketed by Wilcken, as from λογιωτατων following
7 σοι περι bracketed by Kuiper as dittography from 6; Kuiper transposes τον τροπον after αλλα και

---

4. THE KING'S FATHER: Ptolemy I Lagus.   CITY: Regularly for Alexandria, as "country" for Egypt. In dealing with Palestine "city" and "country" naturally stand for Jerusalem and Judaea.
5. THE ISLAND: Hardly Pharos, the scene of the translation, because it is too near; probably Cyprus. On the assumption that Pharos is meant Wendland fixes the *terminus ante quem* as 47 BCE, the year of Julius Caesar's Alexandrine war, after which Pharos was uninhabited.
6. ON A PREVIOUS OCCASION: On the basis of this passage some scholars have suggested that our author is to be identified with the Aristeas or Aristaeus who wrote the *On the Jews* of which Eusebius *Praep. Ev.* 9.25

possesses the greatest usefulness for his countrymen, those with him and those in other places, for the translation of the divine Law, for it exists among them written on parchments in Hebrew characters. ⁴This embassy, then, I undertook with alacrity, when I had seized the opportunity of speaking to the king concerning those who had been transported to Egypt from Judaea by the king's father when he first acquired possession of the city and took over the government of Egypt. It is worth while to inform you of these things also. ⁵I am confident that you in particular, because of your tendency towards holiness and the outlook of those men who live according to the holy Law, will gladly listen to what I purpose to reveal, for you have only lately come over to us from the island and are eager to hear whatever contributes to the soul's edification. ⁶On a previous occasion also I transmitted to you an exposition of matters I deemed worthy of record concerning the race of the Jews which I received from the most erudite High Priests in the most erudite land of Egypt. ⁷To you who are a lover of learning in matters capable of benefiting the mind it is right to communicate these things. Gladly would I communicate them to all who are like-minded, but in particular to you, whose convictions are genuine and who are not only proven my brother german in character but also at one with me in striving for the good.

---

has preserved a fragment. But that fragment is dull in style and follows Scripture closely, and in every respect is different from our author. Perhaps the reference is to another work of our author (Freudenthal, *Hellenistische Studien* 141), or more probably part of the fiction, like the promise of a third work in 322.   PRIESTS ... OF EGYPT: After the profession of reverence for Jewish piety this reliance upon Egyptian priests for information concerning the Jews is odd. It was a literary convention (after Herodotus) to refer to Egyptian priests for such information, and our author doubtless also wishes to emphasize his non-Jewishness: see on 15.

7. The notion that kinship is a spiritual as well as physical affinity occurs in Philo, *De Nobilitate* 195: "Kinship is not measured only by blood, but by similarity of conduct and pursuit of the same objects." This is a development of the idea promulgated by Isocrates (*Panegyricus* 50) and widespread in Hellenistic writers that "Hellene" (as contrasted to "barbarian") is to be defined not by blood but by education.

⁸χρυσοῦ γὰρ χάρις ἢ κατασκευή τις ἄλλη τῶν τετιμημένων παρὰ τοῖς κενοδόξοις ὠφέλειαν οὐκ ἔχει τὴν αὐτήν, ὅσον ἡ παιδείας ἀγωγὴ καὶ ἡ περὶ τούτων φροντίς. ἵνα δὲ μὴ περὶ τῶν προλεγομένων μηκύνοντες ἀδόλεσχόν τι ποιῶμεν, ἐπὶ τὸ συνεχὲς τῆς διηγήσεως ἐπανήξομεν.

⁹Κατασταθεὶς ἐπὶ τῆς τοῦ βασιλέως βιβλιοθήκης Δημήτριος ὁ Φαληρεὺς ἐχρηματίσθη πολλὰ διάφορα πρὸς τὸ συναγαγεῖν, εἰ δυνατόν, ἅπαντα τὰ κατὰ τὴν οἰκουμένην βιβλία· καὶ ποιούμενος ἀγορασμοὺς καὶ μεταγραφὰς ἐπὶ τέλος 10 ἤγαγεν, ὅσον ἐφ' ἑαυτῷ, τὴν τοῦ βασιλέως πρόθεσιν. ¹⁰παρόντων οὖν ἡμῶν ἐρωτηθεὶς Πόσαι τινὲς μυριάδες τυγχάνουσι βιβλίων; εἶπεν Ὑπὲρ τὰς εἴκοσι, βασιλεῦ· σπουδάσω δ' ἐν ὀλίγῳ χρόνῳ πρὸς τὸ πληρωθῆναι πεντήκοντα μυριάδας τὰ λοιπά. προσήγγελται δέ μοι καὶ τῶν Ἰουδαίων νόμιμα μεταγραφῆς ἄξια καὶ τῆς παρὰ σοὶ βιβλιοθήκης εἶναι. ¹¹Τί τὸ κωλῦον οὖν, εἶπεν, ἐστί σε τοῦτο ποιῆσαι; πάντα γὰρ ὑποτέτακταί σοι τὰ πρὸς τὴν χρείαν. ὁ δὲ Δημήτριος εἶπεν Ἑρμηνείας προσδεῖται· χαρακτῆρσι γὰρ ἰδίοις κατὰ τὴν Ἰουδαίων χρῶνται, καθάπερ Αἰγύπτιοι τῇ τῶν γραμμάτων θέσει, καθὸ καὶ φωνὴν ἰδίαν ἔχουσιν. ὑπολαμβάνονται

---

10 σπουδασω Euseb., πληρωσω MSS

8 The "ethical" introduction is a regular feature of Hellenistic historical or "philosophic" treatises, and marks the present work as conforming to accepted literary canons
9–11. DEMETRIUS' PROPOSAL CONCERNING THE TRANSLATION.
9. DEMETRIUS OF PHALERUM: Born ca. 350, pupil of Theophrastus, and himself an author in the Peripatetic tradition as well as a statesman. In 307 he was driven from Athens by Demetrius Poliorcetes and received in Alexandria by Ptolemy I. For the succession Demetrius favored Ptolemy Ceraunus, whereas Ptolemy himself favored Ptolemy Philadelphus, and when the latter ascended the throne (285) he immediately banished Demetrius. It is furthermore certain that Demetrius was never librarian at Alexandria, though he may have been instrumental in bringing the foundation of the library about and may have broached schemes under Ptolemy I which were realized under Ptolemy II. Aristeas is therefore wrong in assigning Demetrius influence over Ptolemy I, though he may have consciously telescoped his story to include two appropriate great names. Demetrius probably figured in the original story of the questions on kingship (see Introd. 40), and Plutarch, *Sayings of Kings and Commanders* 189 D, says that he urged the king to read books in order to find out about king-

⁸For neither the charm of gold nor any other of the embellishments prized by the vainglorious confers as great benefit as education and attention devoted to culture. But not to weary you with a long extended introduction, I shall resume the thread of my narrative.
⁹When Demetrius of Phalerum was put in charge of the king's library he was assigned large sums of money with a view to collecting, if possible, all the books in the world; and by arranging purchases and transcriptions he carried the king's design to completion as far as he was able. ¹⁰When he was asked, in my presence, about how many thousands of books were already collected, he replied, "Above two hundred thousand, Your Majesty; and in a short while I shall exert every effort for the remainder, to round out the number of half a million. I am informed that the laws of the Jews also are worthy of transcription and of being included in your library." ¹¹"What is to prevent you from doing so?" the king replied; "all the necessary means are at your disposal." But Demetrius said, "Translation is required; in the country of the Jews they use a peculiar script, just as the Egyptians employ their arrangement of letters, and they have their own

ship. Josephus, *Against Apion* 2.218, confuses this Demetrius with the Jewish historian of the same name. Philadelphus, on the other hand, was the richest of the Ptolemies, and the greatest patron of learning. Our author's model for the account of the royal gifts may have derived from a similar account associated with Philadelphus: see Introd. 47.   THE KING'S: As is appropriate to a courtier, Aristeas does not mention his king by name, but we soon learn his identity.   PURCHASES AND TRANSCRIPTIONS: These were in fact the methods employed; the tragedies, for example, were transcribed from the official copies kept at Athens.

10. IN MY PRESENCE: Similar claims of direct knowledge are made at 83, 91, 96, 100, 297, and elsewhere.   ABOVE 200,000: Josephus, *Ant.* 12.13, "about 200,000." About 250 the Alexandrian library contained 400,000–500,000 rolls, and eventually 700,000.

11. The king apparently thought the books needed only to be copied, and hence Demetrius finds it necessary to explain that translation is required. The author's desire to elaborate an obvious point, because it is the occasion of his whole work, results in confusion.   LETTER: At 33 we are told that the letter was ordered written as result of Demetrius' memorandum. It looks as if the intervening matter is an interpolation in an account of the translation told through documents.   SYRIAN: Aramaic.

Συριακῇ χρῆσθαι· τὸ δ' οὐκ ἔστιν, ἀλλ' ἕτερος τρόπος. Μεταλαβὼν δὲ ἕκαστα ὁ βασιλεὺς εἶπε γραφῆναι πρὸς τὸν ἀρχιερέα τῶν Ἰουδαίων, ὅπως τὰ προειρημένα τελείωσιν λάβῃ. [12]Νομίσας δὲ ἐγὼ καιρὸν εἶναι περὶ ὧν πολλάκις ἠξιώκειν Σωσίβιόν τε τὸν Ταραντῖνον καὶ Ἀνδρέαν, τοὺς ἀρχισωματοφύλακας, περὶ τῆς ἀπολυτρώσεως τῶν μετηγμένων ἐκ τῆς Ἰουδαίας ὑπὸ τοῦ πατρὸς τοῦ βασιλέως— ἐκεῖνος γὰρ ἐπελθὼν τὰ κατὰ κοίλην Συρίαν καὶ Φοινίκην ἅπαντα, συγχρώμενος εὐημερίᾳ μετὰ ἀνδρείας, τοὺς μὲν μετῴκιζεν, οὓς δὲ ᾐχμαλώτιζε, φόβῳ πάντα ὑποχείρια ποιούμενος· ἐν ὅσῳ καὶ πρὸς δέκα μυριάδας ἐκ τῆς τῶν Ἰουδαίων χώρας εἰς Αἴγυπτον μετήγαγεν, [13]ἀφ' ὧν ὡσεὶ

12–27. THE EMANCIPATION OF THE JEWS OF EGYPT.
12. The manner of introducing this digression, by a nominative participle + de is a noticeable characteristic of similar transitions in III Mac. also. SOSIBIUS: A common name in the Ptolemaic court. The only recorded Sosibius at Alexandria in the reign of Philadelphus was a historian from Sparta, but the name was borne by the notorious minister of Ptolemy IV Philopator (Polybius 15.25 ff.) who figures in III Mac., and also by his son, who, like our Sosibius, was an *archisōmatophulax* "chief of the bodyguard," to Ptolemy Epiphanes. Possibly the name here is a conscious allusion to the later Sosibius, and OF TARENTUM an intentional variation. Tarentum had entered history after the Punic wars, but it is strange to find a Tarentine as an official in the Ptolemaic court. ANDREAS: A less common name, also associated with Ptolemy IV, as physician. He is named as such in Polybius 5.81, and probably in III Mac. 1.4, where the text is altered: see note *ad loc.* in the present series. CHIEFS OF THE BODYGUARD *archisōmatophulakes*: The title is correct, and occurs in third-century papyri. COELE-SYRIA: Aristeas' ordinary designation of Palestine, which he never mentions; the use of the word cannot be documented as a territorial designation before the second century. Where Aristeas uses "Syria" alone or "Phoenicia and Syria" (as in 22; see note there) he is closely following an earlier source. Ptolemy I's siege of Jerusalem is mentioned, on the authority of Agatharchides, by Josephus, *Against Apion* 1.205 ff., and *Ant.* 12.5 ff. The conquest of Syria cannot refer to that after the battle of Ipsus (301), which was concluded by treaty, and must hence refer to either 320 or 312. The former is unlikely, for in that battle Ptolemy commanded the navy and entrusted the land forces to Nicanor. Hence the allusion must be to the expedition of 312, at Gaza. Josephus, *Against Apion* 1.186 ff. quotes Hecataeus of Abdera as saying that after the battle of Gaza many of the inhabitants of Syria "hearing of his kindliness and his humanity, desired to accompany him to Egypt and to associate themselves with his realm," and that among these was "Ezechias, a chief priest of the Jews." On the basis of newly discovered numismatic evidence which corroborates

language. They are supposed to use Syrian, but that is not the case, for theirs is another dialect." When the king learned these particulars he gave word that a letter should be addressed to the High Priest of the Jews, in order that the design above mentioned might be carried to completion.

¹²Now I thought was the opportune moment for proffering the matter concerning which I had often petitioned Sosibius of Tarentum and Andreas, chiefs of the bodyguard, namely, the emancipation of those who had been carried away from Judaea by the king's father. He had overrun the whole of Coele-Syria and Phoenicia, exploiting his good fortune and prowess, and had transplanted some and made others captive, reducing all to subjection by terror; it was on this occasion that he transported more than a hundred thousand persons from the country of the Jews to Egypt. ¹³Of these he

the position of Ezechias, A. T. Olmstead writes, in the *Journal of the American Oriental Society* 56 (1936), 244, "With this unexpected proof that Hecataeus knew more than his critics, we are constrained to accept his other statements, that Jewish soldiers were taken to Egypt by Ptolemy I, given some sort of modified citizenship, and granted lands under military tenure": see Marcus on Josephus, *Ant.* 12.9 (Loeb).   TRANSPLANTED ... MADE CAPTIVE: Aristeas' imperfects indicate repeated action, and may suggest that the movement was voluntary; but at 12.7 Josephus (following Aristeas) indicates the removal was forcible. For detailed discussions of Jewish settlements in Egypt in the early Hellenistic period see L. Fuchs, *Die Juden Aegyptens in Ptolemäischer und Römischer Zeit* (1924), 5 ff., and V. Tcherikover, *The Jews in Egypt in the Hellenistic-Roman Age in the Light of the Papyri* (Hebrew: Jerusalem, 1945), 16 ff.

13. ARMED SOME 30,000: Josephus *Ant.* 11.345 says that Alexander gave the soldiers of Sanaballetes allotments in the Thebaid and ordered them to guard the territory, and there is good papyrus testimony that the Ptolemies followed this practice. *P. Hibeh* 96 (259 BCE), *P. Gurob* 2 (226 BCE), *P. Gurob* 8 (210 BCE), *P. Gurob* 26 (111 BCE) all prove the presence of Jewish garrisons: see Tramontano *ad loc.*   PREVIOUSLY ... EVEN BEFORE THIS: Some may have taken refuge in Egypt from the invasions of the Assyrians (722) or of the Chaldaeans (597).   AUXILIARIES ... PSAMMETICHUS: Aramaic inscriptions on rock tombs in the eastern desert opposite Oxyrhynchus, which also bear references to Psammetichus, are presumably Jewish: see W. M. Flinders Petrie, *The Jews in Egypt*, 27. It is not clear whether the Aristeas reference is to Psammetichus I (671–617), of whom Herodotus (2.151 ff.) says that he was the first Egyptian king to employ Greek mercenaries in foreign campaigns, or Psammetichus II (594–589; Herodotus calls him Psammis) who made war AGAINST THE

τρεῖς μυριάδας καθοπλίσας ἀνδρῶν ἐκλεκτῶν εἰς τὴν χώραν κατῴκισεν ἐν τοῖς φρουρίοις (ἤδη μὲν καὶ πρότερον ἱκανῶν εἰσεληλυθότων σὺν τῷ Πέρσῃ, καὶ πρὸ τούτων ἑτέρων συμμαχιῶν ἐξαπεσταλμένων πρὸς τὸν τῶν Αἰθιόπων βασιλέα μάχεσθαι σὺν Ψαμμιτίχῳ· ἀλλ' οὐ τοσοῦτοι τῷ πλήθει παρεγενήθησαν, ὅσους Πτολεμαῖος ὁ τοῦ Λάγου μετήγαγε)· ¹⁴καθὼς δὲ προείπομεν, ἐπιλέξας τοὺς ἀρίστους ταῖς ἡλικίαις καὶ ῥώμῃ διαφέροντας καθώπλισε, τὸ δὲ λοιπὸν χύμα πρεσβυτέρων καὶ νεωτέρων, ἔτι δὲ γυναικῶν, εἴασεν εἰς τὴν οἰκετίαν, οὐχ οὕτως τῇ προαιρέσει κατὰ ψυχὴν ἔχων, ὡς κατακρατούμενος ὑπὸ τῶν στρατιωτῶν, δι' ἃς ἐπεποίηντο χρείας ἐν τοῖς πολεμικοῖς ἀγῶσιν—ἡμεῖς δὲ ἐπεί τινα παρεύρεσιν εἰς τὴν ἀπόλυσιν αὐτῶν ἀπελάβομεν, καθὼς προδεδήλωται, τοιούτοις ἐχρησάμεθα λόγοις πρὸς τὸν βασιλέα ¹⁵Μήποτε ἄλογον ᾖ ἐλέγχεσθαι ὑπ' αὐτῶν τῶν πραγμάτων, ὦ βασιλεῦ. τῆς γὰρ νομοθεσίας κειμένης πᾶσι τοῖς Ἰουδαίοις, ἣν ἡμεῖς οὐ μόνον μεταγράψαι ἐπινοοῦμεν, ἀλλὰ καὶ διερμηνεῦσαι, τίνα λόγον ἕξομεν πρὸς ἀποστολήν, ἐν οἰκετίαις ὑπαρχόντων ἐν τῇ σῇ βασιλείᾳ πληθῶν ἱκανῶν; ἀλλὰ τελείᾳ καὶ πλουσίᾳ ψυχῇ ἀπόλυσον τοὺς συνεχομένους ἐν ταλαιπωρίαις, κατευθύνοντός σου τὴν βασιλείαν τοῦ τεθεικότος αὐτοῖς θεοῦ τὸν νόμον, καθὼς περιείργασμαι. ¹⁶τὸν γὰρ πάντων ἐπόπτην καὶ κτίστην θεὸν οὗτοι σέβονται,

---

16 Ζηνα και Δια edd., Ζηνα και δια τουτο MSS

KING OF THE ETHIOPIANS (Herodotus 2.161). Our reference is therefore probably to Psammetichus II. Zedekiah, king of Judah at the time, was on terms of hostility with Babylon, and sought assistance from Egypt (Ezek. 17.13 ff.), and it is not unlikely that he sent the Egyptian king auxiliaries for his war against Ethiopia. The Abu Simbel inscriptions dating from the reign of Psammetichus II speak of Greeks and Egyptians and "people of other tongue," and it is likely that the latter were Semites, for besides the names in Greek there are some in Phoenician and Hebrew. WITH THE PERSIAN: Cambyses, son of Cyrus the Great, who conquered Egypt in 525. The Elephantine papyri, dating 494–400, attest the existence in the V century of a Jewish colony originally settled there as mercenaries: see A. E. Cowley, *Jewish Documents of the Time of Ezra; Aramaic Papyri of the Fifth Century B.C.;* Sayce and Cowley, *Aramaic Papyri Discovered at Assuan.* Numbers of Jews (and Samaritans) entered Egypt under

armed some thirty thousand chosen men and settled them in garrisons in the country. Previously many had come into the country along with the Persian, and even before this others had been sent out as auxiliaries to fight in the army of Psammetichus against the king of the Ethiopians; but these were not so numerous a body as Ptolemy son of Lagus transported. ¹⁴As has been said, then, he selected and armed those that were fittest in age and outstanding in ruggedness, but the remaining bulk, those too old and too young and also the women, he reduced to bondage, not out of his own individual choice indeed, but because he was overborne by his soldiers, in return for the services which they had rendered in military action.

Now when I had procured a pretext for their release, as signified above, I addressed arguments to the king somewhat as follows: ¹⁵"Surely it would be illogical, Your Majesty, to be proven inconsistent by our deeds. For inasmuch as the legislation which we propose not only to transcribe but also to translate is laid down for all Jews, what justification shall we have for our mission when a large multitude subsists in slavery in your realm? Rather with a perfect and bountiful spirit release those who are afflicted in wretchedness, for the same God who has given them their law guides your kingdom also, as I have learned in my researches. ¹⁶God, the overseer

Alexander the Great and under the first Ptolemy: see on 12. PTOLEMY SON OF LAGUS: General of Alexander the Great, after whose death (323) he secured Egypt; in 320 he took possession of Phoenicia and Coele-Syria and captured Jerusalem. He abdicated in favor of Philadelphus in 285 and died in 283.
14. AS HAS BEEN SAID: In the preceding paragraph; see on 3. NOT OUT OF . . . CHOICE: A polite addition to spare the memory of the king's father.
15. ILLOGICAL: The logic is that the Jews are a single people because they are subject to a single Law. Courtesies could therefore not be logically extended to one portion of the Jewish people and requests made of them while the king himself was responsible for holding another portion in bondage.
16. ZEUS: The Jewish Hellenistic writers have no objection to describing God by general Greek terms for the gods, but they never apply to God the proper name of any Greek deity; only because Aristeas is represented as a non-Jew and a philosopher can he be made to speak of Zeus as meaning

ὃν καὶ πάντες, ἡμεῖς δέ, βασιλεῦ, προσονομάζοντες ἑτέρως Ζῆνα καὶ Δία· τοῦτο δ' οὐκ ἀνοικείως οἱ πρῶτοι διεσήμαναν, δι' ὃν ζωοποιοῦνται τὰ πάντα καὶ γίνεται, τοῦτον ἁπάντων ἡγεῖσθαί τε καὶ κυριεύειν. ὑπερηρκὼς δὲ σύμπαντας ἀνθρώπους τῇ λαμπρότητι τῆς ψυχῆς ἀπόλυσιν ποίησαι τῶν ἐνεχομένων ταῖς οἰκετίαις. ¹⁷Οὐδὲ πολὺν χρόνον ἐπισχών, καὶ ἡμῶν κατὰ ψυχὴν πρὸς τὸν θεὸν εὐχομένων, τὴν διάνοιαν αὐτοῦ κατασκευάσαι πρὸς τὸ τοὺς ἅπαντας ἀπολυθῆναι (κτίσμα γὰρ ὃν θεοῦ τὸ γένος τῶν ἀνθρώπων καὶ μεταλλοιοῦται καὶ τρέπεται πάλιν ὑπ' αὐτοῦ· διὸ πολλαχῶς καὶ ποικίλως ἐπεκαλούμην τὸν κυριεύοντα κατὰ καρδίαν, ἵνα συναναγκασθῇ, καθὼς ἠξίουν, ἐπιτελέσαι· ¹⁸μεγάλην γὰρ εἶχον ἐλπίδα, περὶ σωτηρίας ἀνθρώπων προτιθέμενος λόγον, ὅτι τὴν ἐπιτέλειαν ὁ θεὸς ποιήσει τῶν ἀξιουμένων· ὃ γὰρ πρὸς δικαιοσύνην καὶ καλῶν ἔργων ἐπιμέλειαν ἐν ὁσιότητι νομίζουσιν ἄνθρωποι ποιεῖν, κατευθύνει τὰς πράξεις καὶ τὰς ἐπιβολὰς ὁ κυριεύων ἁπάντων θεός), ¹⁹ὁ δὲ διανακύψας καὶ προσβλέψας ἱλαρῷ τῷ προσώπῳ Πόσας ὑπολαμβάνεις μυριάδας ἔσεσθαι; ἔφη. παρεστὼς δὲ Ἀνδρέας ἀπεφήνατο Βραχεῖ πλεῖον μυριάδων δέκα. ὁ δέ, Μικρόν γε, εἶπεν, Ἀριστέας ἡμᾶς ἀξιοῖ πρᾶγμα. Σωσίβιος δὲ καὶ τῶν παρόντων τινὲς τοῦτ' εἶπον Καὶ γὰρ ἄξιόν ἐστι τῆς σῆς μεγαλοψυχίας, ὅπως χαριστήριον ἀναθῇ τῷ μεγίστῳ θεῷ τὴν τούτων ἀπόλυσιν. μεγίστως γὰρ τετιμημένος ὑπὸ τοῦ κρατοῦντος τὰ πάντα καὶ δεδοξασμένος ὑπὲρ τοὺς προγόνους, εἰ καὶ μέγιστα ποιήσεις χαριστήρια, καθῆκόν ἐστί σοι.

the same as the God worshipped by the Jews: see Wolfson, *Philo* 1.15. Josephus' paraphrase (*Ant.* 23) has Aristeas say specifically: "It is not because I am related to them by race or am their countryman," etc.
THROUGH WHOM ... LIFE: The two accusative forms of Zeus, *Zena* and *Dia*, are here derived from *zen*, "to live," and *dia*, "through, by means of." Fanciful etymologizing of divine names to show the universal and natural attributes of the Greek gods was common in Stoic and Orphic writings. The Jewish philosopher Aristobulus has a close parallel to our passage: Eusebius, *Praep. Ev.* 13.12.7.
17. PRAYED: Significantly omitted in Josephus; see Introd. 21. RULES THE HEART: *Cf.* Proverbs 21.1, "The king's heart is in the hand of the Lord as the water-courses: He turneth it whithersoever He will." Prayer is

and creator of all things, whom they worship, is He whom all men worship, and we too, Your Majesty, though we address Him differently, as Zeus and Dis; by these names men of old not unsuitably signified that He through whom all creatures receive life and come into being is the guide and lord of all. Surpass all men, then, in magnanimity of spirit, and grant liberty to those oppressed in bondage."

[17]The king refrained himself for a little while, and I prayed inwardly to God to dispose his mind for a general release. Human beings, since they are creatures of God, are by Him turned and swayed; and therefore repeatedly and in various terms I called upon Him who rules the heart that the king might be constrained to fulfill my petition. [18]For I had high hope, in presenting an argument concerning the deliverance of men, that God would effect the fulfillment of my petition; when men piously believe that what they do is for the sake of justice and the promotion of good deeds, then God, who is Lord of all, guides their actions and their designs. [19]The king then raised his head, showing a friendly countenance, and said, "How many thousands do you suppose there will be?" Andreas, who was standing in attendance, declared, "A little more than a hundred thousand." "It is but a small matter indeed," the king said, "that Aristeas asks of us." Sosibius and others of those present said, "Surely it is worthy of your magnanimity that you dedicate the release of these people as a thank-offering to God the Greatest. Greatly as you have been honored by Him who rules all things, and greatly as you have been distinguished above your forefathers, it is fitting if you make your thank-offering very

---

stressed in Aristeas: *cf.* 45, 192, 193, 196, 197, 226, 227, 233, 242, 245, 248, 251, 256, 283, 305.
18. LORD . . . GUIDES: His consistent belief in God's creation of man and control of all his actions (*cf.* 155–156) proves Aristeas is no pagan.
19. THAN 100,000: Josephus, *Ant.* 24, "a little more than 110,000." SMALL MATTER: Slightly ironical, and in keeping with Philadelphus' fabulous lavishness. ARISTEAS: Our principal indication that A. is the author: see Introd. 3.

20 ²⁰Διαχυθεὶς δὲ εὖ μάλα τοῖς ὀψωνίοις εἶπε προσθεῖναι, καὶ σώματος ἑκάστου κομίζεσθαι δραχμὰς εἴκοσι, καὶ περὶ τούτων ἐκθεῖναι πρόσταγμα, τὰς δὲ ἀπογραφὰς ποιεῖσθαι παρ' αὐτά, μεγαλείως χρησάμενος τῇ προθυμίᾳ, τοῦ θεοῦ τὴν πᾶσαν ἐπιτελέσαντος ἡμῶν προαίρεσιν, καὶ συναναγκάσαντος αὐτὸν ἀπολυτρῶσαι μὴ μόνον τοὺς συνεληλυθότας τῷ στρατοπέδῳ τοῦ πατρός, ἀλλὰ καὶ εἴ τινες προῆσαν, ἢ μετὰ ταῦτα παρεισήχθησαν εἰς τὴν βασιλείαν. ὑπὲρ τὰ τετρακόσια τάλαντα τὴν δόσιν ἀπέφαινον εἶναι. ²¹καὶ τοῦ προστάγματος δὲ τὸ ἀντίγραφον οὐκ ἄχρηστον οἴομαι κατακεχωρίσθαι. πολλῷ γὰρ ἡ μεγαλομοιρία φανερωτέρα καὶ εὔδηλος ἔσται τοῦ βασιλέως, τοῦ θεοῦ κατισχύοντος αὐτὸν εἰς τὸ σωτηρίαν γενέσθαι πλήθεσιν ἱκανοῖς. ²²ἦν δὲ τοιοῦτο Τοῦ βασιλέως προστάξαντος—"Ὅσοι τῶν συν-

20 W conjectures a lacuna after βασιλειαν, to be filled by an objection of the courtiers that if others besides Ptolemy I's captives were to be included the sum would be υπερ τα τετρακοσια ταλαντα
21 μεγαλομοιρια MSS, μεγαλομερια W

20. The number and total redemption price of the slaves (19, 20, 27) show discrepancies. In 19–20 the number is 100,000 (approximately) and the price 20 dr. each; the total would therefore be 2,000,000 dr. or 333⅓ talents, reckoning 6000 dr. to the talent. The 66⅔ talents which is the difference between this sum and the 400 talents here mentioned may be accounted for by the additional slaves released, which would then number 20,000. The total set free would then be 120,000 and the cost 400 talents. But at 27 the total redemption money is given as 660 talents, and the 260 talents in excess would account for 78,000 additional slaves, or a total of 198,000. It is difficult to account for the disparity by the inclusion of infants. Josephus says the total amount was over 460 talents; this would mean an addition of only 18,000 and a total of 138,000, which is more credible. Wendland suggests that the 660 at 27 is merely a doubling of 333⅓, using 330 as a round number. Furthermore the price per slave seems improbably low; and perhaps for this reason Josephus makes it 120 dr. instead of 20. W. L. Westermann, *Upon Slavery in Ptolemaic Egypt* (New York, 1929), 60 f., gives a price range of 50–300 dr., and suggests 40 f.) that since we have here a flat rate, including infants and the like, 20 dr. is not a purchase price but simply a token compensation for a great loss. On the other hand, P. Gradewitz 1 (G. Plaumann, *Sitzungsber. Heid. Akad., ph.-hist. Kl.* 5 (1914), seems to refer to a price of 20 dr. each for war prisoners in the eighteenth year of Philadelphus.

21. MUNIFICENCE is in Josephus, but WHOM GOD is not.

22 ff. In the *P. Gradewitz* 1 publication cited on 20 above, U. Wilcken

20 great." ²⁰The king was delighted, and ordered that an addition be made to the soldiers' stipends, that twenty drachmas be paid for each slave, that a decree should be issued concerning these matters, and the registers be constituted forthwith. Generous was the zeal he displayed; God fulfilled our whole desire and constrained him to liberate not only those who had accompanied his father's army, but also any that were there previously or had been brought into the kingdom subsequently. It was pointed out that the donation was in excess of four hundred talents.

²¹I think it not unprofitable to put the text of the decree on record. Thus the munificence of the king, whom God enabled to become a means of deliverance to a numerous multitude, will be far more manifest and explicit. It ran as follows: ²²"All persons who took the field with our father against the regions of Syria and Phoenicia and in the invasion

---

pointed out the keen knowledge of Ptolemaic administrative procedure displayed in the composition of this decree, and in *Archiv für Papyrusforschung* 12 (1937), 221 ff., he pronounced it a genuine official document. The occasion for this judgment was H. Liebesny's publication of *P. Rainer* 24,552, in *Aegyptus* 16 (1936), 257–291, which contains a decree dealing with registration of slaves, which Liebesny attributes to Ptolemy Philadelphus, calling attention to the similarity to our passage. W. L. Westermann, "Enslaved Persons Who Are Free," *American Journal of Philology* 59 (1938), 1–30, denies that ours is an official document, but asserts, on the basis of close parallelism in language, and especially of his use of "Syria" or "Syria and Phoenicia" in the decree where Aristeas otherwise uses "Coele-Syria," that our passage is actually a reworking of the decree of Philadelphus preserved in *P. Rainer* 24,552. Our decree, in turn, shows striking resemblances to those ascribed to Ptolemy IV Philopator in III Mac. 7.1 ff., similarly releasing the Jews of Egypt from a hardship, and III Mac. 3.12 ff., ordering disabilities placed upon the Jews. Our passage is a decree (*prostagma*) in form, whereas the III Mac. documents are circular orders in letter form; the similarities nevertheless seem closer than could be accounted for by the fact that both books follow correct chancellery usage. Philopator's hostile decree insists, as ours does and the genuine decree does not, on the king's generally humanitarian motives, and it orders similar harsh punishment for recalcitrants—a punishment which Josephus' paraphrase of Aristeas significantly omits. Philopator's favorable decree is in spirit very like the present passage, except that where here the king's measures are motivated by enlightened statesmanship, in III Mac. they are motivated by fear of God's retribution. For possible relationship between the two books, see Introd. 33, and Introd. to III Mac. in this series.

ἐστρατευμένων τῷ πατρὶ ἡμῶν εἰς τοὺς κατὰ Συρίαν καὶ
Φοινίκην τόπους ἐπελθόντες τὴν τῶν Ἰουδαίων χώραν
ἐγκρατεῖς ἐγένοντο σωμάτων Ἰουδαϊκῶν καὶ ταῦτα διακε-
κομίκασιν εἴς τε τὴν πόλιν καὶ τὴν χώραν ἢ καὶ πεπράκασιν
ἑτέροις, ὁμοίως δὲ καὶ εἴ τινες προῆσαν ἢ καὶ μετὰ ταῦτά
εἰσιν εἰσηγμένοι τῶν τοιούτων, ἀπολύειν παρὰ χρῆμα τοὺς
ἔχοντας, κομιζομένους αὐτίκα ἑκάστου σώματος δραχμὰς
εἴκοσι, τοὺς μὲν στρατιώτας τῇ τῶν ὀψωνίων δόσει, τοὺς
δὲ λοιποὺς ἀπὸ τῆς βασιλικῆς τραπέζης. ²³νομίζομεν γὰρ
καὶ παρὰ τὴν τοῦ πατρὸς ἡμῶν βούλησιν καὶ παρὰ τὸ καλῶς
ἔχον ἠχμαλωτεῦσθαι τούτους, διὰ δὲ τὴν στρατιωτικὴν
προπέτειαν τήν τε χώραν αὐτῶν κατεφθάρθαι καὶ τὴν τῶν
Ἰουδαίων μεταγωγὴν εἰς τὴν Αἴγυπτον γεγονέναι· ἱκανὴ
γὰρ ἦν ἡ παρὰ τὸ πεδίον γεγονυῖα ἐκ τῶν στρατιωτῶν
ὠφέλεια· διὸ παντελῶς ἀνεπιεικής ἐστι καὶ ἡ τῶν ἀνθρώπων
καταδυναστεία. ²⁴πᾶσιν οὖν ἀνθρώποις τὸ δίκαιον ἀπονέμειν
ὁμολογούμενοι, πολλῷ δὲ μᾶλλον τοῖς ἀλόγως καταδυνασ-
τευομένοις, καὶ κατὰ πᾶν ἐκζητοῦντες τὸ καλῶς ἔχον πρός
τε τὸ δίκαιον καὶ τὴν κατὰ πάντων εὐσέβειαν, προστετά-
χαμεν ὅσα τῶν Ἰουδαϊκῶν ἐστι σωμάτων ἐν οἰκετίαις
<πανταχῇ> καθ' ὁντινοῦν τρόπον ἐν τῇ βασιλείᾳ, κομι-
ζομένους τοὺς ἔχοντας τὸ προκείμενον κεφάλαιον ἀπολύειν,
καὶ μηδένα κακοσχόλως περὶ τούτων μηδὲν οἰκονομεῖν· τὰς
δ'ἀπογραφὰς ἐν ἡμέραις πρισίν, ἀφ' ἧς ἡμέρας ἐκκεῖται τὸ
πρόσταγμα, ποιεῖσθαι πρὸς τοὺς καθεσταμένους περὶ τούτων,
25 καταδεικνύντας εὐθὺ καὶ τὰ σώματα. ²⁵διειλήφαμεν γὰρ
καὶ ἡμῖν συμφέρειν καὶ τοῖς πράγμασι τοῦτ' ἐπιτελεσθῆναι.
τὸν δὲ βουλόμενον προσαγγέλλειν περὶ τῶν ἀπειθησάντων,
ἐφ' ᾧ τοῦ φανέντος ἐνόχου τὴν κυρίαν ἕξειν· τὰ δὲ ὑπάρ-
χοντα τῶν τοιούτων εἰς τὸ βασιλικὸν ἀναληφθήσεται.
²⁶Εἰσδοθέντος τοῦ προστάγματος, ὅπως ἐπαναγνωσθῇ τῷ

---

23 παρα το πεδιον MSS, παρα ποδα Schmidt, παρα πολεμον Naber
24 ομολογουμενοι edd., ομολογουμενως, ομολογουμενοις MSS / πανταχη T, παντι και W, παντι μη MSS
25 εφ' ω edd., εφη MSS; Tramontano suggests εφεικαμεν, "we grant"

23. MILITARY RECKLESSNESS: Apparently another pious touch to save Ptolemy I's reputation.
24. JUSTICE TO ALL MEN: Not an absurd claim for Philadelphus.

of the country of the Jews came into possession of Jewish slaves and have brought them over to our city and country or have sold them to others—and likewise if any such were in the country previously or introduced subsequently—those holding them shall release them straightway, receiving forthwith compensation of twenty drachmas for each slave, the soldiers with the payment of their stipend, and others from the royal bank. [23]For it is our belief that these persons were made prisoner contrary to the will of our father and to propriety, and that it was to military recklessness that the despoliation of their country and the removal of the Jews themselves to Egypt was due. The booty which accrued to the soldiers on the field of battle was sufficient; hence the further oppression of the people was wholly inequitable. [24]Therefore, since it is our professed purpose to award justice to all men, and more particularly to those who are unreasonably tyrannized, and since we strive in every respect to deal fairly with all men in accordance with justice and piety, we have decreed that so many Jewish persons as are held in bondage in whatever manner anywhere in the kingdom their owners shall release upon receipt of the stipulated sum. No one shall be in any way negligent in the discharge of this obligation. Lists shall be submitted to the officials placed in charge of this matter within three days from the posting up of this decree, and the persons involved shall be produced at once. [25]For we have determined that it is advantageous both for ourselves and for the realm for this business to be accomplished. Any who wish may give information concerning recalcitrants, on condition that the informer acquire ownership of the culprit; the property of the defaulters shall be confiscated to the royal purse."

[26]The decree as submitted to be read over to the king con-

---

25. ACQUIRE OWNERSHIP OF THE CULPRIT: Neither in the genuine decree nor in Josephus. It is worth noting that at 166 f. the class of informers is castigated in the severest terms.

26. THE KING HIMSELF . . . MADE THE ADDITION: Westermann, *op. cit.* 22, acutely notes: "It was probably the absence of this provision in the model used by Pseudo-Aristeas in shaping his decree which suggested to the

βασιλεῖ, τὰ ἄλλα πάντ' ἔχοντος πλὴν τοῦ Καὶ εἴ τινες προῆσαν ἢ καὶ μετὰ ταῦτα εἰσηγμένοι εἰσι τῶν τοιούτων, αὐτὸς τοῦτο ὁ βασιλεὺς προσέθηκε, μεγαλομοιρίᾳ καὶ μεγαλοψυχίᾳ χρησάμενος, ἐκέλευσέ τε τῶν διαφόρων δόσιν ἀθρόαν οὖσαν ἀπομερίσαι τοῖς ὑπηρέταις τῶν ταγμάτων καὶ βασιλικοῖς τραπεζίταις. ²⁷οὕτω δοχθὲν ἐκεκύρωτο ἐν ἡμέραις ἑπτά· πλεῖον δὲ ταλάντων ἑξακοσίων ἑξήκοντα ἡ δόσις ἐγεγόνει. πολλὰ γὰρ καὶ τῶν ἐπιμαστιδίων τέκνων σὺν ταῖς μητράσιν ἐλευθεροῦντο. προσανενεχθέντος εἰ καὶ περὶ τούτων εἰκοσαδραχμία δοθήσεται, καὶ τοῦτ' ἐκέλευσεν ὁ βασιλεὺς ποιεῖν, ὁλοσχερῶς περὶ τοῦ δόξαντος ἅπαντ' ἐπιτελῶν.

²⁸Ὡς δὲ κατεπράχθη ταῦτα, τὸν Δημήτριον ἐκέλευσεν εἰσδοῦναι περὶ τῆς τῶν Ἰουδαϊκῶν βιβλίων ἀναγραφῆς. πάντα γὰρ διὰ προσταγμάτων καὶ μεγάλης ἀσφαλείας τοῖς βασιλεῦσι τούτοις διῳκεῖτο, καὶ οὐδὲν ἀπερριμμένως οὐδ' εἰκῇ. διόπερ καὶ τὸ τῆς εἰσδόσεως καὶ τὰ τῶν ἐπιστολῶν ἀντίγραφα κατακεχώρικα, καὶ τὸ τῶν ἀπεσταλμένων πλῆθος καὶ τὴν ἑκάστου κατασκευήν, διὰ τὸ μεγαλομοιρίᾳ καὶ τέχνῃ διαφέρειν ἕκαστον αὐτῶν. τῆς δὲ εἰσδόσεώς ἐστιν ἀντίγραφον τόδε ²⁹Βασιλεῖ μεγάλῳ παρὰ Δημητρίου. προστάξαντός σου, βασιλεῦ, περὶ τῶν ἀπολιπόντων εἰς τὴν συμπλήρωσιν τῆς βιβλιοθήκης βιβλίων, ὅπως ἐπισυναχθῇ, καὶ τὰ διαπεπτωκότα τύχῃ τῆς προσηκούσης ἐπισκευῆς, πεποιημένος οὐ παρέργως τὴν ἐν τούτοις ἐπιμέλειαν, προσανα-

---

28 διῳκεῖτο] some MSS have διῳκητο
(plupf.) or other variations

author the idea that it should be inserted at the special instance of King Ptolemy himself after the *prostagma* had been drafted and presented to him. Artistically this addition is turned into a clever literary device for enhancing that 'munificence and greatness of soul' which prompted Philadelphus to accede to the original proposal of Aristeas regarding the Jewish slaves and, in this particular, even to widen its scope." BANKERS: Banks were a royal monopoly in Egypt: see M. Rostovtzeff, *A Social and Economic History of the Hellenistic World* (Oxford, 1941), 2.1282 ff.

27. SEVEN DAYS: Unexampled and impossible, as Westermann, *op. cit.* 24 f., points out; but the author wishes to represent the whole enterprise, like the actual translation, as being carried out with miraculous dispatch.

tained all the rest with the exception of the clause "If any such were in the country previously or introduced subsequently," and the king himself, indulging his munificence and magnanimity, made the addition. He also ordered that the several amounts be assigned in a lump sum to the paymasters of the forces and to the royal bankers. [27]Thus the matter was decreed and went into force in seven days. The grant amounted to more than six hundred and sixty talents, for many children at the breast were emancipated along with their mothers. When the question was raised whether the sum of twenty drachmas should be paid out for these also, the king ordered that this should be done, so completely did he give effect to his decision in every detail.

[28]Now when this business was finished he bade Demetrius to submit a statement concerning the transcription of the Jewish books. These kings used to administer all their business through decrees and with great precaution; nothing was done negligently or casually. I have therefore put on record copies of the memorial and the letters and also an inventory of the lavish gifts and a description of each, for each was outstanding in magnificence and artistic execution. Here is the copy of the memorial:

[29]"To the great king, from Demetrius: At Your Majesty's bidding with respect to the completion of the collection of books in the library, that those which are wanting should be added to the collection and that those in disrepair should receive the proper attention, my efforts in the charge have not been cursory, and I now submit the following statement

---

660 TALENTS: Josephus says 460; see on 20.

28–33. DEMETRIUS' MEMORANDUM.

28. THESE KINGS USED TO ADMINISTER: A clear indication (but the imperfect tense of the verb is not textually certain) that the events were in fact remote from the author's day, for only *one* Ptolemy preceded Philadelphus; there is also a note of wistful admiration for the better days of old.   THESE KINGS: Could hardly be used under Philadelphus' successors, and perhaps not even under the Ptolemaic dynasty at all. Ptolemy Auletes (the father of Caesar's Cleopatra) was indeed of a new line, and may mark a division. See 288 and Introd. 11.

29. The form of this memorandum seems to follow correct Ptolemaic usage.

110 ΑΡΙΣΤΕΑΣ ΦΙΛΟΚΡΑΤΕΙ 30–32

30 φέρω σοι τάδε. ³⁰τοῦ νόμου τῶν Ἰουδαίων βιβλία σὺν ἑτέροις ὀλίγοις τισὶν ἀπολείπει· τυγχάνει γὰρ Ἑβραϊκοῖς γράμμασι καὶ φωνῇ λεγόμενα, ἀμελέστερον δέ, καὶ οὐχ ὡς ὑπάρχει, σεσήμανται, καθὼς ὑπὸ τῶν εἰδότων προσαναφέρεται· προνοίας γὰρ βασιλικῆς οὐ τέτευχε. ³¹δέον δέ ἐστι καὶ ταῦθ' ὑπάρχειν παρά σοι διηκριβωμένα, διὰ τὸ καὶ φιλοσοφωτέραν εἶναι καὶ ἀκέραιον τὴν νομοθεσίαν ταύτην, ὡς ἂν οὖσαν θείαν. διὸ πόρρω γεγόνασιν οἵ τε συγγραφεῖς καὶ ποιηταὶ καὶ τὸ τῶν ἱστορικῶν πλῆθος τῆς ἐπιμνήσεως τῶν προειρημένων βιβλίων, καὶ τῶν κατ' αὐτὰ πεπολιτευμένων [καὶ πολιτευομένων] ἀνδρῶν, διὰ τὸ ἁγνήν τινα καὶ σεμνὴν εἶναι τὴν ἐν αὐτοῖς θεωρίαν, ὥς φησιν Ἑκαταῖος ὁ Ἀβδηρίτης. ³²ἐὰν οὖν φαίνηται, βασιλεῦ, γραφήσεται πρὸς τὸν ἀρχιερέα τὸν ἐν Ἱεροσολύμοις, ἀποστεῖλαι τοὺς μάλιστα καλῶς βεβιωκότας καὶ πρεσβυτέρους ὄντας ἄνδρας, ἐμπείρους τῶν κατὰ τὸν νόμον τὸν ἑαυτῶν, ἀφ' ἑκάστης φυλῆς ἕξ, ὅπως τὸ σύμφωνον ἐκ τῶν πλειόνων ἐξετάσαντες καὶ λαβόντες τὸ κατὰ τὴν ἑρμηνείαν ἀκριβές, ἀξίως καὶ τῶν πραγμάτων καὶ τῆς σῆς προαιρέσεως, θῶμεν εὐσήμως.

31 αυτα edd., αυτας MSS / και πολιτευομενων bracketed (perhaps wrongly) on the basis of omission in Eus. and Jos.

30. COMMITTED TO WRITING: The entire sentence seems intentionally ambiguous. The important question, for the history of the Greek translation of the Bible, is whether the existing books referred to are carelessly-transmitted Hebrew texts or carelessly-made earlier translations. It seems unnatural for the king to be interested in the state of the Hebrew text, and *sesēmantai* more regularly means "interpreted," *i.e.*, translated. The phrase *oukh hōs huparkhei* is also difficult Greek. P. Kahle, *The Cairo Geniza* (London, 1947), 132 ff., takes this passage as a principal argument for his theory that Aristeas is intended to give authority not to the original translation of the Law into Greek, but to a revision of the original translation. KING'S FORETHOUGHT: Expected flattery, but justified by what the royal librarians were doing for secular texts.
31. LEGISLATION . . . PHILOSOPHICAL: So in IV Mac. Eleazar insists on the philosophical character of the legislation (5.35, 7.7), while Antiochus denies it (5.6, 5.22).   ABSTAINED: The notion that aliens must not deal with Scripture because of its special sanctity is referred to again by Demetrius at 314–316, where he cites the divine deterrents visited upon Theopompus and Theodectes—probably also on the authority of "Hecataeus."   HECATAEUS: A contemporary of Alexander and a familiar at the court of Ptolemy I. Considerable portions of his semi-fabulous history of Egypt (in which he speaks of the Jews favorably as making no images and nurturing their

30 to you. ³⁰The books of the Law of the Jews together with some few others are wanting. It happens that they are written in Hebrew characters and in the Hebrew tongue, and they have been committed to writing somewhat carelessly and not adequately, according to the testimony of experts, for they have never benefited by a king's forethought. ³¹It is necessary that these books too, in an emended form, should be given a place in your library, for their legislation is most philosophical and flawless, inasmuch as it is divine. It is for this reason that authors and poets and the mass of historians have abstained from mentioning these aforesaid books and the men who have lived and are living in accordance with them, because the views set forth in them have a certain holiness and sanctity, as Hecataeus of Abdera says. ³²If it seems good to Your Majesty, therefore, a letter shall be written to the High Priest at Jerusalem requesting him to dispatch elders who have led exemplary lives and are expert in their own law, six from each tribe, so that when we have examined wherein the majority agree and have obtained an accurate translation we may lay it up in a distinguished manner worthy of the subject matter and of your benevolence. Fare well forever."

children carefully) are incorporated in the first book of Diodorus Siculus. His was therefore a suitable name to attach to later works on the history of the Jews and on Abraham (probably the same book) which are cited by Josephus (*Against Apion* 1.182 ff., *Ant.* 1.159). The chief tendency of these works was to demonstrate the high antiquity of Judaism and its influence upon the earliest Greeks. The question would then arise why classical authors failed to mention the Jews, and "Hecataeus" doubtless did provide some such explanation as is here cited. But it is not impossible that the statement here cited is from the real Hecataeus: see on 12.

32. IF IT SEEMS GOOD: The omission of *soi* points to a date after 163 BCE: see Meecham, 332 f.   ELDERS: *I.e.*, authoritative representatives, as is also perhaps the intention of SIX FROM EACH TRIBE (repeated in the king's letter and in Eleazar's reply, 39 and 46). The tribal division had fallen into desuetude, and its use suggests an idealization on the basis of Scripture. The number 72 seems to be Aristeas' own invention, for the title of the LXX and the number of Moses' elders given at Ex. 24.1, 9 would suggest 70. Furthermore the eleventh questions in the last two sessions of table talk (273 and 291) seem extra additions beyond the expected number. See Introd. 42.   FARE WELL FOREVER: *eutukhei* is regularly employed to conclude a letter to a superior, and hence correctly used here. Between equals the formula is *errōso*, as correctly used in 40 and 46.

εὐτύχει διὰ παντός. ³³Τῆς δὲ εἰσδόσεως ταύτης γενομένης, ἐκέλευσεν ὁ βασιλεὺς γραφῆναι πρὸς τὸν Ἐλεάζαρον περὶ τούτων, σημάναντας καὶ τὴν γενομένην ἀπολύτρωσιν τῶν αἰχμαλώτων. ἔδωκε δὲ καὶ εἰς κατασκευὴν κρατήρων τε καὶ φιαλῶν καὶ τραπέζης καὶ σπονδείων χρυσίου μὲν ὁλκῆς τάλαντα πεντήκοντα καὶ ἀργυρίου τάλαντα ἑβδομήκοντα καὶ λίθων ἱκανόν τι πλῆθος—ἐκέλευσε δὲ τοὺς ρισκοφύλακας τοῖς τεχνίταις, ὧν ἂν προαιρῶνται, τὴν ἐκλογὴν διδόναι—καὶ νομίσματος εἰς θυσίας καὶ ἄλλα πρὸς τάλαντα ἑκατόν. ³⁴δηλώσομεν δέ σοι περὶ τῆς κατασκευῆς, ὡς ἂν τὰ τῶν ἐπιστολῶν ἀντίγραφα διέλθωμεν. ἦν δὲ ἡ τοῦ βασιλέως
35 ἐπιστολὴ τὸν τύπον ἔχουσα τοῦτον ³⁵Βασιλεὺς Πτολεμαῖος Ἐλεαζάρῳ ἀρχιερεῖ χαίρειν καὶ ἐρρῶσθαι. ἐπεὶ συμβαίνει πλείονας τῶν Ἰουδαίων εἰς τὴν ἡμετέραν χώραν κατῳκίσθαι γενηθέντας ἀνασπάστους ἐκ τῶν Ἱεροσολύμων ὑπὸ Περσῶν, καθ' ὃν ἐπεκράτουν χρόνον, ἔτι δὲ καὶ συνεληλυθέναι τῷ πατρὶ ἡμῶν εἰς τὴν Αἴγυπτον αἰχμαλώτους,—³⁶ἀφ' ὧν πλείονας εἰς τὸ στρατιωτικὸν σύνταγμα κατεχώρισεν ἐπὶ μείζοσι μισθοφορίαις, ὁμοίως δὲ καὶ τοὺς προόντας κρίνας πιστοὺς φρούρια κτίσας ἀπέδωκεν αὐτοῖς, ὅπως τὸ τῶν Αἰγυπτίων ἔθνος φόβον [μὴ] ἔχῃ διὰ τούτων· καὶ ἡμεῖς δὲ παραλαβόντες τὴν βασιλείαν φιλανθρωπότερον ἀπαντῶμεν τοῖς πᾶσι, πολὺ δὲ μᾶλλον τοῖς σοῖς πολίταις—³⁷ὑπὲρ δέκα μυριάδας αἰχμαλώτων ἠλευθερώκαμεν, ἀποδόντες

---

36 μη bracketed (probably rightly) on basis of omission in Eus. and Jos.

37 επι χρειων edd., επι χειρων MSS, επικρινων Euseb.

33. ELEAZAR: see on 1; at this point Josephus (12.43–44) inserts a note on the genealogy of Eleazar.   SEVENTY TALENTS OF SILVER: Not in Josephus. COINED MONEY: Silver.
34–51. THE LETTERS OF PTOLEMY AND ELEAZAR.
34. I SHALL GIVE YOU AN ACCOUNT: 51–82.
35. KING PTOLEMY TO ELEAZAR THE HIGH PRIEST: Correct usage for an exchange between sovereigns: Bickermann, "Zur Datierung des Pseudo-Aristeas," *Zeitschrift für die neutestamentliche Wissenschaft* 29 (1930), 280–296. It is only thus indirectly that the presumed courtier of Ptolemy Philadelphus identifies his monarch, whom he speaks of, in his own person, as "Your Majesty." The reign of Ptolemy Philadelphus (285–247) was brilliant, and he was in fact a patron of fine arts and learning. His memory was especially dear to the Jews; Philo, *Moses* 2.29 f., eulogizes

³³When this memorial had been submitted, the king bade that a letter be written to Eleazar concerning these matters, informing him also of the liberation of the captives. For the construction of bowls and flagons and a table and libation cups he presented gold fifty talents in weight and seventy talents of silver and a great quantity of stones—he bade the treasurers allow the craftsmen to select the materials they preferred—and for sacrifices and other purposes he presented as much as a hundred talents of coined money.

³⁴Of the construction of the gifts I shall give you an account when I have done with the copies of the letters. The purport of the king's letter was as follows:

35   ³⁵"King Ptolemy to Eleazar the High Priest, greeting and good health. Whereas it is come about that many Jews have been settled in our country, some forcibly removed from Jerusalem by the Persians during their period of power and others who came into Egypt as captives in the train of our father—³⁶of these he enrolled many in the armed forces at higher than ordinary pay, and likewise when he judged their chief men to be loyal he gave them fortresses which he built, so that the native Egyptians might be in awe of them; and we too, since we have assumed the realm, meet all men in a very humane manner but your countrymen to a special degree—³⁷we, then, have given liberty to above a hundred

---

him in the highest terms: see Introd. 23.   BY THE PERSIANS: More prominence is given to the relatively smaller number introduced by the Persians in order to minimize the Ptolemies' injustice.

36. ENROLLED: See on 12 and 13.   CHIEF MEN: The Greek *proontas* may also bear the meaning "those who were already in the country," and so Thackeray takes it.   MIGHT BE IN AWE OF THEM: The MSS insert the negative *mē*, "might *not* be in awe of them," but the parallels in Josephus and Eusebius omit the negative, and the historical context also suggests its omission.

37. HAVE GIVEN LIBERTY . . . PAYING: See on 12 and 22. Commenting on this passage in his "Seleucid Babylonia: Bullae and Seals of Clay with Greek Inscriptions," *Yale Classical Studies* 3 (1932), 68, Professor Rostovtzeff thinks that it reflects an actual measure of Ptolemy Philadelphus. "The Syrian War was ended successfully by Philadelphus and during this war no doubt large quantities of slaves were imported into Egypt and sold there both by the king and by his officers and soldiers, as well as by private

τοῖς κρατοῦσι τὴν κατ' ἀξίαν ἀργυρικὴν τιμήν, διορθούμενοι καὶ εἴ τι κακῶς ἐπράχθη διὰ τὰς τῶν ὄχλων ὁρμάς, διειληφότες εὐσεβῶς τοῦτο πρᾶξαι, καὶ τῷ μεγίστῳ θεῷ χαριστικὸν ἀνατιθέντες, ὃς ἡμῖν τὴν βασιλείαν ἐν εἰρήνῃ καὶ δόξῃ κρατίστῃ παρ' ὅλην τὴν οἰκουμένην διατετήρηκεν· εἴς τε τὸ στράτευμα τοὺς ἀκμαιοτάτους ταῖς ἡλικίαις τετάχαμεν, τοὺς δὲ δυναμένους καὶ περὶ ἡμᾶς εἶναι, τῆς περὶ τὴν αὐλὴν πίστεως ἀξίους, ἐπὶ χρειῶν καθεστάκαμεν. ³⁸βουλομένων δ' ἡμῶν καὶ τούτοις χαρίζεσθαι καὶ πᾶσι τοῖς κατὰ τὴν οἰκουμένην Ἰουδαίοις καὶ τοῖς μετέπειτα, προῃρήμεθα τὸν νόμον ὑμῶν μεθερμηνευθῆναι γράμμασιν Ἑλληνικοῖς ἐκ τῶν παρ' ὑμῶν λεγομένων Ἑβραϊκῶν γραμμάτων, ἵν' ὑπάρχῃ καὶ ταῦτα παρ' ἡμῖν ἐν βιβλιοθήκῃ σὺν τοῖς ἄλλοις βασιλικοῖς βιβλίοις. ³⁹καλῶς οὖν ποιήσεις καὶ τῆς ἡμετέρας σπουδῆς ἀξίως ἐπιλεξάμενος ἄνδρας καλῶς βεβιωκότας πρεσβυτέρους, ἐμπειρίαν ἔχοντας τοῦ νόμου, καὶ δυνατοὺς ἑρμηνεῦσαι, ἀφ' ἑκάστης φυλῆς ἕξ, ὅπως ἐκ τῶν πλειόνων τὸ σύμφωνον εὑρεθῇ, διὰ τὸ περὶ μειζόνων εἶναι τὴν σκέψιν. οἰόμεθα γὰρ ἐπιτελεσθέντος τούτου μεγάλην ἀποίσεσθαι
40 δόξαν. ⁴⁰ἀπεστάλκαμεν δὲ περὶ τούτων Ἀνδρέαν τῶν ἀρχισωματοφυλάκων καὶ Ἀριστέαν, τιμωμένους παρ' ἡμῖν, διαλεξομένους σοι καὶ κομίζοντας ἀπαρχὰς εἰς τὸ ἱερὸν

---

40 κεχαρισμενος Euseb., και χαρισαμενος MSS

dealers who bought the slaves from the victors on the spot. The influx of slaves no doubt required special attention and was handled in his own way by 'the genius of fiscality' that Philadelphus certainly was." IN-JURY... THROUGH... THE MOB: This allusion to Egyptian anti-Semitism is characteristically omitted by Josephus. WORTHY OF THE TRUST OF THE ROYAL COURT: The striking similarity of this expression with a similar expression at I Mac. 10.37 has been adduced as an argument that Aristeas is in part based on I Mac.: see A. Momigliano, *Prime Linee di Storia della Tradizione Maccabaica* (Rome, 1931), 164.
38. TO SHOW FAVOR: In Demetrius' memorandum (29 ff.) the sole motive for the translation was the requirements of the library; from 308 ff. it is quite clear that it was made primarily for the needs of the Jewish community. This passage is an interesting combination of the two motives, and indeed makes the king's interest in the project more credible. ALL THE JEWS IN THE WORLD: This seems to envisage a Greek-speaking diaspora much more widespread that could in fact have existed in the time of

thousand captives, paying their owners proper market prices and making good whatever injury may have been inflicted through the impulses of the mob. Our resolve in this matter was to do a pious deed and to dedicate a thank-offering to God the Most High, who has preserved our kingdom in tranquillity and in the mightiest esteem throughout the inhabited world. Those in the flower of their age, moreover, we have enrolled in our forces, and to those capable of being about our person and worthy of the trust of the royal court we have assigned offices of state. [38]Now since we desire to show favor to these and to all the Jews in the world and to their posterity we have resolved that your Law should be translated into Greek writing from the Hebrew tongue in use among you, so that these writings should find place in our library along with other royal books. [39]It will be a courteous act, therefore, and one worthy of our own zeal if you will choose elders of exemplary life who possess skill in the law and ability to translate, six from each tribe, so that it may be discovered wherein the majority agree, for the investigation concerns a matter of great weight. We think that we shall bear off great renown by the accomplishment of this task. [40]We have sent upon this business Andreas, of the keepers of the bodyguard, and Aristeas, men whom we hold in honor,

---

Ptolemy Philadelphus, and would point to a later date. HEBREW TONGUE IN USE AMONG YOU: The Greek may also bear the translation "the Hebrew tongue as you call it."
39. IT WILL BE A COURTEOUS ACT: Formal language of polite insistence. ELDERS etc.: A compendious statement of the suggestions in Demetrius' memorandum. WHEREIN THE MAJORITY AGREE: A further indication that the product is to have official authority.
40. ARISTEAS: This is the only explicit statement that Aristeas was an official courtier of the king. WHOM WE HOLD IN HONOR: Like the analogous "king's friends" this refers to a specific degree of royal preferment. As far as we know it was only under Ptolemy VI Philometor and Ptolemy VII Euergetes II that Jews, like the generals Onias and Dositheus, played an important role. DEDICATORY OFFERINGS: The Greek *aparkhai* is the regular LXX word for "first-fruits." AND . . . A HUNDRED TALENTS: Perhaps "and" should be deleted, and "hundred talents" taken in apposition to "offerings." For parallels to show that the close of this letter follows correct Ptolemaic usage, see Tramontano 159 f.

ἀναθημάτων καὶ εἰς θυσίας καὶ τὰ ἄλλα ἀργυρίου τάλαντα ἑκατόν. γράφων δὲ καὶ σὺ πρὸς ἡμᾶς περὶ ὧν ἐὰν βούλῃ κεχαρισμένος ἔσῃ, καὶ φιλίας ἄξιόν τι πράξεις, ὡς ἐπιτελεσθησομένων τὴν ταχίστην περὶ ὧν ἂν αἱρῇ. ἔρρωσο. ⁴¹Πρὸς ταύτην τὴν ἐπιστολὴν ἀντέγραψεν ἐνδεχομένως ὁ Ἐλεάζαρος ταῦτα Ἐλεάζαρος ἀρχιερεὺς βασιλεῖ Πτολεμαίῳ φίλῳ γνησίῳ χαίρειν. αὐτός τε ἔρρωσο καὶ ἡ βασίλισσα Ἀρσινόη, ἡ ἀδελφή, καὶ τὰ τέκνα, καλῶς ἂν ἔχοι καὶ ὡς βουλόμεθα, καὶ αὐ οἱ ἐ ὑγιαίνομεν. ⁴²λαβόντες τὴν παρὰ σοῦ ἐπιστολὴν μεγάλως ἐχάρημεν διὰ τὴν προαίρεσίν σου καὶ τὴν καλὴν βουλήν, καὶ συναγαγόντες τὸ πᾶν πλῆθος παρανέγνωμεν αὐτοῖς, ἵνα εἰδῶσιν ἣν ἔχεις πρὸς τὸν θεὸν ἡμῶν εὐσέβειαν. ἐπεδείξαμεν δὲ καὶ τὰς φιάλας ἃς ἀπέστειλας, χρυσᾶς εἴκοσι καὶ ἀργυρᾶς τριάκοντα, κρατῆρας πέντε, καὶ τράπεζαν εἰς ἀνάθεσιν, καὶ εἰς προσαγωγὴν θυσιῶν καὶ εἰς ἐπισκευὰς ὧν ἂν δέηται τὸ ἱερὸν ἀργυρίου τάλαντα ἑκατόν, ⁴³ἅπερ ἐκόμισεν Ἀνδρέας τῶν τετιμημένων παρὰ σοὶ καὶ Ἀριστέας, ἄνδρες καλοὶ καὶ ἀγαθοὶ καὶ παιδείᾳ διαφέροντες καὶ τῆς σῆς ἀγωγῆς καὶ δικαιοσύνης ἄξιοι κατὰ πάντα· οἳ καὶ μετέδωκαν ἡμῖν τὰ παρὰ σοῦ, πρὸς ἃ καὶ παρ' ἡμῶν ἀκηκόασιν ἁρμόζοντα τοῖς σοῖς γράμμασι. ⁴⁴πάντα γὰρ ὅσα σοι συμφέρει, καὶ εἰ παρὰ

---

41 ενδεχουενως MSS, εκδ. Diels
42 δεηται MSS and Jos., προσδεηται
Euseb. (W: "fortasse recte")
43 εκομιζον MSS also have εκομιζεν, εκομισεν, Jos. εκομιζαν
44 τροπους edd.-Euseb., MSS omit

41. AS WELL AS MIGHT BE: A variant, *ekdekhomenōs*, would mean "immediately." *Endekhomenōs* may mean "appropriately" or "to the best of his ability," with the implication that the High Priest used Greek imperfectly. The Josephus paraphrase has "as obligingly as possible." TO HIS TRUE FRIEND: Eleazar addresses the king as an equal. ARSINOE: II, whom coins show to have been an extraordinary beauty, and who had a lurid history. Daughter of Ptolemy I, she was married at 15 to Lysimachus, king of Thrace, displacing a Persian princess, was loved by her husband's 20-year-old son, left her maid dressed in her royal robes to be killed in a battle while she escaped in rags, married Ptolemy Ceraunus, who murdered her children, escaped to Samothrace, and eventually married her younger full brother Ptolemy II, displacing his former wife, Arsinoe I. She enjoyed very great power and esteem in Egypt and the entire Hellenistic world, and was deified, possibly even before her death, as "Philadelphus," which title was only later applied to Ptolemy himself: see G. H. Macurdy, *Hellenistic Queens* (Baltimore, 1932), 11-130. THE CHILDREN: Arsinoe II bore Philadelphus

to converse with you. They bring with them dedicatory offerings for the Temple, and for sacrifices and other purposes a hundred talents of silver. And if you should write us concerning any desires of yours, you would gratify us and act as friendship requires; be assured that your wishes shall be fulfilled most speedily. Farewell."

[41]To this letter Eleazar replied as well as might be in the terms following: "Eleazar the High Priest to his true friend King Ptolemy, greeting. Yourself fare well, and Queen Arsinoe your sister, and the children: so will it be well and as we wish; we too are in good health. [42]When we received your letter we rejoiced greatly because of your resolution and your goodly plan, and we assembled our entire people and read it out to them, in order that they might know the piety you cherish for our God. We displayed also the flagons which you sent, twenty of gold and thirty of silver, the five bowls, the table for dedication, and for the offering of sacrifices and whatever repairs the Temple might require a hundred talents of silver. [43]These gifts were brought by Andreas, who holds a place of honor with you, and by Aristeas, true gentlemen both, outstanding in culture, and in every respect worthy of your own conduct and righteousness. They have also communicated your message to us, and from our lips have heard a reply in accordance with your letter. [44]Whatever

---

no children, but this is not necessarily a slip, for Scholiast on Theocritus 17.128 says that Philadelphus "made over to her the children borne of his former wife."

42. TWENTY . . . THIRTY . . . FIVE: This is in the nature of a receipt, Ptolemy not having itemized his gifts.   TABLE FOR DEDICATION: The table of the shew-bread is meant.

43. COMMUNICATED YOUR MESSAGE . . . HEARD A REPLY: There is probably no real discrepancy with 40, where Ptolemy writes only that the messengers were "to converse with you" (the request for the translators is stated in the latter); but the language of the letters is carefully chosen, and even a slight inconsistency may point to the use, in one case or both, of actual written sources, imperfectly adapted.

44. EVEN IF IT BE CONTRARY TO NATURE: Andrews translates, "even though your request is very unusual," and the expression may simply indicate the High Priest's courteous readiness to accommodate Ptolemy in every particular; on the other hand, we may see a hint of misgivings at the prospect of translating Scriptures into an alien language; see Introd. 81.

φύσιν ἐστίν, ὑπακουσόμεθα· τοῦτο γὰρ φιλίας καὶ ἀγαπήσεως σημεῖόν ἐστι. μεγάλα γὰρ καὶ σὺ καὶ ἀνεπίληστα τοὺς πολίτας ἡμῶν κατὰ πολλοὺς τρόπους εὐηργέτηκας.
45 ⁴⁵εὐθέως οὖν προσηγάγομεν ὑπὲρ σοῦ θυσίας καὶ τῆς ἀδελφῆς καὶ τῶν τέκνων καὶ τῶν φίλων· καὶ ηὔξατο πᾶν τὸ πλῆθος, ἵνα σοι γένηται καθὼς προαιρῇ διὰ παντός, καὶ διασώζῃ σοι τὴν βασιλείαν ἐν εἰρήνῃ μετὰ δόξης ὁ κυριεύων ἁπάντων θεός, καὶ ὅπως γένηταί σοι συμφερόντως καὶ μετὰ ἀσφαλείας ἡ τοῦ ἁγίου νόμου μεταγραφή. ⁴⁶παρόντων δὲ πάντων ἐπελέξαμεν ἄνδρας καλοὺς καὶ ἀγαθοὺς πρεσβυτέρους, ἀφ' ἑκάστης φυλῆς ἕξ, οὓς καὶ ἀπεστείλαμεν ἔχοντας τὸν νόμον. καλῶς οὖν ποιήσεις, βασιλεῦ δίκαιε, προστάξας, ὡς ἂν ἡ μεταγραφὴ γένηται τῶν βιβλίων, ἵνα πάλιν ἀποκατασταθῶσι πρὸς ἡμᾶς ἀσφαλῶς οἱ ἄνδρες. ἔρρωσο. ⁴⁷Εἰσὶ δὲ πρώτης φυλῆς· Ἰώσηφος Ἐζεκίας Ζαχαρίας Ἰωάννης Ἐζεκίας Ἐλισσαῖος. δευτέρας· Ἰούδας Σίμων Σομόηλος Ἀδαῖος Ματταθίας Ἐσχλεμίας. τρίτης· Νεεμίας Ἰώσηφος Θεοδόσιος Βασέας Ὀρνίας Δάκις. ⁴⁸τετάρτης· Ἰωνάθας Ἀβραῖος Ἐλισσαῖος Ἀνανίας Χαβρίας ... πέμπτης· Ἴσακος Ἰάκω-

---

47 Εζεκιας the second occurrence perhaps corrupt; Ιεζεκιας and Εζειας have been suggested / Εσχλεμιας MSS, Σελεμιας Epiphanius

48 Χαβριας MSS, Ζαχαριας Epiphanius. The sixth name is wanting (ζητει is noted on margin of one MS); Χελκιας is supplied by Epiphanius

---

45. FRIENDS: A specific title of preferment in the Egyptian court. For instances of sacrifices in the Temple at Jerusalem on behalf of pagan rulers, see Tramontano ad loc., Schürer 2.302 ff.
46. RESTORED TO US IN SAFETY: Eleazar's concern for the translators is a pleasing trait; cf. 123, 172. Josephus 56 asks for the return of the Law as well as of the translators.   FAREWELL: errōso, the proper term for use between equals.
47. THEIR NAMES: This list is apparently appended to the letter; cf. 51; Josephus 57 says their names "were set down at the end of the letter," and excuses himself from repeating them. Josephus gives the number as 70, but this is probably merely a slip, influenced by the title of the LXX and the number of Moses' elders, for Josephus too speaks of six from each tribe. The tribal division was no longer current in Palestine, but natural to non-Palestinians, who always looked upon Palestine from the point of view of Scripture. Epiphanius, De Mensuris et Ponderibus 3, in his Greek account of the LXX lists the translators' names in Syriac (Wendland's testimonia 142 f., Cahana ad loc.); the list is in general agreement (exceptions

is to your advantage, even if it be contrary to nature, we shall hearken; for to do so is a mark of friendship and affection. You too have vouchsafed our countrymen great and unforgettable benefits in many ways. ⁴⁵We have therefore straightway offered sacrifices on your behalf and on behalf of your sister and children and friends, and the entire multitude prayed that your affairs might always turn out as you desire, and that God Lord of all might preserve your kingdom in peace with honor, and that the transcription of the holy Law might come about to your advantage and with security. ⁴⁶And in the presence of all we selected elders good and true, six from each tribe, with whom we have sent the book of the Law. We shall be obliged to you, righteous king, if you enjoin that when the transcription of the books is completed the men may be restored to us again in safety. Farewell."

⁴⁷"Their names are, of the first tribe, Joseph, Hezekiah, Zechariah, Johanan, Hezekiah, Elisha; of the second, Judah, Simeon, Samuel, Adaiah, Mattathias, Eschlemias; of the third, Nehemiah, Joseph, Theodosius, Besai, Araunah, Dakis; ⁴⁸of the fourth, Jonathan, Heber, Elisha, Hananiah, Zechariah, Hilkiah; of the fifth, Isaac, Jacob, Joshua, Sabbatai,

---

will be noted) with our text. Epiphanius lists the tribes by name, and not, as here, by mere enumeration. Wendland sees in the recurrence of names associated with Hasmonaean heroes (Judah, Simon, Jonathan, Mattathias) an argument for a post-Maccabean date. The names are predominantly Hebrew, and the Greek names such as were common among Jews. They are theophoric, and literal translations of familiar Hebrew names: Theodosius or Dositheus-Mataniah; Theodotus-Nathaniah; Theophilus-Jedediah. Even the Hebrew names are given a Greek form, a usage of which Josephus, *Ant.* 1.129 speaks: "With a view to euphony and my readers' pleasure these names have been Hellenized, the form in which they here appear is not that used in our country." HEZEKIAH occurs twice in the first tribe. ESCHLEMIAS is given as Shelmiah in Epiphanius, like the last name in 48 (*cf.* Jer. 37.13).

48. OF THE FOURTH: Our MSS give Jonathan, Abraios, Elisha, Hananiah, Habrias—or only five names. From the parallel in Epiphanius it appears that Habrias has replaced Hezekiah, and that Hilkiah has fallen out. The occurrence of Hananiah and Hilkiah (Onias and Chelkias), the names of Cleopatra III's Jewish generals in her war against Ptolemy Lathyrus, has been taken (but without real cogency) as evidence for a date not earlier than 100.

ΑΡΙΣΤΕΑΣ ΦΙΛΟΚΡΑΤΕΙ

βος Ἰησοῦς Σαββαταῖος Σίμων Λευίς. ἕκτης· Ἰούδας Ἰώσηφος Σίμων Ζαχαρίας Σομόηλος Σελεμίας. ⁴⁹ἐβδόμης· Σαββαταῖος Σεδεκίας Ἰάκωβος Ἴσαχος Ἰησίας Ναθαῖος. ὀγδόης· Θεοδόσιος Ἰάσων Ἰησοῦς Θεόδοτος Ἰωάννης Ἰωνάθας. ἐνάτης· Θεόφιλος Ἄβραμος Ἄρσαμος Ἰάσων Ἐνδεμίας Δανίηλος. ⁵⁰δεκάτης· Ἰερεμίας Ἐλεάζαρος Ζαχαρίας Βανέας Ἐλισσαῖος Δαθαῖος. ἐνδεκάτης· Σαμούηλος Ἰώσηφος Ἰούδας Ἰωνάθης Χαβεῦ Δοσίθεος. δωδεκάτης· Ἰσάηλος Ἰωάννης Θεοδόσιος Ἄρσαμος Ἀβιήτης Ἐζεκῆλος. οἱ πάντες ἑβδομήκοντα δύο. ⁵¹Καὶ τὰ μὲν πρὸς τὴν τοῦ βασιλέως ἐπιστολὴν τοιαύτης ἐτύγχανεν ἀντιγραφῆς <ὑπὸ> τῶν περὶ τὸν Ἐλεάζαρον.

Ὡς δὲ ἐπηγγειλάμην καὶ τὰ τῶν κατασκευασμάτων διασαφῆσαι, ποιήσω. πολυτεχνίᾳ γὰρ διαφέροντα συνετελέσθη, τοῦ βασιλέως πολλὴν ἐπίδοσιν ποιουμένου καὶ παρ' ἕκαστον ἐπιθεωροῦντος τοὺς τεχνίτας. διὸ παριδεῖν οὐδὲν ἠδύναντο οὐδὲ εἰκῇ συντελέσαι. πρῶτον δέ σοι τὰ περὶ τῆς τραπέζης ἐξηγήσομαι. ⁵²Προεθυμεῖτο μὲν οὖν ὁ βασιλεὺς ὑπερόπλόν τι ποιῆσαι τοῖς μέτροις τὸ κατασκεύασμα. προσέταξε δὲ πυθέσθαι τῶν ἀνὰ τὸν τόπον, πηλίκη τίς ἐστιν ἡ προοῦσα καὶ κειμένη κατὰ τὸ ἱερὸν ἐν Ἱεροσολύμοις. ⁵³ὡς δὲ ἀπεφήναντο τὰ μέτρα, προσεπηρώτησεν, εἰ κατασκευάσει μείζονα. τινὲς μὲν οὖν καὶ τῶν ἱερέων καὶ τῶν ἄλλων ἔλεγον μηδὲν ἐπικωλύειν. ὁ δὲ εἶπε βούλεσθαι καὶ πενταπλῆν τοῖς

---

49 Ενδεμιας is suspect; W suggests Νεεμιας
50 Χαβευ doubtless corrupt, Χαλεβ

Epiphanius
51 υπο edd., υπερ MSS / διασαφησαι ποιησω MSS, διασαφησω Mend. W

---

50. ELIEZER: According to Josippon (122, Günzburg) and Jerahmeel (260, Gaster) this Eliezer was the chief of the translators, and the man whose martyrdom is reported in II Mac. 6.18–31; see Cahana ad loc. Caleb is from Epiphanius' list; our MSS give Chabeu or Chabbon, which is likely corrupt but may represent Cabbon (cf. Josh. 15.40). DOSITHEUS is the namesake of the Jewish general in the service of Ptolemy VI Philometor, and also of the bearer of Esther to Egypt, named in the Greek colophon to that book.
51–82. DESCRIPTION OF THE GIFTS OF PTOLEMY PHILADELPHUS TO THE TEMPLE.
51. I SHALL NOW GIVE A DETAILED DESCRIPTION: Josephus seems to feel that the apparent irrelevance requires justification, and adds (59): "although perhaps my History does not call for such an account, because I believe

Simeon, Levi; of the sixth, Judah, Joseph, Simeon, Zechariah, Samuel, Selemiah; ⁴⁹of the seventh, Sabbatai, Zedekiah, Jacob, Isaac, Jesse, Nattai; of the eighth, Theodosius, Jason, Joshua, Theodotus, Johanan, Jonathan; of the ninth, Theophilus, Abraham, Arsamus, Jason, Endemias, Daniel; ⁵⁰of the tenth, Jeremiah, Eliezer, Zechariah, Baneas, Elisha, Dathaius; of the eleventh, Samuel, Joseph, Judah, Jonathan, Caleb, Dositheus; of the twelfth, Isael, Johanan, Theodosius, Arsamus, Abietes, Ezekiel. In all, seventy-two." ⁵¹Such, then, was the reply to the king's letter given by Eleazar and his colleagues.

I shall now give a detailed description of the works of art, as I promised. They were wrought with extraordinary artistry, for the king made generous grants and supervised the craftsmen at every step, so that they could neglect no part of the work or perform it indifferently. First I shall explain the construction of the table. ⁵²Originally the king was eager to build it up to colossal dimensions, but he ordered inquiries to be made of persons in the locality concerning the size of the previous table which stood in the Temple at Jerusalem, ⁵³and when they reported the proportions he inquired further whether he should build on a larger scale. Some informants, both priests and others, said there was nothing to prevent

---

that in this way I shall bring home to my readers the king's love of art and his magnanimity." THE TABLE: Of shew-bread. The account which follows uses and greatly amplifies the brief description in LXX Ex. 25.23 ff. and 37.10 ff. This proves that the LXX was already in existence, though our book purports to be a contemporary account of its genesis. Even from the LXX description it is difficult to envisage the appearance of the actual table; from Aristeas' description it would seem impossible to make any plausible reconstruction. The description of the bowls and goblets, on the other hand, seems quite intelligible; for possible significances of this difference see Introd. 48.

52. THE PREVIOUS TABLE: There seem to have been four, besides this, in the course of history: that of Moses (Ex. 25.23–29, 35.13); that of Solomon (I Kings 7.48); that of the exiles returned from Babylon (the original table was not restored with the other vessels: see Ezra 1.7 ff.); and that of Judah Maccabee (I Mac. 4.49; Antiochus Epiphanes had plundered the previous table: I Mac. 1.22). The table here referred to would be fourth in the list.

53. PRIESTS: Probably in Egypt.

ΑΡΙΣΤΕΑΣ ΦΙΛΟΚΡΑΤΕΙ

μεγέθεσι ποιῆσαι, διστάζειν δὲ μήποτε ἄχρηστος γένηται πρὸς τὰς λειτουργίας. ⁵⁴οὐ γὰρ αἱρεῖσθαι τὸ κεῖσθαι μόνον ἐν τῷ τόπῳ <τὰ> παρ' αὐτοῦ, πολὺ δὲ μᾶλλον χάριν ἕξειν, ἐὰν τὰς καθηκούσας λειτουργίας ἐπὶ τῶν ὑπ' αὐτοῦ 55 κατεσκευασμένων οἷς καθῆκε ποιῶνται δεόντως. ⁵⁵οὐ γὰρ ἕνεκεν σπάνεως χρυσοῦ τὰ προσυντετελεσμένα βραχύμετρα καθέστηκεν, ἀλλὰ φαίνεται πρός τινα λόγον, εἶπεν, οὕτως συνεστηκέναι τοῖς μέτροις. ἔτι γὰρ ἐπιταγῆς οὔσης οὐθὲν ἂν ἐσπάνιζε· διόπερ οὐ παραβατέον οὐδὲ ὑπερθετέον τὰ καλῶς ἔχοντα. ⁵⁶τῇ μὲν οὖν ποικιλίᾳ τῶν τεχνῶν ἐκέλευσεν ὅτι μάλιστα χρήσασθαι, σεμνῶς ἅπαντα διανοούμενος καὶ φύσιν ἔχων ἀγαθὴν εἰς τὸ συνιδεῖν πραγμάτων ἔμφασιν. ὅσα δ' ἂν ᾖ ἄγραφα, πρὸς καλλονὴν ἐκέλευσε ποιεῖν· ὅσα δὲ διὰ γραπτῶν, μέτρα αὐτοῖς κατακολουθῆσαι. ⁵⁷ΔΤΟ γὰρ ΠΗΧΕΩΝ ΤΟ ΜΗΚΟC, ΤΟ δὲ ΤΨΟC ΠΗΧΕΟC ΚΑΙ ΗΜΙCΟΤC συνετέλουν, ΧΡΤCΙΟΤ ΔΟΚΙΜΟΤ στερεὰν πάντοθεν τὴν ποίησιν ἐργασάμενοι, λέγω δὲ οὐ περί τι περιεπτυγμένου τοῦ χρυσοῦ, τὸν δὲ ἐλασμὸν αὐτὸν ἐπιδεδέσθαι. ⁵⁸CΤΕΦΑΝΗΝ δὲ ἐποίησαν ΠΑΛΑΙCΤΙΑΙΑΝ ΚΤΚΛΟΘΕΝ· τὰ δὲ ΚΤΜΑΤΙΑ CΤΡΕΠΤΑ, τὴν ἀναγλυφὴν ἔχοντα σχοινίδων ἔκτυπον, τῇ τορείᾳ θαυμαστῶς ἔχουσαν ἐκ τῶν τριῶν μερῶν· ἦν γὰρ τριγωνία. ⁵⁹καὶ καθ' ἕκαστον μέρος ἡ διατύπωσις τῆς ἐνεργείας τὴν αὐτὴν διάθεσιν εἶχεν, ὥστε, καθ' ὃ ἂν μέρος στρέφοιτο,

---

54 τα inserted by edd.
55 ετι γαρ επιταγης ουσης edd., επι τα της ουσης MSS
57 After μηκος W inserts πηχεος δε το ευρος from LXX
58 τριγωνια MSS, τριγωνα W following Jos.

54. DEPOSITED: Appropriate for Philadelphus, who might well intend only a museum piece.   IN THE TEMPLE: The Greek has *topos*, "place," regularly so used in III Mac. and other Hellenistic writers; *cf.* Hebrew *maqom*.
55. AUTHORITY: This translation is based on an emendation; see textual note.
56. EXCELLENT NATURAL GIFT: Philadelphus' enthusiastic interest in art is documented by Callixinus of Rhodes, quoted in Athenaeus 5.203 C: "Philadelphus devoted himself with enthusiastic zeal to all his art works."
PRESCRIPTION IN SCRIPTURE: See on 51.
57. TWO CUBITS IN LENGTH AND A CUBIT AND A HALF IN HEIGHT: So in Scripture; both LXX and Josephus' paraphrase add "and a cubit in width." This dimension has evidently fallen out of our text by inadvertence.   OF

him, but he declared that he wished, indeed, to increase the proportions fivefold, but that he doubted whether such a table might be useless for priestly ministrations. ⁵⁴It was not his desire that his offering should merely be deposited in the Temple; it would afford him far greater satisfaction if the appropriate ministrations were duly performed by the proper ⁵⁵ministers upon the furniture which he had provided. ⁵⁵Nor, he added, was it for lack of gold that the proportions of the earlier work had been made small, but it was apparently for some reason that the scale was thus limited. If there had been authority for it, there would have been no skimping. Hence the correct measure must neither be deviated from nor surpassed. ⁵⁶But as for diversity in artistic ingenuity, he ordered that it be applied in lavish measure, for his own conceptions were majestic and he possessed an excellent natural gift for perceiving the effects objects would present. Where there was no prescription in Scripture he ordered the construction to follow principles of beauty; where there were written prescriptions their measurements were to be adhered to.

⁵⁷And so they fashioned a table "two cubits in length and a cubit and a half in height," making the construction "of pure gold" and solid on every side; I mean, gold was not overlaid upon other material, but a solid metal plate was put in place. ⁵⁸And they made "a border of a handbreadth round about," with "rails that revolved" bearing a design of ropes worked in relief, the design being marvelously engraved on the three sides, for the rails were triangular. ⁵⁹Upon each side the fashioning of the design had the same arrangement, so that whichever way they were the appearance they presented

---

PURE GOLD: So in LXX also, as against the Hebrew, where the table is of acacia wood overlaid with gold. I MEAN etc. seems to indicate that Aristeas was aware of another prescription, which he chooses to reject.

58. AND THEY MADE: In these passages LXX gives ἐποίησαν for 'asah, στεφάνη for *misgeret*, and κυμάτια στρεπτά for *zer*. These and other details of the construction of the table remain obscure, even with the somewhat clearer paraphrase of Josephus. RAILS: Thackeray suggests "a triangular rotatory bar turning on pivots at the corners."

τὴν πρόσοψιν εἶναι τὴν αὐτήν, κειμένου δὲ κατὰ τῆς στεφάνης τὸ μὲν εἰς αὐτὴν τὴν τράπεζαν ἀπόκλιμα τὴν διατύπωσιν ἔχειν τῆς ὡραιότητος, τὸ δὲ ἐκτὸς κλίμα πρὸς τὴν τοῦ προσάγοντος εἶναι θεωρίαν. 60διὸ τὴν ὑπεροχὴν ὀξεῖαν εἶναι τῶν δύο κλιμάτων συνέβαινε, μετέωρον ἐπικειμένην, ὡς προειρήκαμεν, τριγώνου κατεσκευασμένου, καθ' ὃ ἂν μέρος στρέφοιτο. λίθων τε πολυτελῶν ἐν αὐτῷ διαθέσεις ὑπῆρχον ἀνὰ μέσον τῶν σχοινίδων· ἕτερος παρὰ ἕτερον πλοκὴν εἶχον ἀμίμητον τῇ ποιήσει. 61πάντες δ' ἦσαν διὰ τρημάτων κατειλημμένοι χρυσαῖς περόναις πρὸς τὴν ἀσφάλειαν. ἐπὶ δὲ τῶν γωνιῶν αἱ κατακλεῖδες συνέσφιγγον [δὲ] πρὸς τὴν συνοχήν. 62ἐκ πλαγίων δὲ κατὰ τὴν στεφάνην κυκλόθεν τὰ πρὸς τὴν ἄνω πρόσοψιν ᾠοθεσία κατεσκεύαστο διάλιθος, †ἐκτύπωσιν ἔχουσα προσοχῆς† συνεχέσιν ἀναγλυφαῖς ῥαβδωταῖς, πυκνὴν ἐχούσαις τὴν πρὸς ἄλληλα θέσιν περὶ ὅλην τὴν τράπεζαν. 63ὑπὸ δὲ τὴν ἐκτύπωσιν τῶν λίθων τῆς ᾠοθεσίας, στέφανον ἐποίησαν οἱ τεχνῖται πάγκαρπον, ἐν ὑπεροχῇ προδήλως ἔχοντα βοτρύων καὶ σταχύων, ἔτι δὲ φοινίκων καὶ μήλων ἐλαίας τε καὶ ῥοῶν καὶ τῶν παραπλησίων. τοὺς δὲ λίθους ἐργασάμενοι πρὸς τὴν τῶν προειρημένων καρπῶν διατύπωσιν, ἔχοντας ἑκάστου γένους τὴν χρόαν, ἀνέδησαν τῷ χρυσίῳ κύκλῳ περὶ ὅλην τὴν τῆς τραπέζης κατασκευὴν κατὰ κρόταφον. 64μετὰ δὲ τὴν τοῦ στεφάνου διάθεσιν, ὁμοίως κατὰ τὴν τῆς ᾠοθεσίας διασκευὴν κατεσκεύαστο, καὶ τὰ λοιπὰ τῆς ῥαβδώσεως καὶ διαγλυφῆς, <διὰ τὸ> κατ' ἀμφότερα τὰ μέρη τὴν τράπεζαν πρὸς τὴν χρῆσιν πεποιῆσθαι, καθ' ὃ ἂν μέρος αἴρωνται, ὥστε καὶ τὴν τῶν κυμάτων θέσιν καὶ τὴν τῆς στεφάνης εἶναι κατὰ τὸ τῶν ποδῶν μέρος. 65ἔλασμα γὰρ ἐποίησαν καθ' ὅλου τοῦ πλάτους τῆς τραπέζης στερεὸν δακτύλων τεσσάρων, ὥστε τοὺς πόδας ἐνίεσθαι εἰς τοῦτο, περόνας <σὺν> κατακλεῖσιν ἔχοντας ἐσφίγχθαι κατὰ τὴν στεφάνην, ἵνα, καθ' ὃ ἂν αἴρωνται μέρος, ἡ χρῆσις ᾖ· τοῦτο δὲ κατὰ ἐπιφάνειαν

---

60 καθ' ο (αν) μερος στρεφοιτο W deletes as dittography from 59
62 εκτυποσιν εχουσα προσοχης corrupt; Kuiper emends to προσεχη,

Schmidt conjectures προοχης
64 After ομοιως W inserts <κατω τα> / <δια το> T; W transposes ωστε from the following line (after

was the same; as the rail rested on the border the slope towards the table itself was beautifully worked, though it was the outward slope which met the eye of one approaching. ⁶⁰Thus it came about that in whichever direction it was turned the bevel where the two slopes met held the uppermost place, since, as we have said, it was constructed in triangular form. There were arrangements of precious stones in the rail itself, between the rope work; set one stone beside another, the braid they formed was inimitable. ⁶¹All were fastened by golden pins through perforations for security, and at the angles clamps bound them firmly in place. ⁶²Along the border round about, slanting upward to the view, an egg pattern set with precious stones was worked; this was excellently modelled with regular embossed flutings arranged close by one another around the whole table. ⁶³Beneath the raised pattern of the egg design the craftsmen made a garland of all kinds of fruit; visibly projecting were clusters of grapes and ears of grain, and also dates and apples, olives and pomegranates, and the like. They worked stones of the colors of the several species to resemble the shapes of the fruits mentioned, and attached them to the gold around the sides of the whole table. ⁶⁴Next to the system of the garland there was work similar to that of the egg pattern and the rest of the fluted and relief work, for the table was made for use on either side according to choice, so that the rail and the border was in position in the portion towards the feet also. ⁶⁵For they made the solid metal sheet, four fingers in thickness over the whole breadth of the table, in such a way that the legs could be inserted in it, these being fitted with pins and clamps to be attached to the border, so that the table might be used on either surface, according to choice. In appearance, then, an identical aspect was presented, the construction being ambivalent.

αιρωνται) / After διασκευην MSS have η / αιρωνται MSS, αιρωνται W

65 περονας <συν> κατακλεισιν T, π. κατα κλεισιν MSS, π. <δε εν> κατακλεισιν W / αιρωνται MSS, αιρωνται W

θεωρεῖται ἀμφοτεροδεξίου τῆς κατασκευῆς οὔσης. ⁶⁶ἐπ' αὐτῆς δὲ τῆς τραπέζης μαίανδρον ἔκτυπον ἐποίησαν, ἐν ὑπεροχῇ λίθους ἔχοντα κατὰ μέσον πολυτελεῖς τῶν <πολυ­ειδῶν>, ἀνθράκων τε καὶ σμαράγδων, ἔτι δὲ ὄνυχος καὶ τῶν ἄλλων γενῶν τῶν διαφερόντων ἐν ὡραιότητι. ⁶⁷μετὰ δὲ τὴν τοῦ μαιάνδρου διάθεσιν ἐπέκειτο σχιστὴ πλοκή, θαυμασίως ἔχουσα, ῥομβωτὴν ἀποτελοῦσα τὴν ἀνὰ μέσον θεωρίαν· ἐφ' ᾗ κρυστάλλου λίθος καὶ τὸ λεγόμενον ἤλεκτρον ἐντετύπωτο, ἀμίμητον θεωρίαν ἀποτελοῦν τοῖς θεωροῦσι. ⁶⁸τοὺς δὲ πόδας ἐποίησαν τὰς κεφαλίδας ἔχοντας κρινωτάς, ἀνάκλασιν κρίνων ὑπὸ τὴν τράπεζαν λαμβανόντων, τὰ δὲ τῆς ἐντὸς προσόψεως ὀρθὴν ἔχοντα τὴν πετάλωσιν. ⁶⁹ἡ δὲ ἐπ' ἐδάφους ἔρεισις τοῦ ποδὸς ἄνθρακος λίθου πάντοθεν παλιστιαία, κρηπῖδος ἔχουσα τάξιν κατὰ τὴν πρόσοψιν, ὀκτὼ δὲ δακτύλων τὸ πλάτος ἔχουσα· ἐφ' ὃν ἐπίκειται τὸ πᾶν ἔλασμα τοῦ ποδός. ⁷⁰κατεσκεύασαν δὲ ἐκφύοντα κισσὸν ἀκάνθῳ πλεκόμενον ἐκ τοῦ λίθου, σὺν ἀμπέλῳ περιειλούμενον κυκλόθεν τῷ ποδὶ σὺν τοῖς βότρυσιν, οἳ λιθουργεῖς ἦσαν, μέχρι τῆς κεφαλῆς. ἡ δ' αὐτὴ διάθεσις ἦν τῶν τεσσάρων ποδῶν, πάντα ἐνεργῶς πεποιημένα καὶ προσηγμένα, τῆς ἐμπειρίας καὶ τέχνης τὰς ὑπεροχὰς ἀπαραλλάκτως ἔχοντα πρὸς τὴν ἀλήθειαν, ὥστε καὶ ῥιπίζοντος τοῦ κατὰ τὸν ἀέρα πνεύματος κίνησιν ἐπιδέχεσθαι τὴν τῶν φύλλων θέσιν, πρὸς τὴν τῆς ἀληθείας διάθεσιν τετυπωμένων ἁπάντων. ⁷¹ἐποίησαν δὲ τριμερὲς τὸ στόμα τῆς τραπέζης, οἱονεὶ τρίπτυχον, πελεκίνοις συναρμοζόμενα γομφωτοῖς πρὸς ἑαυτὰ κατὰ τὸ πάχος τῆς κατασκευῆς, ἀθέατον καὶ ἀνεύρετον τὴν τῶν ἁρμῶν κατασκευάσαντες συμβολήν. ἡμιπηχίου δὲ οὐκ ἐλάσσονος ἦν τὸ πάχος τῆς ὅλης τραπέζης, ὥστε πολλῶν εἶναι ταλάντων τὴν ὅλην διασκευήν. ⁷²ἐπεὶ γὰρ οὐ προῄρητο τοῖς μεγέθεσιν οὐδὲν προσθεῖναι ὁ βασιλεύς, ὅσον ἔδει

---

66 πολυειδων edd., πυλιαδων MSS
70 κατεσκευασαν edd., κατεσκευασε(ν) MSS / περιειλουμενον MSS, περιειλουμενη W / ενεργως MSS, εναργως W / προσηγμενα MSS, προηγμενα W
71 αθεατον edd. (Jos. has αορατον), αθετον MSS / ελασσονος MSS, ελασσον W

⁶⁶On the surface of the table they worked a meander pattern in relief, with precious stones of many sorts projecting in its midst, carbuncles and emeralds and also onyx and other species of outstanding beauty. ⁶⁷Next to the arrangement of the meander there was placed a marvelous design of open net-work, which gave a rhombus-like effect to the middle of the table; inlaid into this were rock-crystal and amber, affording spectators an inimitable sight.

⁶⁸The legs they made with capitals of lily shape, the lilies making a bend underneath the table, and the upright leaves being the part in view. ⁶⁹The base of the leg which rested on the floor was entirely of carbuncle, a handbreadth high and eight fingers in width, having the character of a shoe in appearance; upon it the whole mass of the leg rested. ⁷⁰And they represented ivy intertwined with acanthus growing out of the stone and encircling the leg, together with a grapevine and its clusters, all worked in stone, right up to the top; the style of the four legs was the same. All the parts were carefully made and fitted, the ingenious art corresponding to truth to such a superlative degree that if a breath of wind blew the leaves stirred in their place; so closely was every detail modelled on reality. ⁷¹The face of the table they made in three pieces, as it were a triptych, joined together by dovetailing secured with pegs in the thickness of the construction, and the junctures of the members they made invisible and undiscoverable. The thickness of the whole table was no less than half a cubit, so that the construction of the whole amounted to many talents. ⁷²For since the king was resolved to add nothing to the dimensions, the expenditure that would have been neces-

---

72 οσον MSS, οσα Cohn / απεδεδωκε MSS, απεδωκε W

---

66. OF MANY SORTS: Reading πολυειδῶν for the anomalous πυλιάδων. Josephus 71 has "forms like stars," which rests, as Thackeray suggests, on a reading πλειάδων πολυειδῶν, from which πυλιάδων may have derived.
71. FACE: Literally "mouth."

δαπανηθῆναι κατασκευαζομένων μειζόνων, ταῦτα ἀποδέδωκε πλείονα· καὶ κατὰ τὴν προαίρεσιν αὐτοῦ πάντα ἐπετελέσθη θαυμασίως καὶ ἀξιολόγως ἔχοντα, καὶ ταῖς τέχναις ἀμίμητα, καὶ τῇ καλλονῇ διαπρεπῆ. 73Τῶν δὲ κρατήρων δύο μὲν ἦσαν <χρυσοῖ> τῇ κατασκευῇ, φολιδωτὴν ἔχοντες ἀπὸ τῆς βάσεως μέχρι τοῦ μέσου τὴν διασκευὴν τῇ τορείᾳ, καὶ τὴν τῶν λίθων ἀνὰ μέσον τῶν φολίδων σύνδεσιν πολυτέχνως ἔχοντες. 74εἶτα μαίανδρος ἐπέκειτο πηχυαῖος ὕψει, τὴν δ' ἐκτύπωσιν ἐνυπῆρχε διὰ λιθώσεως ποικίλης, ἐμφαίνων σὺν ὡραιότητι τὸ τῆς τέχνης φιλόπονον. ἐπὶ δὲ τούτου ῥάβδωσις, ἐφ' ᾗ διαπλοκὴ ῥόμβων, δικτυωτὴν ἔχουσα τὴν πρόσοψιν ἕως ἐπὶ τὸ στόμα. 75Τὸ δ' ἀνὰ μέσον ἀσπιδίσκοι λίθων ἑτέρων παρ' ἑτέροις, τοῖς γένεσι παραλλαγὴν ἐχόντων, τετραδακτύλων οὐκ ἔλαττον, ἀνεπλήρουν τὸ τῆς καλλονῆς ἐναργές. ἐπὶ δὲ τῆς στεφάνης τοῦ στόματος κρίνων τύπωσις σὺν ἀνθεμίσι καὶ βοτρύων σχοινιαὶ διάπλοκοι διετυποῦντο κυκλόθεν. 76οἱ μὲν οὖν διὰ τοῦ χρυσοῦ τοιαύτην εἶχον τὴν κατασκευήν, χωροῦντες ὑπὲρ δύο μετρητάς· οἱ δ' ἀργυροῖ λείαν εἶχον τὴν διασκευήν, ἔνοπτρον δὴ γεγονυῖαν πρὸς αὐτὸ τοῦτο θαυμασίως ἔχουσαν, ὥστε πᾶν τὸ προσαχθὲν ἀπαυγάζεσθαι σαφέστερον μᾶλλον ἢ ἐν τοῖς κατόπτροις. 77οὐκ ἐφικτὸν δ' ἐστὶν ἐξηγήσασθαι τὰ προσυντελεσθέντα πρὸς τὴν τῆς ἀληθείας ἔμφασιν. ὡς γὰρ ἐπετελέσθη, τεθέντων τῶν κατασκευασμάτων ἑτέρου παρ' ἕτερον—λέγω δὲ πρῶτον ἀργυροῦ κρατῆρος, εἶτα χρυσοῦ, πάλιν ἀργυροῦ καὶ χρυσοῦ— παντελῶς ἀνεξήγητος ἐγένετο τῆς προσόψεως ἡ διάθεσις, καὶ τῶν πρὸς τὴν θεωρίαν προσιόντων οὐ δυναμένων ἀφίστασθαι διὰ τὴν περιαύγειαν καὶ τὸ τῆς ὄψεως τερπνόν. 78ποικίλη γὰρ ἦν ἡ τῆς ἐπιφανείας ἐνέργεια. προσορώντων γὰρ πρὸς αὐτὴν τὴν τοῦ χρυσίου κατασκευήν, ψυχαγωγία τις ἦν μετὰ θαυμασμοῦ, συνεχῶς ἐφ' ἕκαστον ἐπιβαλλούσης τῆς διανοίας τεχνίτευμα. καὶ πάλιν ὅτε πρὸς τὴν τῶν ἀργυρῶν προσβλέψαι τις θέσιν ἤθελεν, ἀπέλαμπε τὰ πάντα

---

73 <χρυσοί> edd. from Josephus, omitted in MSS
75 σχοινιαί edd., σχοινίω MSS
78 εστηκε MSS, εστηκη W

---

73. BOWLS: The description of these and of the flagons is much more intel-

sary for a larger structure he devoted to greater elaboration; and the whole was completed in a marvelous and memorable style, according to his desire, inimitable in its art and superlative in its beauty.

⁷³Of the bowls two were of gold construction, with a pattern of scales executed in relief from the base halfway up, and with stones artfully set between the scales. ⁷⁴Then above this was a meander a cubit in height, with its surface wrought out of variegated stones, displaying elaborate skill along with beauty. Above this was channeling upon which was a plaiting of lozenges, presenting the aspect of net-work up to the brim. ⁷⁵In the middle were bosses of stones of different sorts, the kinds arranged alternately, not less than four fingers broad, and they were a crowning touch to the manifest beauty. On the crown of the brim a pattern of lilies with their blossoms and interwoven clusters of grapes was fashioned all around. ⁷⁶Such was the construction of the bowls of gold, and they held above twenty gallons each. The silver bowls had a smooth surface, giving the effect, indeed, of a mirror, and remarkable for that very fact, so that anything brought near them was reflected more distinctly than in actual mirrors. ⁷⁷But it is not possible to describe the true impression of the works of art when they had been completed. For when they were finished and the vessels were placed one after the other— I mean first a silver bowl, then a gold, then again a silver and a gold—the character of the spectacle was altogether indescribable, and those who came to view it could not tear themselves from it, so dazzling and entrancing was the sight. ⁷⁸Variety was the keynote of the spectacle's effect. For if one looked at the gold work by itself there was enchantment together with astonishment as the mind was continually directed to each bit of artistry in succession. And again when one wished to turn his gaze to the display of silver vessels, everything around was brilliantly reflected, whatever posi-

---

ligible; for the possible implication of this fact see Introd. 48.
76. TWENTY GALLONS: Literally "two metretes;" the *metretes* was a measure of 39.39 liters. *Cf.* LXX I Kings 18.32.

κυκλόθεν, ὡς ἄν τις ἕστηκε, καὶ διάχυσιν ἐποίει μείζονα τοῖς θεωμένοις· ὥστε παντελῶς ἀνεξήγητον εἶναι τῶν ἐνηργημένων τὴν πολυτεχνίαν. [79]Τὰς δὲ χρυσᾶς φιάλας διετόρευσαν στεφάνοις ἀμπέλου κατὰ μέσον, περὶ δὲ τὰ χείλη κισσοῦ τε καὶ μυρσίνης ἔτι δ' ἐλαίας ἀνέπλεξαν στέφανον ἔκτυπον, πολυτελεῖς ἐνέντες λίθους· καὶ τὰς λοιπὰς δὲ τορείας διηλλαγμένως ἐπετέλεσαν, ἅπαντα φιλοτιμηθέντες εἰς ὑπεροχὴν δόξης τοῦ βασιλέως ποιῆσαι. [80]καθόλου γὰρ οὔτ' ἐν τοῖς βασιλικοῖς ὑπῆρχε ῥισκοφυλακίοις τοιαύτη κατασκευὴ τῇ πολυτελείᾳ καὶ τεχνουργίᾳ, οὔτ' ἔν τινι ἄλλῳ. πρόνοιαν γὰρ οὐ μικρὰν ἐποιεῖτο ὁ βασιλεύς, φιλοδοξῶν εἰς τὰ καλῶς ἔχοντα. πολλάκις γὰρ τὸν δημόσιον χρηματισμὸν παρίει, [81]τοῖς δὲ τεχνίταις παρήδρευεν ἐπιμελῶς, ἵνα καθηκόντως τῷ τόπῳ συντελέσωσιν, εἰς ὃν ἀπεστέλλετο τὰ τῶν ἔργων. διὸ πάντα σεμνῶς ἐγεγόνει, καὶ καταξίως τοῦ τε ἀποστέλλοντος βασιλέως καὶ τοῦ προστατοῦντος ἀρχιερέως τοῦ τόπου. [82]καὶ γὰρ τὸ τῶν λίθων πλῆθος ἄφθονον, καὶ μεγάλοι τοῖς μεγέθεσιν, οὐκ ἔλαττον πεντακισχιλίων· καὶ ταῖς τέχναις κρατιστεύοντα πάντα, ὥστε πενταπλασίως τοῦ χρυσοῦ τιμιωτέραν εἶναι τὴν τῶν λίθων δόσιν καὶ τὴν τῶν τεχνῶν ἐνέργειαν.

79. FLAGONS: The number, not mentioned here, is given by Josephus as 30.
81. FREQUENTLY HE WOULD ... SUPERVISE: Mahaffy, *Greek Life and Thought* (London, 1896), 207 shows that this was actually a trait of Philadelphus.
82. FIVE THOUSAND ... FIVEFOLD: Omitted in Josephus.
83–120. DESCRIPTION OF JERUSALEM AND ITS VICINITY. This and the following sections (120–171), which contain Eleazar's farewell to the translators and his apology of the Law, is omitted in Josephus, without comment, and has been suspected as an interpolation: see Introd. 19. The junctures, both at 83 and 171, do seem awkward, and it is remarkable that there is no word of the deputation's departure from Alexandria, their reception at Jerusalem, and their return to Alexandria. The present section, indeed, sounds like the enthusiastic account of devout but humble pilgrims rather than the report of ambassadors of a great king bringing royal presents and the stunning news of the emancipation of the Jews of Egypt. Two ancient descriptions of Jerusalem which have points of contact with the present account may here be cited. Hecataeus (in Josephus, *Against Apion* 1.197–199) says: "The Jews have many fortresses and villages in different parts of the country, but only one fortified city, which has a circumference of about *fifty* stades and some 120,000 inhabitants; they call it Jerusalem. Nearly in the center of the city stands a stone wall, enclosing an area about 500 feet

tion one took, and produced even greater delight in the spectators. So the artistry manifested in the works is wholly indescribable.

⁷⁹The golden flagons they engraved with vine garlands in the middle, and around the lip they entwined in relief a wreath of ivy and myrtle and olive, setting it with precious stones. The rest of the relief work they carried out in assorted patterns, considering it a point of honor to make everything correspond to the majesty of the king's renown. ⁸⁰In general, neither in the royal treasuries nor in any other was there the like of these works in costliness and artistic skill. No little thought was bestowed upon them by the king, for he loved reputation for things beautifully made. ⁸¹Frequently he would neglect public business and would carefully supervise the craftsmen, so that they might execute their productions in a manner befitting the place to which they were to be sent. Hence everything turned out magnificently, being worthy at once of the king who was sending them and of the High Priest who was the governor of the place. ⁸²For so unstinting was the supply of stones, being large in size and no fewer than five thousand in number, and so supreme was the quality of workmanship in every detail, that the expenditure in stones and artistic workmanship was five-fold the value of the gold.

---

long and a hundred cubits broad, approached by a pair of gates. Within this enclosure is a square altar, built of heaped up stones, unhewn and unwrought; each side is 20 cubits long and the height ten cubits. Beside it stands a great edifice, containing an altar and a lampstand, both made of gold, and weighing two talents; upon these is a light which is never extinguished by night or day" (for a rehabilitation of the general veracity of Hecataeus in these passages see A. T. Olmstead, as cited on 12).

Tacitus, *Histories* 5.12, says: "The temple resembled a citadel, and had its own walls, which were more laboriously constructed than the others. Even the colonnades with which it was surrounded formed an admirable outwork. It contained an inexhaustible spring; there were subterranean excavations in the hills, and tanks and cisterns for holding rain water." Aristeas' description of Jerusalem and the Temple is translated and discussed by Père Vincent, "Jerusalem d'après la Lettre d'Aristée" in *Revue Biblique* 1908, 520–532 and 1909, 555–575. Vincent believes the description proves an early date for Aristeas.

83 Ὑπολαμβάνων οὖν καὶ τούτων τὴν ἀναγραφὴν ἀναγκαίαν εἶναι, δεδήλωκά σοι. τὰ δ' ἑξῆς περιέχει τὴν πρὸς τὸν Ἐλεάζαρον ὁδὸν ἡμῖν γενομένην· τὴν δὲ θέσιν τῆς ὅλης χώρας πρῶτον δηλώσω. Ὡς γὰρ παρεγενήθημεν ἐπὶ τοὺς τόπους, ἐθεωροῦμεν τὴν πόλιν μέσην κειμένην τῆς ὅλης Ἰουδαίων ἐπ' ὄρους ὑψηλὴν ἔχοντος τὴν ἀνάτασιν. 84ἐπὶ δὲ τῆς κορυφῆς κατεσκεύαστο τὸ ἱερὸν ἐκπρεπῶς ἔχον· καὶ οἱ περίβολοι τρεῖς, ὑπὲρ ἑβδομήκοντα δὲ πήχεις τῷ μεγέθει, καὶ τὸ πλάτος ἀκόλουθον καὶ τὸ μῆκος τῆς κατὰ τὸν οἶκον διασκευῆς ὑπῆρχε, μεγαλομοιρίᾳ καὶ χορηγίᾳ κατὰ πάντα 85 ὑπερβαλλούσῃ διῳκοδομημένων ἁπάντων. 85καὶ τοῦ θυρώματος δὲ καὶ τῶν περὶ αὐτὸ συνδέσμων κατὰ τὰς φλιὰς καὶ τῆς τῶν ὑπερθύρων ἀσφαλείας ἔκδηλος ἦν ἡ τῶν χρημάτων γεγονυῖα ἀφειδὴς δαπάνη. 86τοῦ τε καταπετάσματος ἡ διατύπωσις θυρώσει κατὰ πᾶν ὁμοιοτάτη ὑπῆρχε· καὶ μάλιστα διὰ τὴν τοῦ πνεύματος ὑποδρομὴν ἀδιάλειπτον

83 επι τους τοπους T (attested with παραγινεσθαι in inscs. and papyri) επι του * * * και τοπου MSS, επι τουτους τ. τ. Kuiper, επι τους

Ιουδαιων τ. Mend. Fevrier suggests Σκοπος (Jos. B. J. 2.19.4, 5.2.3)
86 θυρωσει MSS also read θυρωσι / κατατεινειν T, κατα MSS

83. WHEN WE REACHED: Note the plural after I HAVE PRESENTED THE DESCRIPTION above. The expression, and the description of the capital as situated on a mountain in the center of the country, suggests the introduction to an account of an ideal country: see Introd. 49.   THE CITY: Jerusalem. Cf. Hab. 2.17; see above.   JUDAEA: The MSS give "of Judaeans," which fits into an idealizing account of an exotic people.
84–87. THE TEMPLE.
84. UPON ITS CREST: Isa. 2.2 (Mic. 4.1) has "The mountain of the Lord's house shall be established on the top of the mountains." Num. 23.9 has ἀπὸ κορυφῆς ὀρέων. Josephus, Ant. 15.11.3 makes a point of the conspicuousness of the Temple, and contrasts it with the humbler situation of its predecessor. Hecataeus (Josephus, Against Apion 1.198) says that the Temple was in the center of the city.   THREE ENCOMPASSING WALLS: Probably not fortifications, but the partitions separating the courts of the gentiles, the Israelites, and the precinct of the altar.   SEVENTY CUBITS: Probably applicable only to the exterior wall; Egyptian cubits were of smaller scale, but even so we should have walls well over 30 yards high.
OF A BREADTH AND LENGTH IN KEEPING: Vincent translates the difficult Greek, sur une largeur proportionnée et une longueur adaptée a la dimension du temple.   LAVISHNESS: See on 85.
85. DOORWAY: The description recalls those in Josephus, Ant. 15.395 ff. and

⁸³I have presented the description of these gifts to you because I believed it was essential. What follows contains an account of our journey to Eleazar; but first I shall describe the position of the whole country. When we reached the region we beheld the city situated in the center of all Judaea upon a mountain which rises to a lofty height. ⁸⁴Upon its crest stood the Temple in its splendor; and there were three encompassing walls, above seventy cubits in height and of a breadth and length in keeping with the structure of the edifice. The whole was built with a lavishness and sumptuousness beyond all precedent. ⁸⁵From the construction of the doorway and its fastenings to the door-posts and the solidity of the lintel it was obvious that no expense had been spared. ⁸⁶The style of the curtain corresponded in every respect to the door; especially when the fabric was kept in unceasing motion by the current of wind beneath, since, the

---

Jewish War 5.212 of the doorway of Herod's Temple, where the point is also made that it surpassed its predecessors; whence critics have deduced that the reference must be to Herod's Temple; but *cf.* I Chronicles 22.3. It is easy to understand the admiration of a visitor, even one accustomed to the architectural triumphs of Alexandria, for the Temple of Herod, which was new when the Alexandrian buildings had grown old; it is less credible that a visitor fresh from Philadelphus' new constructions would be greatly impressed by the ancient and rather humble Temple which preceded. It is to be noted that the implied entry of the ambassadors to the Temple area is not in keeping with their presumed pagan character: see Josephus, *The Jewish War*, 5.144.

86. CURTAIN: Except at Ex. 26.36, LXX regularly uses this word (*katapetasma*) for "curtain"; it denotes a curtain drawn *downward* (*kata-*) from above, whereas the practise in pagan temples was to draw the curtain upwards or to the sides. Since we know from I Mac. 1.22 that Antiochus Epiphanes removed the curtain from the Temple in 170 BCE (it has been ingeniously conjectured that the "curtain of wool dyed with Phoenician purple and worked with Assyrian embroidery" which Pausanias 5.12.4 says Epiphanes presented to the temple of Zeus at Olympia is this same curtain), and since no replacement is mentioned, it has been argued that our passage describes conditions anterior to 169: see Cahana and Tramontano *ad loc*. Vincent (*op. cit.*) is certain, moreover, that ours is surely an eyewitness description. On the other hand, the curtain was regularly spoken of as a central feature of the Temple (*cf.* Ben Sirah 50.5, "the curtained house"), and it was in the tradition of the literary *ekphrasis* (see Introd. 47) to make such descriptions seem eyewitness accounts.

κίνησιν λαμβανούσης τῆς διυφῆς, διὰ τὸ ἀπ' ἐδάφους γινομένης τῆς ὑποδρομῆς <κατατείνειν> τὴν κόλπωσιν μέχρι τῆς ἄνω διατάσεως, ἡδεῖάν τινα καὶ δυσαπάλλακτον τὴν θεωρίαν ἔχοντος τοῦ πράγματος. ⁸⁷Ἥ τε τοῦ θυσιαστηρίου κατασκευὴ <συμμέτρως ἔχουσαν> πρὸς τὸν τόπον καὶ τὰ θύματα διὰ τοῦ πυρὸς ἐξαναλούμενα τὴν διοικοδομὴν εἶχε, τῆς δ' ἀναβάσεως τῆς πρὸς αὐτό, πρὸς τὴν εὐκοσμίαν ἔχοντος τοῦ τόπου καθηκόντως τὸ κλίμα τῶν λειτουργούντων ἱερέων κεκαλυμμένων μέχρι τῶν σφυρῶν BYCCINOIC XITѠCIN. ⁸⁸Ὁ δὲ οἶκος βλέπει πρὸς ἕω, τὰ δ' ὀπίσθια αὐτοῦ πρὸς ἑσπέραν· τὸ δὲ πᾶν ἔδαφος λιθόστρωτον καθέστηκε καὶ κλίματα πρὸς τοὺς καθήκοντας τόπους ἔχει τῆς τῶν ὑδάτων ἐπιφορᾶς ἕνεκεν, ἣ γίνεται διὰ τὴν σμῆξιν τῶν ἀπὸ τῶν θυσιῶν αἱμάτων. πολλαὶ γὰρ μυριάδες κτηνῶν προσάγονται κατὰ τὰς τῶν ἑορτῶν ἡμέρας. ⁸⁹Ὕδατος δὲ ἀνέκλειπτός ἐστι σύστασις, ὡς ἂν καὶ πηγῆς ἔσωθεν πολυρρύτου φυσικῶς ἐπιρρεούσης, ἔτι δὲ θαυμασίων καὶ ἀδιηγήτων ὑποδοχείων ὑπαρχόντων ὑπὸ γῆν, καθὼς ἀπέφαινον πέντε σταδίων κυκλόθεν τῆς κατὰ τὸ ἱερὸν καταβολῆς καὶ ἑκάστου τούτων σύριγγας ἀναριθμους, καθ' ἕκαστον μέρος ἑαυτὰ συναπτόντων τῶν ῥευμάτων· ⁹⁰καὶ πάντα ταῦτα μεμολιβῶσθαι κατ' ἐδάφους καὶ τοῦ τοίχου· ἐπὶ δὲ τούτων κεχύσθαι πολύ τι πλῆθος κονιάσεως, ἐνεργῶς γεγενημένων ἁπάντων· εἶναι δὲ πυκνὰ τὰ στόματα πρὸς τὴν βάσιν, ἀοράτως ἔχοντα τοῖς πᾶσι πλὴν αὐτοῖς οἷς ἐστιν ἡ λειτουργία, ὡς ῥοπῇ καὶ νεύματι

87 συμμετρως εχουσαν edd., συμμετρον εχουσα MSS / After θυματα Mend. inserts τα / λειτουργουντων edd., λειτουργων των MSS
90 εαυτα edd., εαυτας MSS / του
τοιχου MSS, των τοιχων W / κονιασεως edd., κονιας εως MSS
91 πεπεισμενος... αυτος edd., πεπεισμενοις αυτοις MSS

87. ALTAR... SIZE: Cf. dimensions in Hecataeus, cited above.   DECENCY: Cf. Ex. 20.26. The "good order" of the Temple is admired by Ptolemy Philopator in III Mac. 1.10.   COATS OF FINE LINEN: LXX Ex. 36.35 (-39.27).
88-91. THE WATER SUPPLY.
88. LOOKS TOWARDS THE EAST: There is no mention of orientation in the description of Solomon's Temple, but in Ezekiel's vision (47.1) it is so oriented.   SACRIFICES: Hecataeus (in Diodorus Siculus 40.3.4) had noted

current being from below, the curtain bulged out from the bottom to its highest extent, the spectacle was highly agreeable and hard to tear oneself from. ⁸⁷The altar was built in keeping with the size of the place and of the offerings consumed upon it by fire, and the ascent was on a similar scale. The ascent was gradual, from a proper regard for decency, and the ministering priests were swathed in "coats of fine linen" reaching to the ankles. ⁸⁸The edifice looks towards the east, and its back to the west. The entire floor is paved with stones and slopes downward to the appropriate places, to admit of flushing with water in order to wash away the blood of the sacrifices; for many myriads of beasts are offered on the days of the festivals. ⁸⁹The water supply is inexhaustible, for an abundant natural spring pours forth within the Temple area, and there are furthermore marvelous underground reservoirs passing description, to a distance of five stades, as was pointed out, round the foundations of the Temple; of these each had innumerable pipes, so that the various channels converged at the several reservoirs. ⁹⁰The floors and sides of these reservoirs, they explained, were overlaid with lead, and above them a great mass of plaster was laid, everything being made secure. There are numerous outlets, they said, at the foot of the altar, invisible to all except those engaged in the ministration, so that the vast accumulation of sacrificial blood is cleansed away in the twinkling of an eye. ⁹¹I am myself convinced of the system of reservoirs, and I shall show how my belief was confirmed. They took me more than four stades out of the city, and at a certain place bade me bend over and listen to the rushing noise of the meet-

---

that Moses instituted sacrifices of a form different from those prevailing among other peoples.

89. WATER SUPPLY: Its water supply is a stock theme in descriptions of the Temple, as may be seen from Tacitus, *Histories* 5.12; *cf.* the citations in Eusebius, *Praep. Ev.* 9.35–37, and Ben Sirah 50.3.   FIVE STADES: 925 meters.

91. THEY TOOK ME: Février thinks this is obviously part of a cicerone's routine, and hence appropriate to pilgrim-tourists rather than to royal ambassadors.

πάντα καθαρίζεσθαι τὰ συναγόμενα παμπληθῆ τῶν θυμάτων αἵματα. ⁹¹πεπεισμένος δὲ καὶ αὐτὸς τὴν τῶν ὑποδοχείων κατασκευὴν δηλώσω καθὼς ἐπιστώθην. προήγαγον γὰρ πλέον σταδίων τεσσάρων ἐκ τῆς πόλεως, καὶ πρός τινα τόπον ἐκέλευσαν κατακύψαντα συνακοῦσαι τοῦ γινομένου ψόφου τῆς ἀπαντήσεως τῶν ὑδάτων· ὥστε συμφανές μοι γεγονέναι τὸ μέγεθος τῶν ἀγγείων, καθὼς δεδήλωται. ⁹²Τῶν δὲ ἱερέων ἡ λειτουργία κατὰ πᾶν ἀνυπέρβλητός ἐστι τῇ ῥώμῃ καὶ τῇ τῆς εὐκοσμίας καὶ σιγῆς διαθέσει. πάντες γὰρ αὐτοκελεύστως διαπονοῦσι πολλῆς γινομένης κακοπαθείας, καὶ ἑκάστῳ τὸ διατεταγμένον μέλει. καὶ ἀδιαλείπτως ὑπηρετοῦσιν, οἱ μὲν τὴν ξυλείαν, οἱ δὲ ἔλαιον, οἱ δὲ σεμίδαλιν, οἱ δὲ τὰ τῶν ἀρωμάτων, ἕτεροι τὰ τῆς σαρκὸς ὁλοκαυτοῦντες, ἰσχύι διαφερόντως συγχρώμενοι· ⁹³διαλαβόντες γὰρ ἀμφοτέραις τῶν μόσχων τὰ σκέλη, πλεῖον ὄντα ταλάντων δύο σχεδὸν ἑκάστου, ἀναρρίπτουσιν ἑκατέραις θαυμασίως ὕψος ἱκανὸν καὶ οὐχ ἁμαρτάνουσι τῆς ἐπιθέσεως. ὁμοίως δὲ καὶ τὰ τῶν προβάτων ἔτι δ' αἰγῶν τοῖς βάρεσι καὶ πιμελῇ θαυμασίως ἔχει. κατὰ πᾶν γὰρ ἐκλεγομένων οἷς ἐπιμελές ἐστιν ἀμώμητα καὶ τῇ παχύτητι διαφέροντα, τὸ προειρημένον ἐπιτελεῖται. ⁹⁴πρὸς δὲ τὴν ἀνάπαυσιν τόπος αὐτοῖς ἐστὶν ἀποτεταγμένος, οὗ καθίζουσιν οἱ διαναπαυόμενοι. τούτου δὲ γινομένου, τῶν διαλελοιπότων ἐγείρονται πρό-
95 θυμοι, οὐδενὸς ἐπιτάσσοντος τὰ τῆς λειτουργίας. ⁹⁵ἥ τε πᾶσα σιγὴ καθέστηκεν, ὥστε ὑπολαμβάνειν, μηθ' ἕνα ἄνθρωπον ἐν τῷ τόπῳ παρεῖναι, πρὸς τοὺς ἑπτακοσίους παρόντων τῶν λειτουργῶν—καὶ τῶν προσαγόντων δὲ τὰ θύματα πολύ τι πλῆθος—ἀλλὰ φόβῳ καὶ καταξίως μεγάλης θειότητος ἅπαντ' ἐπιτελεῖται. ⁹⁶Μεγάλην δὲ ἔκπληξιν

---

95 ωστε υπολαμβανειν edd., ως τυπον
λαμβανειν MSS

92-95. THE MINISTERING PRIESTS: In this description of the ministrations of the priests the effort to preserve the attitude of the objective spectator is apparent, but it is no less apparent that the writer is himself a devout adherent of the cult. Février points out that the activity here described reflects not the regular daily sacrifices but the much more numerous offerings of the festivals, and regards this as further proof that the writer is

ing of the waters. Thus the size of the cisterns was made evident to me, as I have described them.

⁹²In its exhibition of strength and in its orderly and silent performance the ministration of the priests could in no way be surpassed. All of them, self-bidden, carry out labors involving great toil, and each has his appointed charge. Their service is unceasing, some attending to the wood, others the oil, others the fine wheat flour, others the business of spices, and still others the portions of flesh for burnt offering, employing extraordinary strength in this task. ⁹³For with both hands they grasp the legs of the calves, almost all of which weigh more than two talents each, and then with marvelous deftness they fling them to a considerable height with their two hands, and they never fail of placing the victim correctly. The portions of the sheep and the goats are similarly remarkable for their weight and fat, for always those whose business it is choose beasts that are flawless and especially plump, and then the procedure mentioned is carried out. ⁹⁴For their rest there is a place set apart for them where those who are relieved from duty take seats. When this happens some of those who had had an interval of rest readily rise up, though no one gives an order for them to serve. ⁹⁵Complete silence prevails, so that one might suppose that not a person was present in the place, though those performing the service amount to some seven hundred—besides the great multitude of persons bringing sacrifices to be offered—but everything is done with reverence and in a manner worthy of the great divinity.

⁹⁶We were struck with great astonishment when we beheld

---

a simple pilgrim, in Jerusalem for the festival, and not a royal ambassador.
96–99. THE VESTMENTS OF THE HIGH PRIEST: The description of the vestments of the High Priest makes free use of the phraseology of LXX Ex. 28–29. It may be noted that unless the writer were himself a Jew he could never have approached near enough to observe the details; the vestments were worn only when the High Priest officiated. The High Priest did not himself officiate at ordinary sacrifices (though he may have done so on Sabbaths and New Moons), and this may be a further indication that we are dealing with the account of a participant in a pilgrimage.

ἡμῖν παρέσχεν ὡς ἐθεασάμεθα τὸν Ἐλεάζαρον ἐν τῇ λειτουργίᾳ, τά τε τοῦ στολισμοῦ καὶ τῆς δόξης, ἢ συνίσταται διὰ τὴν ἔνδυσιν οὗ φορεῖ ΧΙΤΩΝΟC καὶ τῶν περὶ αὐτὸν λίθων· ΧΡΥCΟΙ γὰρ ΚΩΔΩΝΕC περὶ τὸν ΠΟΔΗΡΗ εἰσὶν αὐτοῦ, μέλους ἦχον ἀνιέντες ἰδιάζοντα· παρ' ἑκάτερον δὲ τούτων ΑΝΘΕCΙ πεποικιλμένοι ΡΟΙCΚΟΙ, τῇ χρόᾳ θαυμασίως ἔχοντες. ⁹⁷κατέζωστο δὲ διαφόρῳ ΖΩΝΗ διαπρεπεῖ, διυφασμένη καλλίστοις χρώμασιν. ΕΠΙ δὲ ΤΟΥ CΤΗΘΟΥC φορεῖ τὸ λεγόμενον ΛΟΓΙΟΝ, ἐν ᾧ συνεσφιγμένοι ΛΙΘΟΙ ΔΕΚΑΔΥΟ, διαλλάσσοντες, τοῖς γένεσι, χρυσῷ κεκολλημένοι, ΤΑ τῶν φυλάρχων ΟΝΟΜΑΤΑ κατὰ τὴν ἐξ ἀρχῆς διάταξιν γενηθεῖσαν, ἀπαυγάζοντες ἕκαστος ἀνεξήγητον τῆς ἰδιότητος τὴν φυσικὴν χρόαν. ⁹⁸ἐπὶ δὲ τῆς κεφαλῆς ἔχει τὴν λεγομένην ΚΙΔΑΡΙΝ, ἐπὶ δὲ ταύτης τὴν ἀμίμητον ΜΙΤΡΑΝ, τὸ καθηγιασμένον βασίλειον ΕΚΤΥΠΟΥΝ ἐπὶ ΠΕΤΑΛΩ ΧΡΥCΩ γράμμασιν ἁγίοις ὄνομα τοῦ θεοῦ, κατὰ μέσον τῶν ὀφρύων, δόξῃ πεπληρωμένον, ὁ κριθεὶς ἄξιος τούτων ἐν ταῖς λειτουργίαις. ⁹⁹ἡ δὲ συμφάνεια τούτων ἐμποιεῖ φόβον καὶ ταραχήν, ὥστε νομίζειν εἰς ἕτερον ἐληλυθέναι ἐκτὸς τοῦ κόσμου· καὶ διαβεβαιοῦμαι, πάντα ἄνθρωπον προσελθόντα τῇ θεωρίᾳ τῶν προειρημένων εἰς ἔκπληξιν ἥξειν καὶ θαυμασμὸν ἀδιήγητον, μετατραπέντα τῇ διανοίᾳ διὰ τὴν περὶ ἕκαστον ἁγίαν κατασκευήν. ¹⁰⁰Πρὸς γὰρ

97 κατεζωστο MSS-T, κατεζωσται MSS-W
98 δοξη MSS-T, δοξης MSS-W / W marks a lacuna after πεπληρομενον,
for which Mend. suggested something like εν τουτω σχηματι προεισιν
99 εις ετερον κ. τ. λ. W conjectures εις ετερον εκτος τουτου κοσμου

97. WHAT IS CALLED: The expression may indicate the writer's dissatisfaction with the traditional term, or may (more likely) be an effort to maintain his non-Jewish character. THE ORACLE: *logion* is used of sacred or oracular writings, in Herodotus of "oracles," and hence is generally so translated. At 158 it is used of *mezuzot*. In LXX Ex. 28.23, 26 it is used of the High Priest's breastplate HOSHEN. [During the Second Commonwealth the High Priest did not wear a *hoshen* oracle. Hence we must assume that the entire narrative was imaginary. The emissaries could not have seen an oracle on the High Priest as it had been abolished by the Pharisees. Hence it seems likely that the whole story from 83 is a later addition, not a part of the Letter of Aristeas. It was written after the destruction of the Temple, and the author, not knowing that the *hoshen* was no

Eleazar at his ministration, and his apparel, and the visible glory conferred by his being garbed in the "coat" which he wears and the stones that adorn his person. For there are "bells of gold" upon the "skirts of the robe" giving out a peculiar musical sound, and on either side of these are "pomegranates" broidered "with flowers," marvelously corlorful. [97]He was girt with a rich and magnificent "girdle," woven with most beautiful colors. And "upon his breast" he wears what is called the "oracle," in which are set "twelve stones" of various species, soldered with gold, with "the names" of the heads of the tribes, according to their original constitution, each of them flashing forth indescribably with the natural color of its own peculiar character. [98]Upon his head he has the "tiara" as it is called, and on top of this the inimitable "mitre," bearing "engraven" in sacred letters upon a "plate of gold" set between his eyebrows the name of God filled with glory. He is adjudged worthy of these things in his ministrations. [99]The total effect of the whole arouses awe and emotional excitement, so that one would think he had passed to some other sphere outside the world. I venture to affirm positively that any man who witnesses the spectacle I have recounted will experience amazement and astonishment indescribable, and his mind will be deeply moved at the sanctity attaching to every detail.

100   [100]To obtain a thorough knowledge of everything we as-

longer in vogue during the period of the Second Temple, copied the entire story from the Pentateuch. (S. Z.)]
98. THE NAME OF GOD: The circumlocution is apparently an intentional device to avoid using the tetragrammaton.   ADJUDGED WORTHY: Since the office was apparently hereditary under the Hasmonaeans and by nomination under Herod and the Romans, this expression has been taken (by Willrich) to refer to the latter date. The contention is without substance, for even if the literal sense of "adjudged" be pressed, it might still well refer to a hereditary High Priest.
99. PASSED TO SOME OTHER SPHERE: Most translators so understand the expression; it may also bear the meaning given by Andrews: "into the presence of a man who belonged to a different world."
100–104. THE CITADEL: The description of the citadel here given has been taken by scholars to confirm both an early and a late dating of Aristeas (or for this passage, assuming that it is an interpolation or a borrowing),

τὴν ἐπίγνωσιν ἁπάντων ἐπὶ τὴν παρακειμένην ἄκραν τῆς πόλεως ἀναβάντες ἐθεωροῦμεν· ἣ κεῖται μὲν ἐν ὑψηλοτάτῳ τόπῳ, πύργοις ἐξησφαλισμένη πλείοσι, μέχρι κορυφῆς εὐμήκεσι λίθοις ἀνῳκοδομημένων αὐτῶν, ὡς μεταλαμβάνομεν, πρὸς φυλακὴν τῶν περὶ τὸ ἱερὸν τόπων· 101ἵνα, ἐὰν ἐπίθεσίς τις ἢ νεωτερισμὸς ἢ πολεμίων ἔφοδος γένηται, μηθεὶς δύνηται ὁδὸν εἰς τοὺς περιβόλους ποιήσασθαι τοὺς περὶ τὸν οἶκον· ἐπικειμένων καὶ ὀξυβελῶν ἐπὶ τῶν πύργων τῆς ἄκρας καὶ ὀργάνων ποικίλων, καὶ τοῦ τόπου κατὰ κορυφὴν ὄντος τῶν προειρημένων περιβόλων, 102ὡσανεὶ φυλασσομένων τῶν πύργων ὑπὸ τῶν πιστοτάτων ἀνδρῶν καὶ τῇ πατρίδι μεγάλας ἀποδείξεις δεδωκότων· οἵτινες οὐκ εἶχον ἐξουσίαν ἐξιέναι τῆς ἄκρας, εἰ μὴ ταῖς ἑορταῖς, καὶ τοῦτο ἐκ μέρους, οὐδὲ εἰσοδεύειν εἴων οὐδένα. 103μετὰ ἀκριβείας δὲ πολλῆς εἶχον, εἰ καί τις ἐπιταγὴ γένοιτο διὰ τοῦ προκαθηγουμένου πρὸς θεωρίαν εἰσδέξασθαί τινας· οἷον καὶ καθ' ἡμᾶς ἐγεγόνει. μόλις γὰρ ἀνόπλους ὄντας ἡμᾶς δύο παρεδέξαντο πρὸς τὸ κατανοῆσαι τὰ τῶν θυσιῶν. 104ἔλεγον δὲ καὶ δι' ὅρκων πεπιστῶσθαι τὸ τοιοῦτον· τοὺς γὰρ πάντας ὀμωμοκέναι, κατ' ἀνάγκην <ἐπιτελουμένους> θείως τὸ κατὰ τὸν ὁρισμὸν πρᾶγμα, ὄντας πεντακοσίους μὴ παραδέξασθαι πλεῖον ἀνθρώπων πέντε κατὰ τὸ αὐτό· τοῦ γὰρ ἱεροῦ τὴν πᾶσαν εἶναι φυλακὴν τὴν ἄκραν· καὶ τὸν καταβαλλόμενον αὐτὴν

---

104 ἐπιτελουμένους T, ἐπιτελουμένου MSS / τὴν προφυλακὴν T-MSS, πρὸς φυλακὴν W-Schmidt

---

but its evidence seems to be inconclusive; see Introd. 13. The pre-Hasmonaean citadel north of the Temple (Neh. 2.8) was like the present structure adjacent to the Temple and designed for its protection. This citadel the Seleucids pulled down, and built another at a distance south of the Temple, not to protect it but as a garrison for their troops (167–166 BCE; I Mac. 1.33; Josephus, Ant. 12.252). But the citadel rebuilt by the later Hasmonaeans (Josephus, Ant. 15.403) and then again by Herod, who named it Antonia (Ant. 18.91; Jewish War 5.238 ff.) was on the site of the pre-Hasmonaean and not the Seleucid structure; see Ralph Marcus on Ant. 12.252. Our passage then is of little help in dating. Février points out that the tone of the description is again that of pilgrim-tourists and not of high officials.

Josephus' description of the Antonia (Jewish War 5.238–245, quoted in Introd. 12) should be carefully compared for agreements and divergencies.

cended the citadel of the city which lies hard by and looked about. It is situated on a very lofty spot and is fortified with a number of towers which are built of large blocks of stone right up to the very top, as a protection, so we were informed, for the precincts of the Temple, [101]so that in case of any attack or revolution or enemy invasion no one could make his way into the walls which encompass the Temple. On the towers of the citadel are set artillery and various other engines of war, and their lofty eminence commands the aforesaid walls. [102]The towers are guarded, furthermore, by the most loyal of men, who have given demonstrative proof of devotion to their country. These men had orders not to quit the citadel, except on festivals, and then only by turns, nor did they permit anyone to enter. [103]Very scrupulous care was exercised even when they received an order from their leader to admit any visitors as sightseers, as happened in our case, for though we were unarmed and only two, they would barely admit us to study the arrangements for the sacrifices. [104]They said they were pledged to such conduct by oaths: they had all sworn, and of necessity and religious scruple they fulfilled the stipulation of their oath, that though they were five hundred they would not admit more than five persons at the same time; for the citadel was the whole defense of the Temple, and he that founded it had thus secured its protection.

The two descriptions might well be taken to refer to the same structure; but there is no evidence to prove that our passage cannot refer to the pre-Seleucid citadel, which may have been very like Josephus' description and only less elegant. Aristeas, who has a penchant for elegance, is noticeably silent on the subject here.

101. IN CASE OF ... REVOLUTION: Josephus alleges the same motive and uses the same word (νεωτερισμός, νεωτερισθείη).

103. THEIR LEADER: The High Priest, and so at 122.   THEY WOULD BARELY ADMIT US: This is the strongest evidence that the author is a simple pilgrim; on the other hand, since the entire embassy was imaginary, this improbability may merely be a slip of the imagination.

104. FIVE HUNDRED: This corresponds to Josephus' "cohort."   HE THAT FOUNDED IT: Rather an allusion to a well-known personage than an indication of anonymity; if we must choose between Nehemiah and Herod and Judah Maccabee, the last would appear the most likely.

τὴν προφυλακὴν τῶν εἰρημένων οὕτως ἠσφαλίσθαι. 105 Τῆς δὲ πόλεώς ἐστι τὸ χύμα συμμέτρως ἔχον, οἷον τεσσαράκοντα σταδίων ὄντος τοῦ περιβόλου, καθόσον εἰκάσαι δυνατόν. ἔχει δὲ τὴν τῶν πύργων θέσιν θεατροειδῆ, καὶ φαινομένων διόδων—τῶν ὑποκειμένων, τῶν δ' ἐπάνωθεν—<εἰθισμένως>, καὶ τὰς διὰ τούτων διεξόδους. ἀνάκλασιν γὰρ ἔχει τὰ τῶν τόπων, ὡς ἂν ἐπ' ὄρους τῆς πόλεως ᾠκοδομημένης. εἰσὶ δὲ καὶ διαβάθραι πρὸς τὰς διόδους. 106οἱ μὲν γὰρ μετέωροι τὴν ὁδείαν, οἱ δ' ὑπ' αὐτὰς ποιοῦνται, καὶ μάλιστα διεστηκότες τῆς ὁδείας, διὰ τοὺς ἐν ταῖς ἁγνείαις ὄντας, ὅπως μηδενὸς θιγγάνωσιν ὧν οὐ δέον ἐστίν. 107Οὐκ ἀλόγως δὲ τὴν πόλιν συμμετρίᾳ καθηκούσῃ κατεσκεύασαν οἱ πρῶτοι, σοφῶς δὲ ἐπινοήσαντες. τῆς γὰρ χώρας πολλῆς οὔσης καὶ καλῆς, καί τινων μὲν πεδινῶν, τῶν κατὰ τὴν Σαμαρεῖτιν λεγομένην, καὶ τῶν συναπτόντων τῇ τῶν Ἰδουμαίων χώρᾳ, τινῶν δὲ ὀρεινῶν, τῶν <συναπτόντων τῇ τῶν Ἰουδαίων χώρᾳ, χρὴ> πρὸς τὴν γεωργίαν καὶ τὴν ἐπιμέλειαν τῆς γῆς γίνεσθαι συνεχῶς, ἵνα καὶ διὰ τοῦτο οὗτοι τὴν εὐκαρπίαν ἔχωσιν· οὗ καὶ γινομένου γεωργεῖται <πάντα μετὰ> δαψιλείας πολλῆς ἐν πάσῃ τῇ προειρημένῃ χώρᾳ. 108τῶν δὲ πόλεων ὅσαι μέγεθος ἔχουσι καὶ τὴν ἀκόλουθον εὐδαιμονίαν, ταύταις συμβέβηκεν εὐανδρεῖν, ἀμελεῖσθαι δὲ τῆς χώρας, πάντων ἐπὶ τὸ κατὰ ψυχὴν ἱλαροῦσθαι νενευκότων, καὶ τῇ κατασκευῇ πάντας ἀνθρώπους ἐπὶ τὰς ἡδονὰς εὐκατα-

---

105 ειθισμενως T, ηθισμενων W
106 διεστηκοτες T, διεστηκοτας MSS, διεστηκυιας W
107 λεγομενην edd., λεγομενων MSS /

For the lacuna T supplies συναπτοντων τη των Ιουδαιων χωρα χρη, W suggests μεσην την χωραν / παντα μετα edd., μεν παντα MSS

105–111. THE CITY.
105–106. The description of the city seems curiously brief, and notes only a peculiarity which has to do with religious observance. An Alexandrian might in fact be unimpressed by a provincial capital, except for the Temple; and perhaps the justification of its small size has an apologetic motive.
105. MODERATE: Frequent usage and the context suggest this translation, but *summetrōs* may mean "symmetrical." FORTY STADES: Hecataeus (in Josephus, *Against Apion* 187) says 50, and Josephus himself (*Jewish War* 5.159) makes it 33 for the period of Herod Agrippa. TOUCH NOTHING IMPROPER: *Cf.* Lev. 15.22.

105 [105]The extent of the city is moderate, its compass being about forty stades, as far as one may conjecture. In the position of its towers and of the thoroughfares, some of which appear above and some below, with the cross-streets cutting through them, it has the familiar aspects of a theater, for, the city being built upon a mountain, its parts rise one above another, [106]and there are stairs to the thoroughfares. Some persons make their way at the higher level and some underneath, and they are careful to keep apart as they go, so that those in a state of purification may touch nothing improper.

[107]Not without reason did the original founders build their city of convenient proportions, but with wise insight. For the country is large and good, and some parts, those in Samaria so-called and those adjacent to the Idumaeans' country, are level plain, but others, in the center, are mountainous, and unremitting attention to agriculture and care of the soil is essential for these latter parts to obtain crops in plenty also. Since such attention is given, the whole of the aforementioned country is cultivated in various ways and with abundant yield. [108]In cities that have great size and consequently prosperity it has come about that their population is teeming while the countryside is neglected, because everyone is minded to seek enjoyment, all men being con-

---

107-111. The smallness of Jerusalem is justified by a *synkrisis* (see Introd. 50) with Alexandria, and at the same time the sagacity of the Egyptian ruler is approved.
107. SO-CALLED: SAMARIA, unlike THE IDUMAEANS' COUNTRY, is an unfamiliar designation.   ADJACENT TO: If this is to be taken precisely it would indicate a date before *ca.* 126 BCE, when Idumaea was conquered by John Hyrcanus.   BUT OTHERS: All editors mark a lacuna, as indicated in the text; IN THE CENTER translates Wendland's suggested filling of the lacuna; Thackeray suggests "those adjoining the country of Judaea."
108. ALL MEN . . . PRONE TO PLEASURE: The *synkrisis* regularly indulges in philosophic moralization. Aristotle, *Nicomachean Ethics* 1109a, says: "We tend more naturally to pleasures, and hence are more easily carried away towards self-indulgence than towards propriety." The parallel is interesting, for it occurs in the same context of the doctrine of the mean from which 122 seems to be drawn. *Cf.* 222, and see note on 273.

φόρους εἶναι. ¹⁰⁹τοῦτο δὲ ἐγίνετο περὶ τὴν Ἀλεξάνδρειαν ὑπερβάλλουσαν πάσας τῷ μεγέθει καὶ εὐδαιμονίᾳ τὰς πόλεις. οἱ γὰρ ἀπὸ τῆς χώρας εἰς αὐτὴν ἀποξενούμενοι καταμένοντες ἐφ' ἱκανὸν εἰς ἐλάττωσιν ἦγον τὰ τῆς ἐργασίας. ¹¹⁰ὅθεν ὁ βασιλεύς, ἵνα μὴ καταμένωσι, προσέταξε μὴ πλέον εἴκοσιν ἡμερῶν παρεπιδημεῖν· καὶ τοῖς ἐπὶ τῶν χρειῶν ὁμοίως δι' ἐγγράπτων διαστολὰς ἔδωκεν, ἐὰν ἀναγκαῖον ᾖ κατακαλέσαι, διακρίνειν ἐν ἡμέραις πέντε. ¹¹¹πρὸ πολλοῦ δὲ ποιούμενος καὶ χρηματιστὰς καὶ τοὺς τούτων ὑπηρέτας ἐπέταξε κατὰ νομούς, ὅπως μὴ πορισμὸν λαμβάνοντες οἱ γεωργοὶ καὶ προστάται τῆς πόλεως ἐλαττῶσι τὰ ταμιεῖα, λέγω δὲ τὰ τῆς γεωργίας πρόσφορα. ¹¹²Παρεξέβημεν δὲ ταῦτα διὰ τὸ καλῶς ἡμῖν τὸν Ἐλεάζαρον ὑποδεδειχέναι τὰ προειρημένα. μεγάλη γὰρ ἐστὶν ἡ τῶν γεωργουμένων φιλοπονία. καὶ γὰρ ἐλαϊκοῖς πλήθεσι σύνδενδρός ἐστι καὶ σιτικοῖς καρποῖς αὐτῶν ἡ χώρα καὶ ὀσπρίοις, ἔτι δὲ ἀμπέλῳ καὶ μέλιτι πολλῷ. τὰ μὲν τῶν ἄλλων ἀκροδρύων καὶ φοινίκων οὐδ' ἀριθμεῖται παρ' αὐτοῖς. ¹¹³κτήνη τε πολλὰ παμμιγῆ, καὶ δαψιλὴς ἡ τούτων νομή· διὸ καλῶς ἔβλεψαν, ὅτι πολυανθρωπίας οἱ τόποι προσδέονται, καὶ τὴν κατασκευὴν τῆς πόλεως καὶ τῶν κωμῶν ἔθεντο κατὰ λόγον. ¹¹⁴πολὺ δὲ πλῆθος καὶ τῶν ἀρωμάτων καὶ λίθων πολυτελῶν καὶ χρυσοῦ

---

109. ALEXANDRIA: Mentioned by name only here and at 173, elsewhere (4, 22, 11) simply "the city." SURPASSES ALL OTHER CITIES: Including Jerusalem, as even a Jew of Alexandria, however pious, would admit. Philo, *Against Flaccus* 6, says (but with patent exaggeration) that in his day there were a million Jews in Alexandria; it was certainly the most populous city of the Hellenistic world. REMAINING THERE ... REDUCED AGRICULTURE: The depopulation of the countryside and growth of Alexandria suggests a date well below 200; see Lumbroso, *Archiv für Papyrusforschung* 5 (1906), 402. There is a quite remarkable parallel to this passage in Aristotle's account of the regime of Peisistratus in Athens (*Constitution of Athens*, 16): Peisistratus encouraged agriculture, so that people might not dally in cities and neglect the countryside; he instituted local justices, thirty and later forty in number; he himself often went out to the country to settle disputes between individuals "so that they might not come into the city and neglect their farms." In view of our author's familiarity with Aristotelian ideas and expressions it is not impossible that this is an actual echo.

110. IF IT WERE NECESSARY: Normally the jurisdiction of local officials

stitutionally prone to pleasure. [109]This is what happened to Alexandria, which surpasses all other cities in size and wealth. People from the country visiting the city and then remaining there for a long while reduced agriculture to a sorry pass. [110]Hence the king, to prevent their remaining, ordained that their sojourns should not exceed twenty days, and he also issued injunctions in writing to the officials that if it were necessary to summon any their cases were to be decided within five days. [111]Considering the matter of great importance, he ordained that judges of assizes with their bailiffs sit in every district, so that the farmers and their agents might not, while seeking profits, diminish the city's granary, I mean the produce of agriculture.

[112]We have been led to this digression by the admirable exposition of the matters dealt with which we received from Eleazar. The diligence of their agriculturists is indeed great. Their country is plentifully wooded with numerous olive trees, and rich in cereal crops and pulse, and also in vines and honey. Date palms and other fruit trees are beyond reckoning among them. [113]They have plentiful cattle of all varieties, and their pastures are lush. Hence they recognized that the rural districts required a dense population, and they laid the city and the villages out in proportion. [114]A great volume of spices, precious stones, and gold is brought into the region by the

---

sufficed, and the institution of local assizes in the following section may well reflect an ordinance of Philadelphus if it is not merely a literary reminisence of Aristotle.

111. JUDGES OF ASSIZES: *Chrematistai*, literally "experts in a matter," is so used in the papyri. DISTRICT: The Egyptian *nome*.

112. DIGRESSIONS: Namely 108-111, on Egypt, and the patently idealized attractions of Palestine seem almost an apology for the implied praise of Egypt. Meecham (329 f.) calls attention to the similarity to 112-114 of a passage in George Cedrenus, a monk of the XI century, who pretends to be citing Aristotle.

112-120. TOPOGRAPHY AND RESOURCES OF PALESTINE.

113. CITY AND THE VILLAGES: *Cf.* the Hecataeus passage (*Against Apion* 1.197) cited above.

114. LACKS NONE OF THE THINGS: Economic autarky is a regular feature of the ideal city.

παρακομίζεται διὰ τῶν Ἀράβων εἰς τὸν τόπον. ἐργάσιμος
γὰρ καὶ πρὸς τὴν ἐμπορίαν ἐστὶ κατεσκευασμένη ἡ χώρα,
καὶ πολύτεχνος ἡ πόλις, οὐ σπανίζει δὲ οὐδὲν τῶν διακομι-
ζομένων διὰ τῆς θαλάσσης. ¹¹⁵ἔχει γὰρ καὶ λιμένας εὐκαίρους
χορηγοῦντας, τόν τε κατὰ τὴν Ἀσκαλῶνα καὶ Ἰόππην καὶ
Γάζαν, ὁμοίως δὲ καὶ Πτολεμαΐδα τὴν ὑπὸ τοῦ βασιλέως
ἐκτισμένην. μέση δὲ κεῖται πρὸς τοὺς προειρημένους τόπους,
οὐκ ἀπέχουσα τούτων πολύ. ἔχει δὲ πάντα δαψιλῆ κάθυγρος
οὖσα πάντοθεν ἡ χώρα καὶ μεγάλην ἀσφάλειαν ἔχουσα.
¹¹⁶περιρρεῖ δ' αὐτὴν ὁ λεγόμενος Ἰορδάνης ποταμὸς ἀείρρους.
<τῆς δὲ χώρας> οὐκ ἔλαττον ἑξακισχιλίων μυριάδων
ἀρουρῶν κατὰ τὸ ἀρχαῖον οὔσης (μετέπειτα δὲ οἱ γειτνι-
ῶντες ἐπέβησαν αὐτῆς) ἑξήκοντα μυριάδες ἀνδρῶν ἔγκληροι
καθειστήκεισαν ἑκατοντάρουροι. πληρούμενος δὲ ὁ ποταμός,
καθὼς ὁ Νεῖλος, ἐν ταῖς πρὸς τὸν θερισμὸν ἡμέραις, πολλὴν
ἀρδεύει τῆς γῆς· ¹¹⁷ὃς εἰς ἕτερον ποταμὸν ἐκβάλλει τὸ
ῥεῦμα κατὰ τὴν Πτολεμαίων χώραν, οὗτος δὲ ἔξεισιν εἰς
θάλασσαν. ἄλλοι δὲ χείμαρροι λεγόμενοι κατίασι, περι-
λαμβάνοντες τὰ πρὸς τὴν Γάζαν μέρη καὶ τὴν Ἀζωτίων
χώραν. ¹¹⁸περιέχεται δὲ ἀσφαλείαις αὐτοφυέσι, δυσείσ-
βολος οὖσα καὶ πλήθεσιν ἀπραγμάτευτος, διὰ τὸ στενὰς

---

116 της δε χωρας supplied by T / εκατονταρουροι Mahaffy, -οις MSS / επεβησαν T-MSS, υπεβησαν W-MSS
117 εκβαλλει T-MSS, εμβαλλει W-MSS / Πτολεμαιων MSS, W conjectures Πτολεμαεων
118 ασφαλειαις edd., ασφαλες, ασφαλως MSS

---

115. ASCALON etc.: The cities are not in geographical order, for Ascalon is between Joppa and Gaza, and Acco is above all three. Wendland (in *Kautzsch* 3) dates Aristeas to shortly after 96 on the basis of this list, for Joppa was gained in 142 by Simon and Gaza in 96 by Alexander Jannaeus, which gave the Jews control of the coast, though Ascalon and Ptolemais were never taken. If the actual history of the cities is to be pressed one might better argue for a Roman date, for Gaza was not only taken but destroyed, and only rebuilt under Pompey, and Aristeas does not necessarily imply that the Jews owned the ports but only that they used them, which they did under the Romans. But the imaginative character of the book makes such exegesis futile (see Introd. 58), and even the fact that the Jews held none of the ports before Simon need not preclude an early Maccabean date, and certainly not a date when the Ptolemies controlled Palestine. Coins of Philadelphus struck at Ptolemais begin from 261, the 25th year of his reign. WELL WATERED: A patent exaggeration. SECURITY:

Arabs. For the country is adapted for commerce as well as agriculture, and the city is rich in crafts and lacks none of the things imported by sea. ¹¹⁵It also has harbors well situated to supply its needs, those at Ascalon, Joppa, and Gaza, and likewise Ptolemais, which was founded by the king. It is centrally located with reference to the places just mentioned, and not far distant from them. The country enjoys everything in abundance, being well watered everywhere and possessing great security. ¹¹⁶Around it flows the river called Jordan, whose stream never fails. Originally the country comprised no less than six million aroura (but afterwards the neighboring peoples encroached upon it), and six hundred thousand men each became holders of hundred-aroura lots. About the time of harvest the river rises, like the Nile, and irrigates much of the land. ¹¹⁷The stream empties into another river in the district of Ptolemais, and this flows into the sea. Other mountain torrents, as they are called, flow down and take in the parts about Gaza and the district of Azotus. ¹¹⁸The country is encircled by natural defenses, so that it is hard to penetrate and impracticable for large numbers, because the passes are narrow, being flanked by steep cliffs and deep

---

possibly as being sheltered from the winds by the mountains.
116. AROUND IT: So easily verifiable a distortion marks this passage as intentionally following a Utopian pattern; see Introd. 50.   SIX MILLION: Hecataeus (Josephus, *Against Apion* 1.195) says: "They occupy almost three million arourae of the most excellent and fertile soil, productive of every variety of fruits. Such is the extent of Judaea."   AROURA: A section of plow-land, measuring, according to Herodotus 2.168, 100 Egyptian cubits (52.5 meters) square.   ENCROACHED: Reading *epebēsan*, though a well-attested reading is *hupebēsan*, "retired;" "encroached" suits the context better.   600,000: The number that went up from Egypt: Ex. 12.37, Num. 11.12.   HOLDERS OF HUNDRED-AROURA LOTS: "A 100 aroura man" occurs frequently in the Petrie papyri of the veterans of Ptolemy Philadelphus who received allotments in the Fayyum.   THE RIVER RISES: *Cf.* Josh. 3.15: "For the Jordan overfloweth all its banks all the time of harvest."
117. PTOLEMAIS: MSS read "of the Ptolemaeans," which would mean "Egyptians" and is therefore irrelevant; the change requires the insertion of only a single letter.   THE SEA: The Mediterranean.
118. NATURAL DEFENSES: Like economic autarky, a regular feature of the ideal state.

εἶναι τὰς παρόδους, κρημνῶν παρακειμένων καὶ φαράγγων βαθέων, ἔτι δὲ τραχείας οὔσης πάσης τῆς περιεχούσης πᾶσαν τὴν χώραν ὀρεινῆς. [119]Ἐλέγετο δὲ καὶ ἐκ τῶν παρακειμένων ὀρέων τῆς Ἀραβίας μέταλλα χαλκοῦ καὶ σιδήρου συνίστασθαι πρότερον. ἐκλέλειπται δὲ ταῦτα, καθ' ὃν ἐπεκράτησαν Πέρσαι χρόνον, τῶν τότε προστατούντων ποιησαμένων διαβολήν, ὡς ἄχρηστος ἡ κατεργασία γίνεται καὶ πολυδάπανος, [120]ὅπως μὴ διὰ τὴν μεταλλείαν τῶν εἰρημένων συμβῇ καὶ τὴν χώραν καταφθείρεσθαι, καὶ σχεδὸν διὰ τὴν ἐκείνων δυναστείαν ἀλλοτριωθῆναι, παρεύρεσιν λαβόντων εἰς τοὺς τόπους εἰσόδου, διὰ τὸ τὴν διαβολὴν γεγονέναι ταύτην.

Ὅσον οὖν καὶ περὶ τούτων ἔδει, κεφαλαιωδῶς σεσήμαγκά σοι, ὦ Φιλόκρατες ἀδελφέ· τὰ δὲ τῆς ἑρμηνείας ἑπομένως δηλώσομεν. [121]Ἐπιλέξας γὰρ τοὺς ἀρίστους ἄνδρας καὶ παιδείᾳ διαφέροντας, ἅτε δὴ γονέων τετευχότας ἐνδόξων, οἵτινες οὐ μόνον τὴν τῶν Ἰουδαϊκῶν γραμμάτων ἕξιν περιεποίησαν αὑτοῖς, ἀλλὰ καὶ τῆς τῶν Ἑλληνικῶν ἐφρόντισαν οὐ παρέργως κατασκευῆς· [122]διὸ καὶ πρὸς τὰς πρεσβείας εὔθετοι καθεστήκεισαν, καὶ τοῦτ' ἐπετέλουν ὅτε δέοι, καὶ

---

122 καθεστηκεισαν MSS, W conjectures
καθειστηκεισαν

---

119. MINES OF COPPER AND IRON: Clearly an echo of Deut. 8.9: "A land whose stones are iron, and out of whose hills thou mayest dig brass"—just as the idealized picture of Palestine generally (even the division into tribes) is seen through the film of Scripture. Josephus (*Jewish War* 4.454) speaks of a "so-called Iron Mountain" in a range "stretching into Moab," but this has not been identified. Adad-Nirari IV of Assyria mentions a tax of iron from Aram-Damascus. Ancient quarries have been found in Carmel and Wadi Eglon in Transjordan. On the copper and iron ore of Edom see N. Glueck, *Bull. Am. School of Oriental Research* 63 (1936), 4 ff.

120-127. ELEAZAR'S FAREWELL TO THE TRANSLATORS

120. TO PREVENT THE COUNTRY FROM BEING SPOILED: The historical conjuncture apparently alluded to has not been and probably cannot be identified. What we have may be a reflection of some Utopia, where temptations to foreign invasion were deliberately suppressed.

DEAR BROTHER: It is usual in treatises of this sort for the name of the danressee to be repeated at the ends of long sections: *cf.* 171, 295. *Brother* deed not imply a blood relationship.   IN WHAT FOLLOWS . . . TRANSLATION: Very little of what follows is in fact concerned with the translation,

ravines; the whole mountain range which surrounds the entire country is rugged.

¹¹⁹It was also said that there were originally mines of coppe and iron in the adjacent mountains of Arabia. But these mine fell into disuse at the time of the Persian rule, those in charge at the time spreading the false report that their exploitation was unprofitable and extravagant, ¹²⁰in order to prevent the country from being spoiled for the sake of mining the said metals and possibly being expropriated by the power of the Persians; by raising the false report they removed the occasion for their entering those regions.

I have now given you such a summary description of these matters as was essential, my dear brother Philocrates, and in what follows I shall give you an account of the translation. ¹²¹Eleazar, then, selected men most excellent and of outstanding scholarship, to be expected in persons of such distinguished parentage. They had not only acquired proficiency in the literature of the Jews, but had bestowed no slight study on that of the Greeks also. ¹²²They were therefore well qualified to be sent on embassies, and performed this office when-

---

and we seem to have the indications of a framework which was filled out with such disparate insertions as Eleazar's discourse and the table talk of the translators.

121. STUDY ... OF THE GREEKS: A natural point for a Hellenized apologist to make. Greek was in fact much more familiar to Palestinians than was formerly thought to be the case: see S. Lieberman, *Greek in Jewish Palestine* (New York, 1942).

122. EMBASSIES: This is documented by the frequent embassies, not only to Syrian kings and pretenders, but to Rome and Sparta, mentioned in I and II Maccabees: see especially I Mac. 8, 12.1–28, 14.16–24, 15.15–24, and the corresponding passages in Josephus, *Ant.* 12 and 13.   TALENT FOR CONFERENCES AND DISCUSSIONS PERTAINING TO THE LAW ... ESCHEWING A CRUDE AND UNCOUTH DISPOSITION: This passage is of central importance in illustrating Aristeas' latitudinarian view of the proper relationship of Jews to their environment, as contrasted with such views as those of III Mac. see Introd. 37. Aristeas wishes to show that expertness in and devotion to the Law is not incompatible with harmonious relations with the outside world. The translators listened attentively, replied appropriately, did not assume superiority, and in these traits reflected the conduct of the High Priest himself.   CULTIVATED THE QUALITY OF THE MEAN: A clear Aristotelian echo: *cf.* 111, 223, 256. There are interesting parallels in Philo: "He

πρὸς τὰς ὁμιλίας καὶ τὰς ἐπερωτήσεις τὰς διὰ τοῦ νόμου μεγάλην εὐφυίαν εἶχον, τὸ μέσον ἐζηλωκότες κατάστημα (τοῦτο γὰρ κάλλιστόν ἐστιν), ἀποτεθειμένοι τὸ τραχὺ καὶ βάρβαρον τῆς διανοίας, ὁμοίως δὲ καὶ τὸ κατοίεσθαι καὶ νομίζειν ὑπερφρονεῖν ἑτέρους ὑπερβεβηκότες, τὴν δ' ὁμιλίαν καὶ τὸ συνακούειν καὶ πρὸς ἕκαστον ἀποκρίνεσθαι δεόντως παραδεδεγμένοι, καὶ πάντες ταῦτα συντηροῦντές καὶ μᾶλλον ἐν τούτοις βουλόμενοι ὑπερφέρειν ἕτερος ἑτέρου, καὶ τοῦ καθηγουμένου πάντες ἄξιοι καὶ τῆς περὶ αὐτὸν ἀρετῆς. 123νοῆσαι δ' ἦν, ὡς ἠγάπησαν τὸν Ἐλεάζαρον δυσαποσπάστως ἔχοντες, καὶ ἐκεῖνος αὐτούς· χωρὶς καὶ τοῦ πρὸς τὸν βασιλέα γεγραφέναι περὶ τῆς ἀποκαταστάσεως αὐτῶν πολλὰ παρεκάλεσε τὸν Ἀνδρέαν ποιῆσαι, συναντιλαμβάνεσθαι παρακαλῶν, καθ' ὃ ἂν δυνώμεθα. 124καὶ ἡμῶν ἐπαγγελλομένων <εὖ φροντίσειν> περὶ τούτων, ἔφη καὶ λίαν διαγωνιᾶν· εἰδέναι γάρ, ὅτι φιλάγαθος ὢν ὁ βασιλεὺς πάντων μέγιστον ἡγεῖται τὸ μεταπέμπεσθαι, καθ' ὃν ἂν τόπον ὀνομασθῇ τις ἄνθρωπος διαφέρων ἀγωγῇ καὶ φρονήσει παρ' ἑτέρους. 125μετείληφα γὰρ καλῶς αὐτὸν λέγειν, ὅτι περὶ ἑαυτὸν ἔχων ἄνδρας δικαίους καὶ σώφρονας τὴν μεγίστην ἂν φυλακὴν τῆς βασιλείας ἕξειν, συμβουλευόντων παρρησίᾳ πρὸς τὸ συμφέρον τῶν φίλων· ὃ δὴ σύνεστι τοῖς ἀποστελλομένοις ὑπ' αὐτοῦ. 126καὶ δι' ὅρκων ἐπιστοῦτο, μὴ προΐεσθαι τοὺς ἀνθρώπους, εἴ τις ἑτέρα χρεία πρὸς τὰ κατ' ἰδίαν αὐτῷ κατεπείγοι, πρὸς δὲ τὴν κοινὴν πᾶσι τοῖς πολίταις ἐπανόρθωσιν ἐξαποστέλλειν αὐτούς. τὸ γὰρ καλῶς ζῆν ἐν τῷ τὰ νόμιμα συντηρεῖν εἶναι· 127τοῦτο δὲ ἐπιτελεῖσθαι διὰ τῆς ἀκροάσεως πολλῷ μᾶλλον ἢ διὰ τῆς ἀναγνώσεως. προτιθέμενος οὖν ταῦτα καὶ τὰ τούτοις παραπλήσια φανερὸς ἦν τὴν διάθεσιν, ὃς ἦν πρὸς αὐτούς.

---

123 και εκεινος αυτους· χωρις MSS, και εκεινος αυτος χωρις W / ποιησαι T-MSS, και ημας Mend. W
124 <ευ φροντισειν> edd., αφροντισειν MSS
128 <δια> edd. / νομιζω edd., νομιζειν MSS / τους πολλους T, τοις πολλοις MSS

---

approved neither of rigorous austerity, like the Spartan legislator, nor of dainty living, like him who introduced the Ionians and Sybarites to luxuri-

ever there was need. They possessed great natural talent for conferences and discussions pertaining to the Law. They zealously cultivated the quality of the mean (and that is the best course), and eschewing a crude and uncouth disposition, they likewise avoided conceit and the assumption of superiority over others. In conversation it was their principle to listen attentively and to reply appropriately to every question. All of them observed this behavior, and it was in such conduct that they most desired to surpass one another; all were worthy of their leader and of his virtue. [123]One could see how they loved Eleazar and he them from the distress of their parting. Besides writing the king on the subject of their safe return, Eleazar besought Andreas and me too to exert our efforts in the matter as far as we were able. [124]And though we promised to take careful heed of the matter he said he was still deeply distressed, for he knew how the king in his love of excellence regarded it a very great gain, wherever he heard of a man surpassing others in culture and intellect, to summon him to himself. [125]Indeed I have heard of a fine saying of his, that by having about himself just and prudent men he would have the greatest protection for his kingdom, for friends frankly advise what is best. This was surely true of the men Eleazar sent. [126]And he pledged his word on oath that he would not let the men go if it were any other need of a private nature that impelled him; it was only for the common benefit of all his countrymen that he was sending them on this mission. [127]A good life, he said, consists in the observance of the laws, and this is attained by hearkening much better than by reading. From these and similar remarks that he added it is evident what his disposition towards these men was.

---

ous and voluptuous practices. Instead he opened up a path midway between the two." (*On Special Laws* 4.17.102, *cf.* 4.27.144; see H. A. Wolfson, *Philo* (Harvard, 1947), 2.273.)

123–127. Eleazar's concern for the safe return of the translators is phrased to throw the most favorable light possible on the motives and character of both the High Priest and the king.

127. HEARKENING: The Greek word suggests "heeding" as well as "listening."

128"Ἄξιον δὲ ἐπιμνησθῆναι <διὰ> βραχέων τῶν ὑποδειχθέντων ὑπ' αὐτοῦ πρὸς τὰ δι' ἡμῶν ἐπιζητηθέντα. νομίζω γὰρ τοὺς πολλοὺς περιεργίαν ἔχειν τινὰ τῶν ἐν τῇ νομοθεσίᾳ περί τε τῶν βρωτῶν καὶ ποτῶν καὶ τῶν νομιζομένων ἀκαθάρτων εἶναι κνωδάλων. 129πυνθανομένων γὰρ ἡμῶν, διὰ τί, μιᾶς καταβολῆς οὔσης, τὰ μὲν ἀκάθαρτα νομίζεται πρὸς βρῶσιν, τὰ δὲ καὶ πρὸς τὴν ἀφήν (δεισιδαιμόνως γὰρ τὰ πλεῖστα τὴν νομοθεσίαν ἔχειν, ἐν δὲ τούτοις †πάνυ† δεισιδαιμόνως) πρὸς ταῦτα οὕτως ἐνήρξατο 130Θεωρεῖς, ἔφη, τὰς ἀναστροφὰς καὶ τὰς ὁμιλίας, οἷον ἐνεργάζονται πρᾶγμα, διότι κακοῖς ὁμιλήσαντες διαστροφὰς ἐπιλαμβάνουσιν ἄνθρωποι, καὶ ταλαίπωροι δι' ὅλου τοῦ ζῆν εἰσιν· ἐὰν δὲ σοφοῖς καὶ φρονίμοις συζῶσιν, ἐξ ἀγνοίας ἐπανορθώσεως εἰς τὸν βίον ἔτυχον. 131διαστειλάμενος οὖν τὰ τῆς εὐσεβείας καὶ δικαιοσύνης πρῶτον ὁ νομοθέτης ἡμῶν, καὶ διδάξας ἕκαστα περὶ τούτων, οὐκ ἀπαγορευτικῶς μόνον ἀλλ' ἐνδεικτικῶς, καὶ τὰς βλάβας προδήλους καὶ τὰς ὑπὸ τοῦ θεοῦ γινομένας ἐπιπομπὰς τοῖς αἰτίοις—προϋπέδειξε γὰρ πάντων πρῶτον, ὅτι μόνος ὁ θεός ἐστι, 132καὶ διὰ πάντων ἡ δύναμις αὐτοῦ φανερὰ γίνεται, πεπληρωμένου παντὸς τόπου τῆς

---

129 πανυ MSS, W conjectures παντελως, Schmidt παντaπασι, Euseb. and some MSS have παλιν πανυ which Tramontano favors

131 ενδεικτικως Euseb.-edd., ενδικως MSS / προδηλους MSS-Euseb., προδηλωσας Schmidt followed by W, who also conjectures προδηλους θεις

128–171. ELEAZAR'S APOLOGY FOR THE LAW.
128. EXPLANATIONS HE GAVE IN REPLY TO OUR INQUIRIES: It is to be noticed that no previous meeting of the High Priest with the ambassadors is mentioned; the section is omitted in Josephus. The allegorical interpretation credited to Eleazar in 128–171 can be parallelled only in Philo, and constitutes one of the principal arguments for a late dating of this passage if not of the whole of Aristeas: see Introd. 15. FOOD AND DRINK AND ANIMALS REGARDED AS UNCLEAN: The order is that of LEV. 11, where food is dealt with at 1–23, and unclean animals 24-end. Drink comes in only at 34, with reference to that contained in unclean vessels.
129. THINGS REGARDED AS UNCLEAN: Naturally the sore point in relationships between Jews and gentiles, and hence one demanding explanation; the allegorical explanations supplied would be the one most appealing to the heathen, and least insistent on Jewish superiority. SCRUPULOUS: The Greek word *deisidaimonia* is sometimes used in a pejorative sense ("superstitious"); DOUBLY rests upon an emendation.

¹²⁸It is worth while to mention briefly the explanations he gave in reply to our inquiries, for I believe that most men feel some curiosity concerning passages in the law dealing with food and drink and animals regarded as unclean. ¹²⁹When we inquired, then, why it was that, creation being one, some things are regarded as unclean for food and some even to the touch (for the Law is scrupulous in most things, but in these doubly scrupulous), he began his reply as follows: ¹³⁰"You observe what far-reaching effects are exercised by conversation and association; by associating with the evil, men become perverted and are miserable through all of life; but if they consort with the wise and prudent, then from a state of ignorance they acquire amendment for their lives. ¹³¹Our lawgiver, then, in the first place laid down the principles of piety and justice and expounded them point by point, not alone by prohibitions but by commandments, and he made clear the discomfitures and visitations that would be inflicted by God upon the guilty. ¹³²But first of all he taught that God is one, and that His power is made manifest in all

130. YOU OBSERVE: Eleazar's proem has a dignified *ex cathedra* tone appropriate to his position.   BY ASSOCIATING: *Cf.* Philo, *On Joseph* 83, "For, even as those who consort with the good are improved in character by the pleasure they take in their associates, so those who live with the bad take on some impression of their vice"; Prov. 13.20, "He that walketh with the wise man shall be wise; but the companion of fools shall smart for it." *Cf.* also Menander, Frag. 218 K, "Evil companionships corrupt good morals," which is echoed in I Cor. 15.33.   WISE AND PRUDENT: Speculative and practical wisdom, an Aristotelian distinction.
131. OUR LAWGIVER etc.: Moses is credited with three things—he established principles, expounded them in theory, and taught retribution.   PIETY AND JUSTICE: Philo, *On the Planting* 28.122, says that humanity (an aspect of justice) and piety are the leaders of the virtues, and in *On the Decalogue* 12.52 he says "piety is the beginning of the virtues"; see Wolfson, 2.215, 220; *cf.* also 189 below. See also Introd., Note 22.
132. BUT FIRST OF ALL HE TAUGHT: Moses is credited with teaching three things—the unity, the omnipotence, and the omniscience of God.   POWER: Used in the sense of immanent power; *cf.* Philo, *On the Posterity of Cain* 5.14: "Though transcending and being beyond what He has made, none the less has He filled the universe with Himself; for He has caused His powers to extend themselves throughout the universe to its utmost bounds and in accordance with the laws of harmony has knit each part of each" (*cf.* Wolfson, 1.344).

δυναστείας, καὶ οὐθὲν αὐτὸν λανθάνει τῶν ἐπὶ γῆς γινομένων ὑπ' ἀνθρώπων κρυφίως, ἀλλ' ὅσα ποιεῖ τις αὐτῷ φανερὰ καθέστηκε, καὶ τὰ μέλλοντα γίνεσθαι— [133]ταῦτ' οὖν ἐξεργαζόμενος ἀκριβῶς καὶ πρόδηλα θεὶς ἔδειξεν ὅτι, κἂν ἐννοηθῇ τις κακίαν ἐπιτελεῖν, οὐκ ἂν λάθοι, μὴ ὅτι καὶ πράξας, διὰ πάσης τῆς νομοθεσίας τὸ τοῦ θεοῦ δυνατὸν ἐνδεικνύμενος. [134]ποιησάμενος οὖν τὴν καταρχὴν ταύτην, καὶ δείξας ὅτι πάντες οἱ λοιποὶ παρ' ἡμᾶς ἄνθρωποι πολλοὺς θεοὺς εἶναι νομίζουσιν, αὐτοὶ δυναμικώτεροι πολλῷ καθεστῶτες ὧν σέβονται ματαίως— [135]ἀγάλματα γὰρ ποιήσαντες ἐκ λίθων καὶ ξύλων, εἰκόνας φασὶν εἶναι τῶν ἐξευρόντων τι πρὸς τὸ ζῆν αὐτοῖς χρήσιμον, οἷς προσκυνοῦσι, παρὰ πόδας ἔχοντες τὴν ἀναισθησίαν. [136]εἴ τι γὰρ κατ' ἐκεῖνό τις <θεὸς εἴη>, κατὰ τὴν ἐξεύρεσιν, παντελῶς ἀνόητον· τῶν γὰρ ἐν τῇ κτίσει λαβόντες τινὰ συνέθηκαν καὶ προσυπέδειξαν εὔχρηστα, τὴν κατασκευὴν αὐτῶν οὐ ποιήσαντες αὐτοί· διὸ κενὸν καὶ μάταιον τοὺς ὁμοίους ἀποθεοῦν. [137]καὶ γὰρ ἔτι καὶ νῦν εὑρεματικώτεροι καὶ πολυμαθέστεροι τῶν ἀνθρώπων τῶν πρίν εἰσι πολλοί, καὶ οὐκ ἂν φθάνοιεν αὐτοὺς προσκυνοῦντες. καὶ νομίζουσιν οἱ ταῦτα διαπλάσαντες καὶ μυθοποιήσαντες τῶν Ἑλλήνων οἱ σοφώτατοι καθεστάναι. [138]τῶν γὰρ ἄλλων πολυματαίων τί δεῖ καὶ λέγειν, Αἰγυπτίων τε καὶ τῶν παραπλησίων, οἵτινες ἐπὶ θηρία καὶ τῶν ἑρπετῶν τὰ πλεῖστα καὶ κνωδάλων τὴν

---

136 ει τι T-MSS, ειτε W-MSS / θεος
ειη T, θειη MSS, W conjectures
θεωθειη, Tramontano suggests
θεοι / ανοητον T-Euseb., ανοητοι

W-MSS
138 πολυματαιων MSS-T πολυ ματαιων W

133. HE COULD NOT ESCAPE NOTICE: *Cf.* Ben Sirah 16.17, 17.19 f., 23.18 f., 42.20, *Wisdom of Solomon* 1.6 ff.
134–138, on the folly of paganism, is really parenthetical to the main course of the thought. The outspoken criticism is of the nature of a *chreia*: see Introd. 51.
135. PERSONS WHO MADE DISCOVERIES USEFUL IN LIFE . . . THEY WORSHIP: This is the view of Euhemerism, which held that the gods were originally men who had contributed greatly to the welfare of mankind; Euhemerus was a courtier of Cassander in Macedonia, *ca.* 316, and the author of the utopian *Hiera Anagraphē*. Cicero, *De Natura Deorum* 15.38, reports that Persaeus, a disciple of Zeno, said that "they who have made discoveries

things, and that every place is filled with His sovereignty, and that nothing done by men on earth secretly escapes His notice, but that all that anyone does and all that is to be is manifest to Him. ¹³³When he had elaborated these points and made them plain he showed that even if a man but think of compassing some evil, and not alone if he actually do it, he could not escape notice; thus throughout the Law he displayed the power of God.

¹³⁴"After he set down these premises he showed that all other men except ourselves believe that there are many gods, though they are themselves much more powerful than the gods they vainly revere. ¹³⁵They make idols of stone and wood and declare that these are images of persons who made discoveries useful in life, and these they worship, though their senselessness is obvious. ¹³⁶That anyone should be made a god because of some invention he has contrived is altogether foolish; for such persons only took things already created and put them together and showed that they possessed further usefulness, but they did not themselves create the objects. Hence to deify men like themselves is idle and foolish. ¹³⁷Even at this day there are many who are more inventive and more learned than the men of old, and yet they would never hasten to worship them. And yet those who devise and fashion such fables consider that they are the wisest of the Greeks. ¹³⁸What need even to speak of other infatuated people, Egyptians and their like, who have put their reliance in wild beasts and most creeping creatures and animals, and

---

of great service to the life of man should be esteemed as gods."
136. ONLY TOOK THINGS ALREADY CREATED AND PUT THEM TOGETHER: They made useful combinations of things already constructed, whereas God constructed them; but this does not necessarily imply that God's creation was *ex nihilo*: see Wolfson, 1.303.
137. WISEST OF THE GREEKS: This scornful expression, deriving from Euhemerus, was therefore not shocking on the lips of a High Priest.
138. OTHER INFATUATED PEOPLES, EGYPTIANS AND THEIR LIKE: Such denigration of Egyptian worship is startling on the part of a man who professes to be an Egyptian courtier; but the words are attributed to the High Priest, who might be allowed the license of the *chreia*: see Introd. 51.

ἀπέρεισιν πεποίηνται, καὶ ταῦτα προσκυνοῦσι, καὶ θύουσι τούτοις καὶ ζῶσι καὶ τελευτήσασι;— ¹³⁹συνθεωρήσας οὖν ἕκαστα σοφὸς ὢν ὁ νομοθέτης, ὑπὸ θεοῦ κατεσκευασμένος εἰς ἐπίγνωσιν τῶν ἁπάντων, περιέφραξεν ἡμᾶς ἀδιακόποις χάραξι καὶ σιδηροῖς τείχεσιν, ὅπως μηθενὶ τῶν ἄλλων ἐθνῶν ἐπιμισγώμεθα κατὰ μηδέν, ἁγνοὶ καθεστῶτες κατὰ σῶμα καὶ κατὰ ψυχήν, ἀπολελυμένοι ματαίων δοξῶν, τὸν μόνον θεὸν καὶ δυνατὸν σεβόμενοι παρ' ὅλην τὴν πᾶσαν 140 κτίσιν. ¹⁴⁰ὅθεν οἱ Αἰγυπτίων καθηγεμόνες ἱερεῖς, ἐγκεκυφότες εἰς πολλὰ καὶ μετεσχηκότες πραγμάτων, ἀνθρώπους θεοῦ προσονομάζουσιν ἡμᾶς· ὃ τοῖς λοιποῖς οὐ πρόσεστιν, εἰ μή τις σέβεται τὸν κατὰ ἀλήθειαν θεόν, ἀλλ' εἰσὶν ἄνθρωποι βρωτῶν καὶ ποτῶν καὶ σκέπης· ¹⁴¹ἡ γὰρ πᾶσα διάθεσις αὐτῶν ἐπὶ ταῦτα καταφεύγει. τοῖς δὲ παρ' ἡμῶν ἐν οὐδενὶ ταῦτα λελόγισται, περὶ δὲ τῆς τοῦ θεοῦ δυναστείας δι' ὅλου τοῦ ζῆν ἡ σκέψις αὐτοῖς ἐστιν. ¹⁴²ὅπως οὖν μηθενὶ συναλισγούμενοι μηδ' ὁμιλοῦντες φαύλοις διαστροφὰς λαμβάνωμεν, πάντοθεν ἡμᾶς περιέφραξεν ἁγνείαις καὶ διὰ βρωτῶν καὶ ποτῶν καὶ ἀφῶν καὶ ἀκοῆς καὶ ὁράσεως νομικῶς. ¹⁴³τὸ γὰρ καθόλου πάντα πρὸς τὸν φυσικὸν λόγον ὅμοια καθέστηκεν, ὑπὸ μιᾶς δυνάμεως οἰκονομούμενα, καὶ καθ' ἓν ἕκαστον ἔχει λόγον βαθύν, ἀφ' ὧν ἀπεχόμεθα κατὰ τὴν χρῆσιν, καὶ οἷς συγχρώμεθα. χάριν δὲ ὑποδείγματος

---

139 πασαν W brackets
140 πραγματων MSS-T, W approves Diels' γραμματων

142 ουν edd.-Euseb., εν MSS / συναλισγουμενοι MSS, συναλισγομενοι Euseb., συμμισγομενοι W following Wilcken

---

139. FENCED US ABOUT: *Cf.* Abot 1.1 "Make a hedge about the Torah"; Job 1.10, "Hast thou not made a hedge about him?" *Cf.* also LXX Isa. 5.2, Prov. 28.4, and 142 below. REVERING ... GOD: Contrast 16, where Zeus is accepted as an equivalent.
140. MEN OF GOD: Moses is so designated in LXX (Deut. 33.1 and elsewhere), as is Elijah (I Kings 17.18). After the plague of the first-born even the Egyptians confessed that the Israelites were children of God (Wisd. 18.13). THE REST: Humanity is here divided into two categories, men of food, and men who revere the true God; the universalist implications of the second category, especially as coming from the High Priest, are in marked contrast to the nationalist emphasis of III Maccabees.

worship these, and to these offer sacrifice, whether alive or dead?

139"When therefore our lawgiver, equipped by God for insight into all things, had surveyed each particular, he fenced us about with impregnable palisades and with walls of iron, to the end that we should mingle in no way with any of the other nations, remaining pure in body and in spirit, emancipated from vain opinions, revering the one and mighty God above the whole of creation. 140Whence the priests who are the guides of the Egyptians, have looked closely into many things and are conversant with affairs, have named us 'men of God,' a title applicable to none others but only to him who reveres the true God. The rest are men of food and drink and raiment, 141for their whole disposition has recourse to these things. With our countrymen, however, these things are reckoned as of nothing worth, but throughout the whole of life their contemplation is of the sovereignty of God. 142And therefore, so that we should be polluted by none nor be infected with perversions by associating with worthless persons, he has hedged us about on all sides with prescribed purifications in matters of food and drink and touch and hearing and sight. 143In general all things are to the natural reason similarly constituted, being all administered by a single power, and yet in each and every case there is a profound logic for our abstinence from the use of some things and our participation in the use of others. For the sake of illustration I will run over one or two details and provide an explanation.

---

141. THEIR CONTEMPLATION IS OF THE SOVEREIGNTY OF GOD: The essential, in this presentation of Judaism, is a "philosophical" belief, and
142. PRESCRIBED PURIFICATIONS IN MATTERS OF FOOD AND DRINK are presented as ancillary, to protect and foster the philosophical belief; cf. Philo, *Quod det. pot.* 4-7. This seems to be a specific reply to charges of separatism such as are adduced at Esther 3.8 and III Maccabees 3.4.
143. The High Priest now proceeds to show that the prohibitions are not ends in themselves but calculated to promote a spiritual view. ADMINISTERED BY A SINGLE POWER: See Introd., note 20.

ἐν ἦ δεύτερον ἐπιδραμών σοι σημανῶ. ¹⁴⁴Μὴ γὰρ εἰς τὸν καταπεπτωκότα λόγον ἔλθης, ὅτι ΜΥΩΝ καὶ ΓΑΛΗC ἢ τῶν τοιούτων χάριν περιεργίαν, ποιούμενος ἐνομοθέτει ταῦτα Μωϋσῆς· ἀλλὰ πρὸς ἁγνὴν ἐπίσκεψιν καὶ τρόπων ἐξαρτισμὸν δικαιοσύνης ἕνεκεν σεμνῶς πάντα ἀνατέτακται. ¹⁴⁵τῶν γὰρ πτηνῶν, οἷς χρώμεθα, πάντα ἥμερα καθέστηκε καὶ διαφέρει καθαριότητι, πυροῖς καὶ ὀσπρίοις χρώμενα πρὸς τὴν τροφήν, οἷον περιστεραὶ τρυγόνες ΑΤΤΑΚΟΙ πέρδικες ἔτι δὲ χῆνες καὶ τὰ ἄλλα ὅσα τοιαῦτα. ¹⁴⁶περὶ ὧν δὲ ἀπηγόρευται πτηνῶν, εὑρήσεις ἄγριά τε καὶ σαρκοφάγα καὶ καταδυναστεύοντα τῇ περὶ ἑαυτὰ δυνάμει τὰ λοιπά, καί τὴν τροφὴν ἔχοντα δαπάνησιν τῶν προειρημένων ἡμέρων μετὰ ἀδικίας· οὐ μόνον δὲ ταῦτα, ἀλλὰ καὶ τοὺς ἄρνας καὶ ἐρίφους ἀναρπάζουσι, καὶ τοὺς ἀνθρώπους δὲ ἀδικοῦσι νεκρούς τε καὶ ζῶντας. ¹⁴⁷παράσημον οὖν ἔθετο διὰ τούτων, ΑΚΑΘΑΡΤΑ προσονομάσας, ὅτι δέον ἐστὶ κατὰ ψυχήν, οἷς ἡ νομοθεσία διατέτακται, δικαιοσύνῃ συγχρῆσθαι καὶ μηδένα καταδυναστεύειν, πεποιθότας ἰσχύι τῇ καθ' ἑαυτούς, μηδὲ ἀφαιρεῖσθαι μηδέν, ἀλλ' ἐκ δικαίου τὰ τοῦ βίου κυβερνᾶν, ὡς τὰ τῶν προειρημένων πτηνῶν ἥμερα ζῷα τὰ φυόμενα τῶν ὀσπρίων ἐπὶ γῆς δαπανᾷ, καὶ οὐ καταδυναστεύει πρὸς τὴν ἐπαναίρεσιν τῶν συγγενικῶν. ¹⁴⁸διὰ τῶν τοιούτων οὖν παραδέδωκεν ὁ νομοθέτης σημειοῦσθαι τοῖς συνετοῖς, εἶναι δικαίους τε καὶ μηδὲν ἐπιτελεῖν βίᾳ, μηδὲ τῇ περὶ ἑαυτοὺς ἰσχύι πεποιθότας ἑτέρους καταδυναστεύειν. ¹⁴⁹ὅπου γὰρ οὐδ' ἅψασθαι καθῆκε τῶν προειρημένων διὰ τὴν περὶ ἕκαστα διάθεσιν, πῶς οὐ φυλακτέον παντάπασι τοὺς τρόπους

---

144 παντα MSS-T, ταυτα MSS-W / ανατεκταται MSS, W conjectures κατατεκταται
145 και (after καθεστηκε) edd. from Euseb. / αττακοι MSS, ατταγαι Euseb.

147 πεποιθοτας edd.-Eus., πεποιθοτες MSS / επαναιρεσιν των συγγενικων MSS, επαναιρεσιν ουτε των υποβεβηκοτων ουτε των συγγενικων W-Euseb.

---

144. EXPLODED: Others render "degrading" (Andrews) or "vulgar" (Tramontano). Some regard this an echo of Greek ridicule of the Mosaic law, such as is answered in *Against Apion*, and hence deduce a later dating. MICE ... WEASEL: *Cf.* Lev. 11.29. MOSES: Named only here; elsewhere

¹⁴⁴"Do not accept the exploded idea that it was out of regard for 'mice' and the 'weasel' and other such creatures that Moses ordained these laws with such scrupulous care; not so, these laws have all been solemnly drawn up for the sake of justice, to promote holy contemplation and the perfecting of character. ¹⁴⁵For of the winged creatures of which we make use all are gentle and distinguished by cleanliness and they feed on grain and pulse, such as pigeons, doves, 'locusts,' partridges, and also geese and all similar fowl. ¹⁴⁶But of the winged creatures which are forbidden you will find that they are wild and carnivorous and with their strength oppress the rest and procure their food with injustice at the expense of the tame fowl mentioned above. And not only these, but they also seize lambs and kids, and they do violence to men too, both the dead and the living. ¹⁴⁷Through these creatures then, by calling them 'unclean,' he set up a symbol that those for whom the legislation was drawn up must practise righteousness in spirit and oppress no one, trusting in their own strength, nor rob anyone of anything, but must guide their lives in accordance with justice, just as the gentle creatures among the birds above mentioned consume pulses that grow upon the earth and do not tyrannize to the destruction of their kindred.

¹⁴⁸"By such examples, then, the lawgiver has commended to men of understanding a symbol that they must be just and achieve nothing by violence, nor, confiding in their own strength, must they oppress others. ¹⁴⁹For if it is lawful not even to touch the creatures aforementioned because of their several natures, how must we not in every way guard our

---

(131, 139, 148, 312) referred to as "the lawgiver."
145. LOCUSTS: *attakoi, cf.* Lev. 11.22. But they seem odd in a list of domesticated fowl, and Cahana *ad loc.* desiderates "hens." Eusebius read *attagai*, a species of moor-fowl, which suggests that he had our reading, and felt its incongruity.
148. BE JUST AND ACHIEVE NOTHING BY VIOLENCE: Apparently an answer to pagan charges of Jewish misanthropy and disregard of non-Jews, such as are cited in Diodorus Siculus 40.3 f., 34.1, Tacitus, *Histories* 5.5.

150 εἰς τοῦτο κατακλασθῆναι; ¹⁵⁰πάντα οὖν τὰ τῆς συγχωρήσεως ἡμῖν ἐπὶ τούτων καὶ τῶν κτηνῶν τροπολογῶν ἐκτέθειται. τὸ γὰρ ΔΙΧΗΛΕΥΕΙΝ καὶ διαστέλλειν ΟΠΛΗϹ ΟΝΥΧΑϹ σημεῖόν ἐστι τοῦ διαστέλλειν ἕκαστα τῶν πράξεων ἐπὶ τὸ καλῶς ἔχον· ¹⁵¹ἡ γὰρ ἰσχὺς τῶν ὅλων σωμάτων μετ' ἐνεργείας ἀπέρεισιν ἐπὶ τοὺς ὤμους ἔχει καὶ τὰ σκέλη. μετὰ διαστολῆς οὖν ἅπαντα ἐπιτελεῖν πρὸς δικαιοσύνην ἀναγκάζει †τὸ σημειοῦσθαι† διὰ τούτων· ἔτι δὲ καὶ διότι παρὰ πάντας ἀνθρώπους διεστάλμεθα. ¹⁵²οἱ γὰρ πλείονες τῶν λοιπῶν ἀνθρώπων ἑαυτοὺς μολύνουσιν ἐπιμισγόμενοι, συντελοῦντες μεγάλην ἀδικίαν, καὶ χῶραι καὶ πόλεις ὅλαι σεμνύνονται ἐπὶ τούτοις. οὐ μόνον γὰρ <προάγουσι> τοὺς ἄρσενας, ἀλλὰ καὶ τεκούσας ἔτι δὲ θυγατέρας μολύνουσιν. ἡμεῖς δὲ ἀπὸ τούτων διεστάλμεθα. ¹⁵³περὶ ὃν δὲ ἐστὶν ὁ προειρημένος τῆς διαστολῆς τρόπος, περὶ τοῦτον εἶναι καὶ τὸν τῆς μνήμης κεχαρακτήρικεν. ΠΑΝΤΑ γὰρ ΟϹΑ ΔΙΧΗΛΕΙ καὶ ΜΗΡΥΚΙϹΜΟΝ ΑΝΑΓΕΙ σαφῶς τοῖς νοοῦσιν ἐκτίθεται τὸ τῆς μνήμης. ¹⁵⁴ἡ γὰρ ἀναμηρύκησις οὐθὲν ἕτερον, ἀλλὰ τῆς ζωῆς καὶ συστάσεως ἐπίμνησις. τὸ γὰρ
155 ζῆν διὰ τῆς τροφῆς συνεστάναι νομίζει. ¹⁵⁵διὸ παρακελεύεται καὶ διὰ τῆς γραφῆς ὁ λέγων οὕτως· ΜΝΕΙΑ ΜΝΗϹΘΗϹΗ ΚΥΡΙΟΥ ΤΟΥ ΠΟΙΗϹΑΝΤΟϹ ΕΝ ϹΟΙ ΤΑ ΜΕΓΑΛΑ ΚΑΙ ΘΑΥΜΑϹΤΑ. κατανοούμενα γὰρ καὶ ΜΕΓΑΛΑ ΚΑΙ ΕΝΔΟΞΑ φαίνεται· πρῶτον μὲν ἡ σύμπηξις τοῦ σώματος καὶ ἡ τῆς τροφῆς διοίκησις καὶ ἡ περὶ ἕκαστον μέλος διαστολή· ¹⁵⁶πολλῷ δὲ μᾶλλον ἡ τῶν αἰσθήσεων διακόσμησις, διανοίας ἐνέρ-

---

150 παντα ουν τα της edd.-Euseb., παντων της MSS
151 το σημειουσθαι MSS, τω σ. W, T conjectures ο σημειουται
152 προαγουσι τους αρσενας T, προσαγουσι τ. α. MSS, προς αρσενας

προσαγουσι W-Euseb.
153 κεχαρακτηρικεν edd.-Euseb., κεχαρακτηρικεναι MSS / εκτιθεται edd.-Euseb., εκτιθεμαι MSS
156 περιεχει τροπον MSS, παρεχει τοπον Mend.

---

150. PARTING OF THE HOOF: Lev. 11.2–8, Deut. 14.4–8. *Cf.* Philo, *Spec. Laws* 4.106 ff.
152. MOST OF THE REST: A softening of "all men" above. PROMISCUOUS UNIONS: The implied condemnation of brother-sister marriages is even stranger in a self-styled courtier of Philadelphus and Arsinoe than the condemnation of theriolatry. At 45 the same High Priest says he offered sacrifice for Ptolemy and his sister-wife.

150 characters from degenerating to a similar state? 150All the regulations concerning what is permissible with reference to these and other creatures, then, he has set forth by way of allegory. For the 'parting of the hoof' and the 'cloven foot' is a symbol to discriminate in each of our actions with a view to what is right; 151for the strength of the whole body and its energy depend upon the shoulders and legs. He constrains us, by taking note through these symbols, to do all things with discrimination and with a view to righteousness. An additional signification is that we are set apart from all men. 152For most of the rest of mankind defile themselves by their promiscuous unions, working great unrighteousness, and whole countries and cities pride themselves on these vices. Not only do they have intercourse with males, but they even defile mothers and daughters. But we have been kept apart from such things.

153"Further, men who possess the aforementioned trait of separation the lawgiver has characterized as possessing the trait of memory also. For 'whatsoever parteth the hoof and cheweth the cud' to thinking men clearly signifies memory. 154For the chewing of the cud is nothing else than recalling life and its subsistence, since life appears to subsist through taking food. 155And therefore does he admonish us through Scripture, when he says, 'Thou shalt well remember what great and marvelous things the Lord thy God did in thee'; when clearly understood they do indeed appear 'great and glorious.' In the first place there is the articulation of the body and the means for digesting food, and the distribution of the members; 156but much more does the orderly arrangement of the senses, the working and invisible movement of the intellect, its acuteness in conforming action to any situa-

---

154. FOR THE CHEWING OF THE CUD: Rumination is made to symbolize memory in Philo also (*Spec. Laws*, 4.106 ff.).
155. SCRIPTURE: Perhaps the earliest use of *hē graphē* for the Bible. The quotation is a combination of LXX Deut. 7.18 and 10.21; IN THEE is referred to the human body, "in thy body."
156-157. The human body demonstrates God's handiwork, and must in turn admonish men of God's sovereignty and providence.

γῆμα καὶ κίνησις ἀόρατος, ἥ τε ὀξύτης τοῦ πρὸς ἕκαστόν τι πράσσειν καὶ τεχνῶν εὕρεσις ἀπέραστον περιέχει τρόπον. 157διὸ παρακελεύεται μνείαν ἔχειν, ὡς συντηρεῖται τὰ προειρημένα θείᾳ δυνάμει σὺν κατασκευῇ. πάντα γὰρ χρόνον καὶ τόπον ὥρικε πρὸς τὸ διὰ παντὸς μνημονεύειν τοῦ κρατοῦντος θεοῦ καὶ συντηροῦντος. 158καὶ γὰρ ἐπὶ τῶν βρωτῶν καὶ ποτῶν ἀπαρξαμένους εὐθέως τότε †συγχρῆσθαι† κελεύει. καὶ μὴν καὶ ἐκ τῶν περιβολαίων παράσημον ἡμῖν μνείας δέδωκεν, ὡσαύτως δὲ καὶ ΕΠΙ ΤΩΝ ΠΤΛΩΝ καὶ θυρῶν προστέταχε μὲν ἡμῖν τιθέναι τὰ λόγια, πρὸς τὸ μνείαν εἶναι θεοῦ· 159καὶ ΕΠΙ ΤΩΝ ΧΕΙΡΩΝ δὲ διαρρήδην τὸ σημεῖον κελεύει ΠΕΡΙΗΦΘΑΙ, σαφῶς ἀποδεικνὺς ὅτι πᾶσαν ἐνέργειαν μετὰ δικαιοσύνης ἐπιτελεῖν δεῖ, μνήμην ἔχοντας τῆς ἑαυτῶν κατασκευῆς, ἐπὶ πᾶσι δὲ τὸν περὶ θεοῦ φόβον. 160κελεύει δὲ ΚΑΙ ΚΟΙΤΑΖΟΜΕΝΟΥΣ ΚΑΙ ΔΙΑΝΙΣΤΑΜΕΝΟΥΣ μελετᾶν τὰς τοῦ θεοῦ κατασκευάς, οὐ μόνον λόγῳ, ἀλλὰ διαλήψει θεωροῦντας τὴν κίνησιν καὶ ὑπόληψιν ἑαυτῶν, ὅταν εἰς ὕπνον ἔρχωνται, καὶ τὴν ἔγερσιν, ὡς θεία τίς ἐστι καὶ ἀκατάληπτος τούτων ἡ μετάθεσις. 161Δέδεικται δέ σοι καὶ τὸ περισσὸν τῆς λογίας τῆς κατὰ τὴν διαστολὴν καὶ μνείαν, ὡς ἐξεθέμεθα τὴν διχηλίαν καὶ τὸν μηρυκισμόν. οὐ γὰρ εἰκῆ καὶ κατὰ τὸ ἐμπεσὸν εἰς ψυχὴν νενομοθέτηται, πρὸς δ' ἀλήθειαν καὶ σημείωσιν ὀρθοῦ λόγου. 162διατάξας γὰρ ἐπὶ βρωτῶν καὶ ποτῶν καὶ τῶν κατὰ τὰς ἁφὰς ἕκαστα, κελεύει μηθὲν εἰκῆ μήτε πράσσειν μήτε ἀκούειν, μήτε τῇ τοῦ λόγου δυναστείᾳ συγχρωμένους ἐπὶ τὴν ἀδικίαν τρέπεσθαι. 163καὶ ἐπὶ τῶν κνωδάλων δὲ ταὐτόν ἐστιν εὑρεῖν. κακοποιητικὸς γὰρ ὁ τρόπος ἐστὶ καὶ ΓΑΛΗΣ καὶ ΜΥΩΝ καὶ τῶν τούτοις ὁμοίων, ὅσα διηγόρευται. 164πάντα γὰρ λυμαίνονται καὶ κακοποιοῦσι μύες, οὐ μόνον πρὸς τὴν ἑαυτῶν

---

158 συγχρησθαι edd.-Euseb., συγχωρησαι MSS
159 της εαυτων κατασκευης edd.-Euseb., MSS omit, ημων συστασεως Schard
160 After διανισταμενους W inserts και πορευομενους from Euseb. (cf. Deut. 6.7), omitted in MSS
161 λογιας single MSS also read ευλογιας, αλογιας, whence Cohn conjectures απολογιας
164 εις το edd.-Euseb., omitted in MSS

---

158. CLOTHING: Clearly the "fringes": Num. 15.38, Deut. 22.12.   CHAP-

tion and its discovery of arts, indicate infinite scope. [157]Therefore he exhorts us to bear in mind that the capacities mentioned are preserved in their ordering by divine power. For every time and every place he has appointed for calling to mind continually God the ruler and preserver. [158]For instance, in the case of food and drink he bids us partake of them after having first offered a portion as sacrifice. Yes, and he has set us a mark of remembrance in our clothing, and similarly he has ordained for us that we place the chapters 'upon our door-posts and gates' to serve as a remembrance of God. [159]And he has expressly bidden us to 'bind them for a sign upon the hands,' signifying plainly that every action must be carried out with justice and that we must retain remembrance of our composition and above all fear of God. [160]He bids us to meditate upon God's devisings 'when thou liest down and when thou risest up,' not in word only but in reviewing in thought also the movement and impression men receive when they come to a state of sleep, and then their awakening, reflecting what a divine and incomprehensible thing this interchange is.

[161]"You have now received demonstration of the high worth of the doctrine concerning separation and memory, according to our exegesis of the parting of the hoof and the chewing of the cud. The legislation was not laid down at random or by some caprice of the mind, but with a view to truth and as a token of right reason. [162]For by detailed injunctions concerning food and drink and touch he bids us to do nothing and hearken to nothing heedlessly, and not, by misusing the power of reason, to resort to injustice. [163]In the case of animals too the same principle may be discovered. The character of 'the weasel and the mouse' and the rest of those enumerated is injurious. [164]Mice ravage and injure everything, not only for their own feeding but in such a way that whatever they

---

TERS: *ta logia*, cf. on 97; clearly the *mezuzah* is meant: Deut. 6.4–9, 11.13–21.
159. BIND THEM FOR A SIGN: *Tefillin*, Deut. 6.8. As regularly in this passage, the spiritual implication of ritual observances is stressed.
163. ANIMALS: The context shows that "creeping things" is intended.

τροφήν, ἀλλὰ καὶ εἰς τὸ παντελῶς ἄχρηστον γίνεσθαι ἀνθρώπῳ, ὅ τι ἂν δή ποτ' οὖν ἐπιβάληται κακοποιεῖν. [165]τό τε τῆς γαλῆς γένος ἰδιάζον ἐστί· χωρὶς γὰρ τοῦ προειρημένου ἔχει λυμαντικὸν κατάστημα· διὰ γὰρ τῶν ὤτων συλλαμβάνει, τεκνοποιεῖ δὲ τῷ στόματι. [166]καὶ διὰ τοῦτο ὁ τοιοῦτος τρόπος τῶν ἀνθρώπων ἀκάθαρτός ἐστιν· ὅσα γὰρ δι' ἀκοῆς λαβόντες, ταῦτα τῷ λόγῳ σωματοποιήσαντες, κακοῖς ἑτέρους ἐνεκύλισαν, ἀκαθαρσίαν οὐ τὴν τυχοῦσαν ἐπετέλεσαν, μιανθέντες αὐτοὶ παντάπασι τῷ τῆς ἀσεβείας μολυσμῷ. καλῶς δὲ ποιῶν ὁ βασιλεὺς ὑμῶν τοὺς τοιούτους ἀναιρεῖ, καθὼς μεταλαμβάνομεν.— [167]'Εγὼ δ' εἶπα Τοὺς ἐμφανιστὰς οἴομαί σε λέγειν· καὶ γὰρ αἰκίαις καὶ θανάτοις ἐπαλγέσιν αὐτοὺς περιβάλλει συνεχῶς.—Ὁ δὲ Τούτους γὰρ καὶ λέγω· ἡ γὰρ ἐπαγρύπνησις ἀνθρώπων ἀπωλείᾳ ἀνόσιος. [168]ὁ δὲ νόμος ἡμῶν κελεύει μήτε λόγῳ μήτε ἔργῳ μηδένα κακαποιεῖν. καὶ περὶ τούτων οὖν, ὅσον ἐπὶ βραχὺ <διεξῆλθον, προσυποδείξας> σοι διότι πάντα κεκανόνισται πρὸς δικαιοσύνην, καὶ οὐδὲν εἰκῆ κατατέτακται διὰ τῆς γραφῆς οὐδὲ μυθωδῶς, ἀλλ' ἵνα δι' ὅλου τοῦ ζῆν καὶ ἐν ταῖς πράξεσιν ἀσκῶμεν δικαιοσύνην πρὸς πάντας ἀνθρώπους, μεμνημένοι τοῦ δυναστεύοντος θεοῦ. [169]περὶ βρωτῶν οὖν καὶ τῶν ἀκαθάρτων ἑρπετῶν καὶ κνωδάλων καὶ πᾶς λόγος ἀνατείνει πρὸς δικαιοσύνην καὶ τὴν τῶν ἀνθρώπων συν-

---

168 διεξηλθον προσυποδειξας T, διεξελθειν προσυποδειξαντα MSS-W, Euseb. merely simplifying has ουν διεξηλθον βραχυ, δεικνυων σοι οτι κ. τ. λ.,

Schmidt al. keep διεξελθειν and read προσυπεδειξα (or προσυπεδειξαμεν) / μυθωδως edd., θυμωδως MSS

---

165. CONCEIVE THROUGH THE EARS: Such odd theories were widespread; Aristotle, *On the Generation of Animals* 3.6.5, takes the trouble to explain that the weasel does not conceive through the mouth: its organs are of ordinary structure, but the young being very small the mother carries them about in the mouth, and hence the false explanation arose. Barnabas 10.8 still declares that the weasel gives birth through the mouth. The ear as an organ of generation survived at least in the comic writers; Pantagruel was so born, and the innocent Agnes in Moliere's *École des Femmes* thinks children are so born.

166. SIMILAR CHARACTERISTIC: The procreation of the weasel is taken to symbolize informers.

have set about injuring they make wholly useless to man. 165 ¹⁶⁵The breed of weasels is peculiar, for besides the propensity mentioned they have a defiling characteristic: they conceive through the ears and give birth through the mouth. ¹⁶⁶And hence a similar characteristic in man is impure: when they have given body in speech to what they have received through hearing and have entangled others in evils, they have engendered no ordinary uncleanness and are themselves utterly tainted with the pollution of their impiety. Your king is quite right in putting such persons to death, as I am informed he does."

¹⁶⁷And I said, "I suppose you mean the informers; he does indeed consistently visit torments and painful forms of death upon them." "Yes," he replied, "it is these men I mean. To watch for the destruction of men is an unholy thing. ¹⁶⁸Our law forbids us to injure anyone, by word or deed."

The points I have briefly run over have shown you that all these norms have been regulated with a view to justice and that nothing has been set down through Scripture heedlessly or in the spirit of myth, but rather in order that throughout our life and in our actions we may practise justice towards all men, being mindful of the sovereignty of God. ¹⁶⁹All that is said of food, then, and of unclean creeping things and of animals is directed toward justice and just intercourse among men.

---

167. INFORMERS: Graetz saw in this an allusion to the execution of *delatores* by Tiberius in 33 CE (Tacitus, *Annals* 6.19) and dated Aristeas accordingly.

The term *emphanistae* does occur in Ptolemaic papyri, but they are not so severely punished as is here suggested: see Introd. 15. At 25, it is to be noted, informers are regarded as legitimate.

168. TO INJURE ANYONE: Refuting charges of Jewish misanthropy.   JUSTICE TOWARDS ALL MEN: The true aim of legislation which the uninitiate might think SET DOWN HEEDLESSLY OR IN A SPIRIT OF MYTH. Justice is similarly stressed as the principal content of the Law in *Sibylline Oracles* 3.719 "And let us all pay heed to the law of God most high, who is the most just of all on the earth;" so also in Pseudo-Phocylides.

169. ALL THAT IS SAID OF FOOD: So far from being antisocial in intention IS DIRECTED TOWARDS JUSTICE AND JUST INTERCOURSE AMONG MEN.

170 ἀναστροφὴν δικαίαν. ¹⁷⁰'Εμοὶ μὲν οὖν καλῶς ἐνόμιζε περὶ ἑκάστων ἀπολογεῖσθαι· καὶ γὰρ ἐπὶ τῶν προσφερομένων ἔλεγε μόσχων τε καὶ κριῶν καὶ χιμάρων, ὅτι δεῖ ταῦτα ἐκ βουκολίων καὶ ποιμνίων λαμβάνοντας ἥμερα θυσιάζειν, καὶ μηθὲν ἄγριον, ὅπως οἱ προσφέροντες τὰς θυσίας μηθὲν ὑπερήφανον ἑαυτοῖς συνιστορῶσι, σημειώσει κεχρημένοι τοῦ διατάξαντος. τῆς γὰρ ἑαυτοῦ ψυχῆς τοῦ παντὸς τρόπου τὴν προσφορὰν ποιεῖται ὁ τὴν θυσίαν προσάγων. ¹⁷¹καὶ περὶ τούτων οὖν νομίζω τὰ τῆς ὁμιλίας ἄξια λόγου καθεστάναι· διὸ τὴν σεμνότητα καὶ φυσικὴν διάνοιαν τοῦ νόμου προῆγμαι διασαφῆσαί σοι, Φιλόκρατες, δι' ἣν ἔχεις φιλομάθειαν.

¹⁷²Ὁ δὲ Ἐλεάζαρος ποιησάμενος θυσίαν καὶ τοὺς ἄνδρας ἐπιλέξας καὶ πολλὰ δῶρα τῷ βασιλεῖ κατασκευάσας προέπεμψεν ἡμᾶς μετὰ ἀσφαλείας πολλῆς. ¹⁷³ὡς δὲ παρεγενήθημεν εἰς Ἀλεξάνδρειαν, προσηγγέλη τῷ βασιλεῖ περὶ τῆς ἀφίξεως ἡμῶν. <παρειμένοι> δ' εἰς τὴν αὐλὴν Ἀνδρέας τε καὶ ἐγώ, φιλοφρόνως ἠσπασάμεθα τὸν βασιλέα καὶ τὰς ἐπιστολὰς ἀποδεδώκαμεν τὰς παρὰ τοῦ Ἐλεαζάρου. ¹⁷⁴περὶ πολλοῦ δὲ ποιούμενος τοῖς ἀπεσταλμένοις ἀνδράσιν ἐντυχεῖν, ἐκέλευσε τοὺς λοιποὺς πάντας ἀπολῦσαι τοὺς 175 ἐπὶ τῶν χρειῶν, καλεῖν δὲ τοὺς ἀνθρώπους. ¹⁷⁵οὗ πᾶσι παραδόξου φανέντος—διὰ τὸ κατὰ ἔθος εἶναι, πεμπταίους εἰς πρόσωπον ἔρχεσθαι βασιλεῖ τοὺς περὶ χρήσιμον ἀφικνουμένους, τοὺς δὲ παρὰ βασιλέων ἢ πόλεων ἐν ὑπεροχαῖς μόλις ἐν τριάκοντα εἰς τὴν αὐλὴν παρίεσθαι—τοὺς δὲ ἥκοντας τιμῆς καταξιῶν μείζονος, καὶ τὴν ὑπεροχὴν κρίνων τοῦ πέμψαντος, ἀπολύσας οὓς ἐνόμιζε περισσούς, ὑπέμενε

---

170 ενομιζε MSS, WT conjecture ενομιζετο / δει edd.-Euseb., αει MSS / κεχρημενοι T-Euseb., κεχρημενου W-MSS
171 αξια λογου MSS-Euseb., αξιολογου MSS

173 <παρειμενοι> edd., παρειμεν MSS
175 εθος edd., εθνος MSS / περι χρησιμον MSS, Wilcken conjectures προς χρηματισμον, W περι χρειων

---

170. SACRIFICE: As well as dietary regulations, has an ethical *symbolic* meaning.
171. INHERENT CHARACTER: *Physikēn dianoian*, probably in allusion to the allegorical interpretation. Wendland renders "the deeper sense," and

170 [170]To me he seemed to make a defense in every respect excellent. With reference to the calves and rams and he-goats which were brought for sacrifice he added, moreover, that men must take these from the herds and flocks, and must sacrifice tame animals and nothing wild, so that those who offer the sacrifices, bearing in mind the symbolic meaning of the legislator, might be conscious of no arrogance in themselves. For it is of the entire character of his own soul that he who brings a sacrifice makes offering. [171]His discourse on these matters too I believe it is worth while to set down. And therefore have I been induced, knowing your love of learning, my dear Philocrates, to clarify the sanctity and the inherent character of the law.

[172]And so Eleazar, after he had offered sacrifice and had chosen the men and prepared many gifts for the king, sent us on our way in great security. [173]When we reached Alexandria word of our arrival was brought to the king. Upon our admission to the court Andreas and I gave friendly greeting to the king and delivered the letters from Eleazar. [174]Being very eager to receive the delegates, the king gave orders that all the other officials be dismissed, and that the men be summoned. [175]This procedure struck everyone as strange, for it was the custom that those who came on official business gained access to the royal presence on the fifth day, while visitors from kings and prominent cities were barely admitted to the court in thirty days. But he thought that these men who had come were worthy of higher honor and rightly judged the eminence of him who had sent them, and so, dismissing all persons he considered superfluous, he waited,

---

Thackeray and Andrews "the natural meaning"—which the author probably feels the allegorical interpretation to be.
172–186. THE RETURN TO ALEXANDRIA. Josephus' paraphrase resumes at this point (*Ant.* 12.85 ff.).
172. IN GREAT SECURITY: Seems to imply that Eleazar sent a military escort for the caravan through the desert.
173. DELIVERED THE LETTERS: Josephus adds (86), "and reported to him all that the High Priest had suggested that they should convey by word of mouth," but the text is uncertain.

περιπατῶν, ἕως ἂν παραγινομένους ἀσπάσηται. ¹⁷⁶παρελθόντων δὲ σὺν τοῖς ἀπεσταλμένοις δώροις καὶ ταῖς διαφόροις διφθέραις, ἐν αἷς ἡ νομοθεσία γεγραμμένη χρυσογραφίᾳ τοῖς Ἰουδαϊκοῖς γράμμασι, θαυμασίως <εἰργασμένου τοῦ ὑμένος>, καὶ τῆς πρὸς ἄλληλα συμβολῆς ἀνεπαισθήτου κατεσκευασμένης, ὡς εἶδεν ὁ βασιλεὺς τοὺς ἄνδρας, ἐπηρώτα περὶ τῶν βιβλίων. ¹⁷⁷ὡς δὲ ἀπεκάλυψαν τὰ τῶν ἐνειλημάτων καὶ τοὺς ὑμένας ἀνείλιξαν, πολὺν ἐπιστὰς χρόνον καὶ προσκυνήσας σχεδὸν ἑπτάκις εἶπεν Εὐχαριστῶ μέν, ἄνδρες, ὑμῖν, τῷ δ' ἀποστείλαντι μᾶλλον, μέγιστον δὲ τῷ θεῷ, οὗτινός ἐστι τὰ λόγια ταῦτα. ¹⁷⁸ὁμοθυμαδὸν δὲ πάντων εἰπόντων ὑπὸ μίαν φωνήν, τῶν τε παραγεγονότων καὶ τῶν συμπαρόντων, Εὖ βασιλεῦ, προήχθη δακρῦσαι τῇ χαρᾷ πεπληρωμένος. ἡ γὰρ τῆς ψυχῆς ἔντασις καὶ τὸ τῆς τιμῆς ὑπερτεῖνον δακρύειν ἀναγκάζει κατὰ τὰς ἐπιτυχίας. ¹⁷⁹κελεύσας δὲ εἰς τάξιν ἀποδοῦναι τὰ τεύχη, τὸ τηνικαῦτα ἀσπασάμενος τοὺς ἄνδρας εἶπε Δίκαιον ἦν, θεοσεβεῖς ἄνδρες, ὧν χάριν ὑμᾶς μετεπεμψάμην, ἐκείνοις πρῶτον σεβασμὸν ἀποδοῦναι, μετὰ ταῦτα τὴν δεξιὰν ὑμῖν προτεῖναι· διὸ πεποίηκα τοῦτο πρῶτον. ¹⁸⁰μεγάλην δὲ τέθειμαι τὴν ἡμέραν

---

176 διαφοροις W brackets, Jos. omits / γασμενης της υμενου MSS
ειργασμενου του υμενος edd., ειρ-

---

176. PRECIOUS PARCHMENTS: The adjective is omitted in Josephus. LETTERS . . . OF GOLD: Perhaps only the names of God, of which we have allusions that they were written in gold in Egyptian Torah scrolls. *Cf. Sopherim* 1.10. JEWISH LETTERS: [It is strange that in v. 3 the author uses the phrase "Hebrew characters." In the letter from Demetrius to Ptolemy he writes that the Laws of the Jews "are written in Hebrew characters [ancient Hebrew script] and in the Hebrew tongue." In the letter from Ptolemy to Eleazar, the High Priest, the term "Hebrew tongue" (characters) is again used by the author. The same expressions are employed by Josephus and Eusebius. The problem that confronts us is why the author uses here the term "Jewish letters" (*i.e.*, the square script) instead of "Hebrew characters" which he had employed heretofore. It would seem that these passages do not belong to the original Letter of Aristeas, but were added much later after the destruction of the Second Temple when the Jewish characters, (the square script) were used much more than the ancient Hebrew script. (S. Z.)]
IMPERCEPTIBLE: From this passage Azariah de Rossi, *Meor Enayim* 145, deduced that, unlike current practice, the sheets were joined by a kind of glue.

walking to and fro, to greet them on their arrival. [176]They entered, then, with the gifts which had been sent and the precious parchments in which the Law was inscribed in Jewish letters with writing of gold, the material being wonderfully worked and the joinings of the leaves being made imperceptible; and when the king saw the men he began to put questions concerning the books. [177]When they had uncovered the rolls and had unrolled the parchments the king paused for a considerable space, and after bowing deeply some seven times said, "I thank you, good sirs, and him that sent you even more, but most of all I thank God whose holy words these are." [178]And when all with one accord, both those newly come and those already present, exclaimed in a single voice, "Excellent, Your Majesty!" he was moved to tears out of the fullness of his joy. For the strain of the spirit and the tension of honor constrain to tears upon attainment of success. [179]He bade them put the rolls back in their places, and only then did he greet the men, saying, "It was right, my God-fearing friends, first to pay homage to those treasures for whose sake I summoned you, and thereafter to extend the right hand to you; therefore have I done this thing first. [180]This day upon which you have come I regard as a great

177. BOWING DEEPLY SOME SEVEN TIMES: Omitted in Josephus.   WHOSE HOLY WORDS: *Logia*, used above of the High Priest's breastplate (97) and of the "chapters" of the *mezuzah* (158). Aristeas always stresses the divine origin of the Law, which here even the king acknowledges; *cf.* 313.
178. FOR THE STRAIN OF THE SPIRIT: Josephus (91) has a different psychological explanation: "since it is natural for great joy to be expressed by the same signs as grief."
179. PUT THE ROLLS BACK IN THEIR PLACES: Josephus (92) has "to be given to those in charge of the records," which may be merely a misunderstanding of Aristeas, but is more likely correct; see Marcus' note *ad loc.*
180. EACH YEAR: Philo (see Introd. 25) says that in his day an annual festival at Pharos celebrated the translation of the LXX.   VICTORY OVER ANTIGONUS: Antigonus Gonatas, son of Demetrius Poliorcetes. If our reading is correct (it is followed by Josephus) Aristeas is guilty of a grave error. In the only known sea battle between Philadelphus and Antigonus, fought at Cos *ca.* 258, the Egyptians were badly defeated. Another sea battle between an Antigonus and a Ptolemy was fought at Andros some years later, but neither the identity of the protagonists nor the issue of the battle is known; and in any case both battles were fought after 269, the year of

ταύτην, ἐν ᾗ παραγεγόνατε, καὶ κατ' ἐνιαυτὸν ἐπίσημος ἔσται πάντα τὸν τῆς ζωῆς ἡμῶν χρόνον· συντέτυχε γὰρ καὶ τὰ κατὰ τὴν νίκην ἡμῖν προσπεπτωκέναι τῆς πρὸς Ἀντίγονον ναυμαχίας. διὸ καὶ δειπνῆσαι σήμερον μεθ' ὑμῶν βουλήσομαι. [181]πάντα <δ' ὑμῖν>, εἶπε, παρέσται καθηκόντως, οἷς συγχρήσησθε, κἀμοὶ μεθ' ὑμῶν. τῶν δὲ ἀσμενισάντων ἐκέλευσε καταλύματα δοθῆναι τὰ κάλλιστα πλησίον τῆς ἄκρας αὐτοῖς, καὶ τὰ κατὰ τὸ συμπόσιον ἑτοιμάζειν.

[182]Ὁ δὲ <ἀρχεδέατρος> Νικάνωρ Δωρόθεον προσκαλεσάμενος, ὃς <ἦν> ἐπὶ τούτων ἀποτεταγμένος, ἐκέλευσε τὴν ἑτοιμασίαν εἰς ἕκαστον ἐπιτλεῖν. ἦν γὰρ οὕτω διατεταγμένον ὑπὸ τοῦ βασιλέως, ἃ μὲν ἔτι καὶ νῦν ὁρᾷς· ὅσαι γὰρ πόλεις εἰσίν, <αἳ τοῖς αὐτοῖς> συγχρῶνται πρὸς τὰ ποτὰ καὶ βρωτὰ καὶ στρωμνάς, τοσοῦτοι καὶ προεστῶτες ἦσαν· καὶ κατὰ τοὺς ἐθισμοὺς οὕτως ἐσκευάζετο, ὅταν παραγένοιντο πρὸς τοὺς βασιλεῖς, ἵνα κατὰ μηθὲν δυσχεραίνοντες ἱλαρῶς διεξάγωσιν· ὃ καὶ περὶ τούτους ἐγεγόνει. [183]προσεχέστατος γὰρ ὢν ἄνθρωπος ὁ Δωρόθεος εἶχε τὴν τῶν τοιούτων προστασίαν. συνέστρωσε δὲ πάντα τὰ δι' αὐτοῦ χειριζόμενα, πρὸς τὰς τοιαύτας ὑποδοχὰς διαμεμερισμένα. διμερῆ τε ἐποίησε τὰ τῶν κλισιῶν, καθὼς προσέταξεν ὁ βασιλεύς· τοὺς γὰρ ἡμίσεις ἐκέλευσεν ἀνὰ χεῖρα κατακλῖναι,

---

181 παντα <δ' υμιν> edd., παντα δυναμιν MSS
182 αρχεδεατρος edd., αρχιητρος MSS / ην edd., ων MSS / εισιν <αι τοις αυτοις> T, εισιν οις MSS, εθεσιν ιδιοις W, εθισμοις ιδιοις Cohn
183 ανα χειρα edd.-Jos., αναρχα MSS

Arsinoe II's death, and Arsinoe is presumed to be still alive in Aristeas. Bickermann, "Zur Datierung etc.," suggests that an error has crept into the archetype of our (and Josephus') MSS, "Antigonus" replacing "Antiochus," against whom Philadelphus made a naval expedition in 280.

181. IN KEEPING WITH YOUR USAGES, AND FOR ME ALSO ALONG WITH YOU: *I.e.*, observance of dietary regulations need not prevent social intercourse or provoke ridicule, as against the narrower views of *e.g.* III Mac. NEAR THE CITADEL: Appropriate, as being the residential quarter (called Lochias) assigned to the Jews by Alexander the Great, and a choice site; see *Against Apion* 2.33 ff. with Thackeray's note, and *Jewish War* 2.488.

182. SENESCHAL: The MSS have *archietros*, "chief physician," but *archedeatros* is confirmed by inscriptional evidence as the title of a major-domo.

day, and each year through all the length of my life it shall be held in high esteem. It happens, moreover, to fall on the day of our victory over Antigonus in the battle at sea. Therefore I shall also wish to dine with you this day. [181]Everything," he added, "shall be prepared in keeping with your usages, and for me also along with you." When they had shown their satisfaction he ordered the best lodgings to be assigned to them, near the citadel, and the banquet to be made ready.

[182]And so the seneschal Nicanor summoned Dorotheus, in whose province these visitors fell, and ordered him to carry out the preparation in every particular. For such was the arrangement instituted by the king, which you may observe in use even now. For as many states as there are which employ special usages in drink and food and mode of reclining, so many officials were assigned, and then whenever guests visited the reigning king preparations were made according to their usages, so that there should be nothing to discomfort them and they could pass the time in good cheer. This practice was followed in the case of these visitors. [183]The man Dorotheus was extremely attentive in his charge. He laid out all the stores under his administration which were set apart for the receptions of such guests. The couches he arranged in two rows, as the king had bidden; for he had ordered him to have half the men recline at his right and the others

---

The title *deatros*, of Persian origin, originally designated the official who tasted the dishes before they were served to the king. Josephus (94) paraphrases "the officer in charge of the reception of guests." The name *Nicanor* occurs in Ptolemaic papyri as well as in II Mac. and elsewhere; *Dorotheus* is of the theophoric type favored by Jews.   WHICH YOU MAY OBSERVE IN USE EVEN NOW: A clear indication of the elapse of a considerable interval; see Introd. 7. On the other hand, since ambassadors are received, Egypt must still have an independent dynasty, which it did not have after the Roman conquest in 30 BCE.
183. EXTREMELY ATTENTIVE: Josephus (95) says "because of his exactness in the details of living."   AFTER HIS OWN COUCH: At his left; this seating, AS THE KING HAD BIDDEN, being better calculated TO SHOW THE MEN HONOR than if they were seated opposite, as was done *e.g.* with Philopator's guests at III Mac. 5.16.

τοὺς δὲ λοιποὺς μετὰ τὴν ἑαυτοῦ κλισίαν, οὐδὲν ἐλλιπὼν εἰς τὸ τιμᾶν τοὺς ἄνδρας. [184]Ὡς δὲ κατεκλίθησαν, ἐκέλευσε τῷ Δωροθέῳ τοῖς ἐθισμοῖς οἷς χρῶνται πάντες οἱ παραγινόμενοι πρὸς αὐτὸν ἀπὸ τῆς Ἰουδαίας, οὕτως ἐπιτελεῖν. διὸ τοὺς ἱεροκήρυκας καὶ θύτας καὶ τοὺς ἄλλους, οἷς ἔθος ἦν τὰς κατευχὰς ποιεῖσθαι, παρῃτήσατο· τῶν δὲ παραγεγονότων σὺν ἡμῖν Ἐλισσαῖον ὄντα τῶν ἱερέων πρεσβύτερον παρεκάλεσε ποιήσασθαι κατευχήν, ὃς ἀξιολόγως στὰς εἶπε [185]Πληρώσαι σε, βασιλεῦ, πάντων τῶν ἀγαθῶν ὧν ἔκτισεν ὁ παντοκράτωρ θεός· καὶ δῴη σοι ταῦτ' ἔχειν καὶ γυναικὶ καὶ τέκνοις καὶ τοῖς ὁμονοοῦσι πάντα ἀνέκλειπτα τὸν τῆς ζωῆς χρόνον. [186]Εἰπόντος δὲ ταῦτα τούτου κατερράγη κρότος μετὰ κραυγῆς καὶ χαρᾶς εὐφροσύνου πλείονα χρόνον· καὶ τὸ τηνικαῦτα πρὸς τὸ τέρπεσθαι διὰ τῶν ἡτοιμασμένων ἐτράπησαν, τῶν λειτουργιῶν ἁπασῶν διὰ τῆς τοῦ Δωροθέου συντάξεως ἐπιτελουμένων· ἐν οἷς καὶ βασιλικοὶ παῖδες ἦσαν, καὶ τῶν τιμωμένων ὑπὸ τοῦ βασιλέως.

[187]Ὅτε δὲ καιρὸν ἔλαβεν ἐκ διαστήματος, ἠρώτησε τὸν ἔχοντα τὴν πρώτην ἀνάκλισιν (ἦσαν γὰρ καθ' ἡλικίαν τὴν ἀνάπτωσιν πεποιημένοι) Πῶς ἂν τὴν βασιλείαν μέχρι τέλους ἄπταιστον ἔχων διατελοῖ; [188]βραχὺ δὲ ἐπισχὼν

---

184 Ελισσαιον   add.-Jos.,   Ελεαζαρον   ομογενεσι
MSS   188 Schmidt inserts η before καθως /
185 ομονοουσι   MSS, W conjectures   και W brackets

184. ELISHA: The reading of Josephus (97), who is not likely in error here. The slip is probably due to confusion with the name of the High Priest, especially as the officiant is here called "eldest." In the list of translators (47-50) there are three Elisha's and one Eleazar.   OF THE PRIESTS: It is probable (the alleged distribution by tribes notwithstanding) that all or most of the translators would be priests.
185. ALMIGHTY: *Pantokratōr*, frequent in LXX. The blessing seems Jewish in spirit, though no exact parallel suggests itself; cf. Isaac's blessings in Gen. 27, or perhaps better Ps. 20.5: "Grant thee according to thine own heart, and fulfill all thy counsel."
186. BURST OF APPLAUSE: To second the benediction as well as approve the officiant.   JOYFUL JUBILATION: Throughout the entertainments there is an effort to convey an atmosphere of easy gaiety.   ADDRESSED THEMSELVES: The same expression is used of similar circumstances in III Mac. 5.3, 13, 36.   SERVICE PERFORMED BY . . . ROYAL PAGES: Significantly omitted in Josephus.

after his own couch, leaving nothing undone to show the men honor.

¹⁸⁴When they had taken their places he bade Dorotheus to carry out the practices used by all his visitors from Judaea. He therefore declined the services of the sacred heralds and the sacrificial ministers and the others who usually offered prayers, and called upon Elisha, the eldest of the priests who had come with us, to offer a prayer, and he arose and spoke these memorable words: ¹⁸⁵"May Almighty God fill Your Majesty full of the good things which He has created, and grant uninterrupted and lifelong possession of them to you and your wife and children and those like-minded with you."
¹⁸⁶At these words there was a burst of applause, and shouts and joyful jubilation continued for a considerable time. Then they addressed themselves to the enjoyment of what had been prepared. All the table service was performed by Dorotheus' staff, among whom were royal pages and persons who had been honored by the king.

¹⁸⁷When, after an interval, an opportunity offered, the king asked the man who occupied the first place at table (their positions at table were arranged according to seniority) how he might preserve his kingdom unimpaired to the end. ¹⁸⁸He paused for a moment and replied, "You would main-

---

187–300. QUESTIONS AND ANSWERS DURING THE KING'S ENTERTAINMENT. The section from 187 to 292 is omitted in the paraphrase of Josephus, who, after the matter of 186, inserts the following sentence (99): "But the king. after waiting for what seemed a sufficiently long time, began to philosophize and asked each one of them about problems of nature, and when, after considering the questions, they gave precise explanations concerning every single problem suggested to them for discussion, he was delighted with them and made the banquet last for twelve (sic) days, so that anyone who wishes to find out the details of the questions discussed at the banquet can learn them by reading the book which Aristaeus (sic) composed on this account." For the nature of the questions and answers and their relationship to similar non-Jewish works see Introd. 41. It is to be noticed that there is nothing specifically Jewish in the questions or answers, and that the pious expressions mentioning the name of God in the answers are usually easily detachable.

188. MORE GENTLY THAN THEY DESERVE: Among the king's virtues which the Egyptian priests were required to recite during sacrifice, Diodorus

εἶπεν Οὕτως ἂν μάλιστα διευθύνοις, μιμούμενος τὸ τοῦ θεοῦ διὰ παντὸς ἐπιεικές. μακροθυμίᾳ γὰρ χρώμενος, καὶ βλιμάζων τοὺς ἀξίους ἐπιεικέστερον, καθώς εἰσιν ἄξιοι, μετατιθεὶς ἐκ τῆς κακίας καὶ εἰς μετάνοιαν ἄξεις. [189]'Επαινέσας δὲ ὁ βασιλεὺς τὸν ἐχόμενον ἠρώτα Πῶς ἂν ἕκαστα πράττοι; ὁ δὲ ἀπεκρίθη Τὸ δίκαιον εἰ πρὸς ἅπαντας διατηροῖ, ἑαυτῷ καλῶς τὰ ἕκαστα πράξει, διαλαμβάνων ὅτι πᾶν ἐννόημα σαφές ἐστι θεῷ· καταρχὴν δὲ θείου φόβου λαμβάνων ἐν οὐδενὶ διαπίπτοις. [190]Καὶ τοῦτον δὲ εὖ μάλα παραδεξάμενος ἕτερον ἐπηρώτα Πῶς ἂν ὁμοίους ἑαυτῷ ἔχοι τοὺς φίλους; κἀκεῖνος εἶπεν Εἰ θεωροίησαν πολλήν σε πρόνοιαν ποιούμενον ὧν ἄρχεις ὄχλων· σὺ δὲ τοῦτο πράξεις ἐπιβλέπων ὡς ὁ θεὸς εὐεργετεῖ τὸ τῶν ἀνθρώπων γένος, ὁ ὑγείαν αὐτοῖς καὶ τροφὴν καὶ τὰ λοιπὰ κατὰ καιρὸν παρασκευάζων ἅπαντα. [191]Συνεπιμαρτυρήσας δὲ τούτῳ τὸν ἐχόμενον ἠρώτα Πῶς ἂν ἐν τοῖς χρηματισμοῖς καὶ διακρίσεσιν εὐφημίας <τυγχάνοι> καὶ ὑπὸ τῶν ἀποτυγχανόντων; ὁ δὲ εἶπεν Εἰ πᾶσιν ἴσος γένοιο τῷ λόγῳ, καὶ μηδὲν ὑπερηφάνως μηδὲ τῇ περὶ σεαυτὸν ἰσχύι πράσσοις κατὰ τῶν ἁμαρτανόντων. [192]τοῦτο δὲ ποιήσεις τὴν διάταξιν βλέπων τὴν ὑπὸ τοῦ θεοῦ· τὰ γὰρ ἱκετευόμενα συντελεῖσθαι τοῖς ἀξίοις, τοῖς δὲ ἀποτυγχάνουσιν ἢ δι' ὀνείρων ἢ πράξεων σημαίνεσθαι τὸ βλαβερὸν αὐτοῖς, οὐ κατὰ τὰς ἁμαρτίας οὐδὲ <κατὰ> τὴν μεγαλωσύνην τῆς ἰσχύος τύπτοντος αὐτούς, ἀλλ' ἐπιεικείᾳ χρωμένου τοῦ θεοῦ. [193]Εὖ δὲ καὶ

---

189 After εκαστα W inserts καλλιστα / W suggests απο before θειου
191 τυγχανοι edd., τυγχανω MSS
193 οχλοις MSS, οπλοις MS

Siculus 1.70.6 reports, was the assertion "that he punished crimes less severely than they deserved and rendered to his benefactors a gratitude exceeding the benefaction." The entire Diodorus passage probably derives from an *On Kingship;* see Introd. 45. This and the two questions following imply an assertion of the principle of equality, which receives special emphasis in Philo; see Wolfson, 2.393.
189. STARTING-POINT: This attitude, throughout the questions, is the specifically Jewish addition; at 235 it is directly stated that the sages were "in advance of the philosophers" precisely because "they made their starting-point from God." FEAR OF GOD: *Cf.* Prov. 1.7, "The fear of the Lord is the beginning of knowledge," and numerous parallels, especially in Ben Sirah 1, and *Abot* 1.3 (Antigonus of Sokho).

tain it best by imitating the constant gentleness of God. For by exercising long-suffering patience and dealing with those who merit punishment more gently than they deserve, you will turn them from wickedness and bring them to repentance."

¹⁸⁹The king commended him, and asked the next man what was his best course in all his actions. And he answered that if he observed justice to all men he would in each case act for the best for himself, reflecting that every thought is clear to God. "By making your starting-point the fear of God you would nowhere fail."

¹⁹⁰Him too he gave his cordial assent, and asked the next man how he might keep his friends like-minded with himself. And this man said, "If they observe you taking great forethought for the multitudes over whom you rule. This you will do by noticing how God acts beneficently to the human race, providing them with health and food and all other things in due season."

¹⁹¹He expressed his approval of this, and asked his neighbor how, in his audiences and judicial decisions, he might obtain good report even from those who failed in their suits. And he said, "If you show yourself impartial to all in speech and never deal arrogantly or tyrannically with offenders. ¹⁹²This you will do if you regard the methods of God. Their petitions are fulfilled for the worthy, and for those who fail the harmfulness of their petitions is made clear to them by dreams or events; God does not smite them according to their shortcomings or according to the greatness of His strength, but He uses forbearance."

¹⁹³He complimented him warmly also, and then asked the

---

190. PROVIDING . . . IN DUE SEASON: *Cf.* Ps. 104.27, "That Thou mayest give them their food in due season." Philo, *On Special Laws* 4.73 says there is nothing better than to imitate God.
193. TRUST IN NUMBERS AND STRENGTH: *Cf.* Ps. 20.8–9, "Some trust in chariots, and some in horses; but we will make mention of the name of the Lord our God. They are bowed down and fallen; but we are risen, and stand upright;" I Mac. 2.61, "None that put their trust in Him shall want for strength;" 3.19, "Victory in battle standeth not in the multitude of a host;

τοῦτον κατεπαινέσας ἠρώτα τὸν ἑξῆς Πῶς ἂν ἐν ταῖς πολεμικαῖς χρείαις ἀήττητος εἴη; ὁ δὲ εἶπεν Εἰ μὴ πεποιθὼς ὑπάρχοι τοῖς ὄχλοις μηδὲ ταῖς δυνάμεσιν, ἀλλὰ τὸν θεὸν ἐπικαλοῖτο διὰ πάντων, ἵνα τὰς ἐπιβολὰς αὐτῷ κατευθύνῃ δικαίως διεξάγοντι πάντα. ¹⁹⁴ Ἀποδεξάμενος δὲ καὶ τοῦτον τὸν ἕτερον ἠρώτα Πῶς ἂν φοβερὸς εἴη τοῖς ἐχθροῖς; ὁ δὲ εἶπεν Εἰ τῇ τῶν ὅπλων καὶ δυνάμεων παρασκευῇ πολλῇ χρώμενος <εἰδείη> ταῦτα ὄντα κενὰ ἐπὶ πλείονα χρόνον πρὸς τὸ συμπέρασμα δρᾶν τι· καὶ γὰρ ὁ θεὸς διδοὺς ἀνοχὰς καὶ ἐνδεικνύμενος τὸν τῆς δυναστείας φόβον ἐγκατασκευάζει πάσῃ διανοίᾳ. ¹⁹⁵ Καὶ τοῦτον δὲ ἐπαινέσας εἶπε πρὸς τὸν ἐχόμενον Τί κάλλιστον αὐτῷ πρὸς τὸ ζῆν ἂν εἴη; κἀκεῖνος ἔφη Τὸ γινώσκειν ὅτι θεὸς δυναστεύει τῶν ἁπάντων, καὶ ἐπὶ τῶν καλλίστων πράξεων οὐκ αὐτοὶ κατευθύνομεν τὰ βουλευθέντα· θεὸς δὲ τελειοῖ τὰ πάντων καὶ καθηγεῖται δυναστεύων. ¹⁹⁶ Ἐπιφωνήσας δὲ καὶ τούτῳ καλῶς λέγειν τὸν ἕτερον ἠρώτα Πῶς ἂν ἀκέραια συντηρήσας ἅπαντα τοῖς ἐγγόνοις τὴν αὐτὴν παραδιδοῖ διάθεσιν ἐπὶ τέλει; ὁ δὲ εἶπεν Εὐχόμενος ἀεὶ πρὸς τὸν θεὸν ἀγαθὰς ἐπινοίας λαμβάνειν πρὸς τὰ μέλλοντα πράσσεσθαι, καὶ τοῖς ἐγγόνοις παρακελευόμενος μὴ ἐκπλήττεσθαι τῇ δόξῃ μηδὲ τῷ πλούτῳ· θεὸν γὰρ εἶναι τὸν χαριζόμενον ταῦτα, καὶ οὐ δι' ἑαυτοὺς ἔχειν τὴν ὑπεροχὴν ἁπάντων. ¹⁹⁷ Ἐπιμαρτυρήσας δὲ τούτοις τοῦ μετὰ ταῦτα ἐπυνθάνετο Πῶς ἂν τὰ συμβαίνοντα μετρίως φέροι; ἐκεῖνος δὲ ἔφησεν Εἰ πρόληψιν λαμβάνοις, ὅτι γέγοναν ὑπὸ τοῦ θεοῦ πάντες ἄνθρωποι μετασχεῖν τῶν μεγίστων κακῶν, ὡσαύτως δὲ καὶ ἀγαθῶν, καὶ οὐκ ἔστιν ἄνθρωπον

---

194 ειδειη edd., ειη ει δε ειη MSS / δραν τα W
τι W conjectures ορωντι / τον MSS,

but strength is from heaven." On the other hand the Greeks too believed that divine help would make up for weak forces in a just cause: so the Melians against the Athenians at the end of Thucydides 5.
194. GRANTING REPRIEVES: Cf. Ps. 130.4, "For with Thee there is forgiveness, that Thou mayest be feared." Our passage may, but need not, be a quotation of this verse. If it is, it is not from LXX, and since LXX Psalms cannot be later than the second half of the second century BCE this would be evidence that Aristeas is earlier; see Abrahams in *Journal of Theological Studies* 21.179 f.

man next in order how he might be invincible in warfare. And he answered, "If he did not place his trust in numbers and strength but called always upon God to direct his undertakings, while he himself followed justice in all his dealings."

[194]He welcomed this saying, and asked of the next man how he might be formidable to his enemies. He replied, "If, while maintaining large preparations in arms and forces, he would realize that these were ineffective for producing any conclusive result over a long period; for God also, by granting reprieves and displaying His sovereign power, implants awe into every mind."

[195]He commended him also, and asked his neighbor what would be the highest good for his life. And that man declared, "The realization that God rules all things, and that in our fairest achievements it is not we ourselves who accomplish our intentions, but God in His sovereignty consummates and guides the actions of us all."

[196]He agreed that this man too had spoken well, and asked the next how he might preserve all his status intact and in the end transmit it unaltered to his descendants. And he said, "By praying always to God to receive good impulses for future actions, and by admonishing your descendants not to be dazzled by fame and by wealth, for it is God who bestows these gifts, and it is not through themselves that they have pre-eminence over all."

[197]He expressed his agreement with these sentiments, and inquired of the man who followed how he could endure whatever befell with equanimity. That man declared, "If you adopt the notion that all men have been fashioned by God to share in the greatest evils as in the greatest good, and it is

---

195. GOD RULES: The main theologic doctrine of Aristeas. *Cf.* Wisd. 12.17-18, 13.9; Philo, *Cherubim* 31, "The purified intellect rejoices in nothing more than in confessing that it has for its master Him who is the Lord of all."

197. NOTION: *Prolepsis*, a word particularly favored by the Stoics, though used by other philosophers also. The mutability of fortune is a commonplace in pagan as in Jewish thought.

ὄντα τούτων ἀμιγῆ γενέσθαι· ὁ θεὸς δὲ τὴν εὐψυχίαν δίδωσιν, ὃν ἱκετεύειν ἀναγκαῖον. [198]Φιλοφρονηθεὶς δὲ καὶ τοῦτον καλῶς εἶπεν ἅπαντας ἀποφαίνεσθαι· ἐπερωτήσας δὲ ἔτι ἕνα καταλήξω τὸ νῦν ἔχον, ἵνα καὶ πρὸς τὸ τέρπεσθαι τραπέντες ἡδέως διεξάγωμεν. ἐν δὲ ταῖς μετὰ ταῦτα ἓξ ἑξῆς ἡμέραις καὶ παρὰ τῶν λοιπῶν ἑξῆς μαθήσομαί τι πλέον. [199]εἶτ' ἐπηρώτα τὸν ἄνδρα Τί πέρας ἀνδρείας ἐστίν; ὁ δὲ εἶπεν Εἰ τὸ βουλευθὲν ὀρθῶς ἐν ταῖς τῶν κινδύνων πράξεσιν ἐπιτελοῖτο κατὰ πρόθεσιν. τελειοῦται δὲ ὑπὸ τοῦ θεοῦ πάντα σοι καλῶς βουλευομένῳ, βασιλεῦ, συμφερόντως. [200]Ἐπιφωνησάντων δὲ πάντων καὶ κρότῳ σημηναμένων πρὸς τοὺς φιλοσόφους εἶπεν ὁ βασιλεὺς (οὐκ ὀλίγοι γὰρ παρῆσαν τούτοις) Οἴομαι διαφέρειν τοὺς ἄνδρας ἀρετῇ καὶ συνιέναι πλεῖον, οἵτινες ἐκ τοῦ καιροῦ τοιαύτας ἐρωτήσεις λαμβάνοντες, ὡς δέον ἐστὶν ἀποκέκρινται, πάντες ἀπὸ θεοῦ τοῦ λόγου τὴν καταρχὴν ποιούμενοι. [201]Μενέδημος δὲ ὁ Ἐρετριεὺς φιλόσοφος εἶπε Ναί, βασιλεῦ. προνοίᾳ γὰρ τῶν ὅλων διοικουμένων, καὶ ὑπειληφότων ὀρθῶς τοῦτο, ὅτι θεόκτιστόν ἐστιν ἄνθρωπος, ἀκολουθεῖ πᾶσαν δυναστείαν καὶ λόγου καλλονὴν ἀπὸ θεοῦ κατάρχεσθαι. [202]τοῦ δὲ βασιλέως ἐπινεύσαντος τὰ περὶ τούτων ἔληξεν, ἐτράπησαν δὲ πρὸς εὐφροσύνην. ἐπιλαβούσης δὲ τῆς ἑσπέρας τὸ συμπόσιον ἐλύθη.

[203]Τῇ δὲ μετὰ ταῦτα πάλιν κατὰ τὴν αὐτὴν διάταξιν τὰ τῆς ἀναπτώσεως καὶ συμποσίας ἐπετελεῖτο. καθὸ δὲ ἐνόμιζεν ὁ βασιλεὺς εὔκαιρον εἶναι πρὸς τὸ πυνθάνεσθαί τι τῶν ἀνδρῶν, ἐπηρώτα τοὺς ἑξῆς τῶν ἀποκεκριμένων τῇ

198 εξης W brackets

198. SIX SUCCEEDING DAYS: Josephus (99) unaccountably says the entertainment lasted 12 days.
199. COURAGE: A cardinal Stoic virtue, and the answer also follows Stoic teaching.
200. MAKING GOD THE STARTING-POINT: Cf. on 189, 235. Ben Sirah 7.5 should be translated "Do not play the sophist in the presence of a king," and perhaps the present statement is intended to show that the sages were not being merely sophistical.
201. MENEDEMUS OF ERETRIA (in Boeotia): A friend of Antigonus Gonatas (see W. W. Tarn, *Antigonus Gonatas* [Oxford, 1913] 22 f.), was a Socratic,

not possible for a human being to be without a part in these things. But God gives stout-heartedness, and Him one must supplicate."

[198]This man too the king complimented warmly, and said that all had approved themselves well. "I shall put a question to yet one more," he added, "and then stop for the present, so that we may address ourselves to enjoyment and pass the time agreeably. In the six succeeding days I shall gain further instruction from each in turn of those that remain." [199]Thereupon he asked the man, "What is the goal of courage?" And he replied, "To carry out correct counsels in the hour of danger in accordance with one's purpose. But your counsels, Your Majesty, are all good, and are carried out by God to your advantage."

[200]When all had expressed approval and signified it by applause, the king said to the philosophers, of whom not a few were present, "I think the virtue of these men is extraordinary and their understanding very great, for having questions of such a sort addressed to them they have given proper replies on the spur of the moment, all of them making God the starting-point of their reasoning." [201]And the philosopher Menedemus of Eretria said, "True, Your Majesty; for inasmuch as all things are governed by providence, and these men are right in holding that man is a creature of God, it follows that all power and beauty of discourse have their starting-point from God." [202]The king expressed his assent, the speeches ceased, and they turned to festivity. And when evening drew on the party broke up.

[203]On the day following the seating and the program of the banquet were carried out according to the same arrangement. When the king thought the time had come for putting queries to the men, he asked questions of the men next in order to

---

and hence here quite consistently credited with belief in divine providence. But his dates (ca. 350–287) make his presence in Alexandria at this juncture very improbable, though Diogenes Laertius (2.140) says that he "was sent as envoy to Ptolemy and Lysimachus"; on the other hand, Diogenes is not reliable. Tertullian, *Apology* 18 calls him *providentiae vindex*.

προτέρᾳ ἡμέρᾳ. πρὸς τὸν ἐνδέκατον δὲ ἤρξατο τὴν κοινολογίαν ποιεῖσθαι· ²⁰⁴δέκα γὰρ ἦσαν οἱ ἠρωτημένοι τῇ προτέρᾳ. σιγῆς δὲ γενομένης ἐπυνθάνετο Πῶς ἂν πλούσιος 205 διαμένοι; ²⁰⁵βραχὺ δὲ ἐπισχὼν ὁ τὴν ἐρώτησιν ἐκδεχόμενος εἶπεν Εἰ μηδὲν ἀνάξιον τῆς ἀρχῆς μηδὲ ἀσελγὲς πράσσοι, μηδὲ δαπάνῃ εἰς τὰ κενὰ καὶ μάταια συντελοῖ, τοὺς <δὲ> ὑποτεταγμένους εὐεργεσίᾳ πρὸς εὔνοιαν ἄγοι τὴν ἑαυτοῦ· καὶ γὰρ ὁ θεὸς πᾶσιν αἴτιος ἀγαθῶν ἐστιν, ᾧ κατακολουθεῖν ἀναγκαῖον. ²⁰⁶Ἐπαινέσας δὲ ὁ βασιλεὺς τοῦτον ἕτερον ἐπηρώτα Πῶς ἂν τὴν ἀλήθειαν διατηροῖ; ὁ δὲ πρὸς τοῦτο ἀπεκρίθη Γινώσκων ὅτι μεγάλην αἰσχύνην ἐπιφέρει τὸ ψεῦδος πᾶσιν ἀνθρώποις, πολλῷ δὲ μᾶλλον τοῖς βασιλεῦσιν· ἐξουσίαν γὰρ ἔχοντες ὃ βούλονται πράσσειν, τίνος ἕνεκεν ἂν ψεύσαιντο; προσλαμβάνειν δὲ δεῖ τοῦτό σε, βασιλεῦ, διότι φιλαλήθης ὁ θεός ἐστιν. ²⁰⁷Ἀποεξάμενος δὲ εὖ μάλα καὶ τοῦτον ἐπιβλέψας εἶπεν Τί ἐστι σοφίας διδαχή; ὁ δὲ ἕτερος ἀπεφήνατο Καθὼς οὐ βούλει σεαυτῷ τὰ κακὰ παρεῖναι, μέτοχος δὲ τῶν ἀγαθῶν ὑπάρχειν ἁπάντων, εἰ πράσσοις τοῦτο πρὸς τοὺς ὑποτεταγμένους καὶ τοὺς ἁμαρτάνοντας, εἰ τοὺς καλοὺς καὶ ἀγαθοὺς τῶν ἀνθρώπων ἐπιεικέστερον νουθετοῖς· καὶ γὰρ ὁ θεὸς τοὺς ἀνθρώπους ἅπαντας ἐπιεικείᾳ ἄγει. ²⁰⁸Ἐπαινέσας αὐτὸν τῷ μετ' αὐτὸν εἶπε Πῶς ἂν φιλάνθρωπος εἴη; κἀκεῖνος ἔφη Θεωρῶν ὡς ἐν πολλῷ χρόνῳ καὶ κακο-

205 δαπανη MSS-T, δαπανην W
206 προλαμβανειν MSS, προσλ. W
207 Before επιβλεψας W inserts επι
τον ετερον and brackets the following ετερος
208 χρονω W conjectures πονω

204. TEN: Questions to foreign sages by Hellenistic kings regularly came in groups of ten; see Introd. 41.
206. TRUTH: The moral quality of sincerity, as I have rendered the same word at 260. There are naturally many Jewish parallels (of which the nearest in language is LXX Prov. 24.22), but as is the case with other general ethical maxims in these questions the virtue is not exclusively Jewish. Coins of Laodicea bear the legend "Zeus lover of truth," Arrian in the preface to his *Anabasis* says it is "more shameful for the king himself (Alexander) than for another to lie," and, more significantly for our passage, Diodorus reports (1.70.6) that veracity was one of the royal virtues which the Egyptian priests were required to rehearse.
207. JUST AS YOU DO NOT WISH: Perhaps the closest parallel to this form of expressing the golden rule is that cited from Philo in Eusebius, *Praep.*

those who had given answers on the preceding day. ²⁰⁴He began by addressing the conversation to the eleventh man, for those who had been questioned the day previous were ten. When silence obtained, he asked how he might remain rich. ²⁰⁵The man to whom this question was directed paused for a little and then said, "If he did nothing unworthy of his rule, never behaved licentiously, never incurred expenses for empty and foolish things, but by benefactions drew his subjects to be well disposed towards him; for God is the author of blessings to all men, and His example must be followed."

²⁰⁶The king commended this man, and asked the next how he might observe truth. To this he responded, "By recognizing that lying brings great disgrace upon all men, but to a far greater degree upon kings. For since they have authority to do what they choose, to what end should they lie? And this Your Majesty must take to heart, that God is a lover of truth."

²⁰⁷This too he gave his warm approval, and directing his glance at another asked, "What is the teaching of wisdom?" And the next man replied, "Just as you do not wish evils to befall you, but to participate in all that is good, so you should deal with those subject to you and with offenders, and you should admonish good men and true very gently, for God deals with all men with gentleness."

²⁰⁸He commended him, and asked of the man next after

Ev. 8.7.6, which has exact Rabbinic parallels. But again the sentiment is familiar enough in Greek, from Socrates onwards, and quite precisely in Isocrates 3.61: "Do not do unto others that which angers you when others do it unto you." Expressions of the Golden Rule in Rabbinic and early Christian texts are listed in Meecham, *Oldest Version* 292; see also Strack and Billerbeck 1.459 f.

208. HUMANE ... MERCY: A familiar enough Jewish idea, the closest parallel to the present passage being perhaps Sirah 18.11 ff. but *philanthropia* and related virtues were much stressed by the Hellenistic philosophers, and especially with reference to rulers; *cf.* Max Mühl, *Die Antike Menschheitsidee etc.* (Leipzig, 1928). SUFFERING: Learning through suffering is an idea found in *e.g.* Wisd. 16.11, Psalms of Solomon 10.1–4, 16.4, but *pathemata mathemata* is very prominent in Greek thought, and central in tragedy.

παθείαις μεγίσταις αὔξει τε καὶ γεννᾶται τὸ τῶν ἀνθρώπων γένος· ὅθεν οὔτε εὐκόπως δεῖ κολάζειν, οὔτε αἰκίαις περιβάλλειν· γινώσκων ὅτι τὸ τῶν ἀνθρώπων ζῆν ἐν ὀδύναις τε καὶ τιμωρίαις καθέστηκεν. ἐπινοῶν οὖν ἕκαστα πρὸς τὸν ἔλεον τραπήσῃ· καὶ γὰρ ὁ θεὸς ἐλεήμων ἐστίν. ²⁰⁹Ἀποδεξάμενος δὲ τοῦτον ἐπυνθάνετο τοῦ κατὰ τὸ ἑξῆς Τίς ἀναγκαιότατος τρόπος βασιλείας; Τὸ συντηρεῖν, εἶπεν, αὑτὸν ἀδωροδόκητον, καὶ νήφειν τὸ πλεῖον μέρος τοῦ βίου, καὶ δικαιοσύνην προτιμᾶν, καὶ τοὺς τοιούτους φιλοποιεῖσθαι· 210 καὶ γὰρ ὁ θεὸς φιλοδίκαιός ἐστιν. ²¹⁰Ἐπισημήνας καὶ τοῦτον πρὸς τὸν ἕτερον εἶπε Τί τὸ τῆς εὐσεβείας ἐστὶ κατάστημα; ἐκεῖνος δὲ ἔφη Τὸ διαλαμβάνειν ὅτι πάντα διὰ παντὸς ὁ θεὸς ἐνεργεῖ καὶ γινώσκει, καὶ οὐθὲν ἂν λάθοι ἄδικον ποιήσας ἢ κακὸν ἐργασάμενος ἄνθρωπος· ὡς γὰρ θεὸς εὐεργετεῖ τὸν ὅλον κόσμον, οὕτως καὶ σὺ μιμούμενος ἀπρόσκοπος ἂν εἴης. ²¹¹Ἐπιφωνήσας δὲ τούτῳ πρὸς τὸν ἕτερον εἶπε Τίς ὅρος τοῦ βασιλεύειν ἐστίν; ὁ δὲ ἔφη Τὸ καλῶς ἄρχειν ἑαυτοῦ, καὶ μὴ τῷ πλούτῳ καὶ τῇ δόξῃ φερόμενον ὑπερήφανον καὶ ἄσχημόν τι ἐπιθυμῆσαι, εἰ καλῶς λογίζοιο. πάντα γάρ σοι πάρεστιν ὡς οὐδέν. ὁ θεὸς δὲ ἀπροσδεής ἐστι καὶ ἐπιεικής. καὶ σὺ καθόσον ἄνθρωπος ἐννόει, καὶ μὴ πολλῶν ὀρέγου, τῶν δὲ ἱκανῶν πρὸς τὸ βασιλεύειν. ²¹²Κατεπαινέσας δὲ αὐτόν, ἐπηρώτα τὸν ἕτερον Πῶς ἂν τὰ κάλλιστα διαλογίζοιτο; ἀπεκρίθη δὲ ἐκεῖνος Εἰ τὸ δίκαιον ἐπὶ παντὸς προβάλλοι συνεχῶς, καὶ νομίζοι τὴν

211 ως ουδεν W conjectures οσα δεον

209. TO KEEP ONESELF INCORRUPTIBLE . . . TO HONOR JUSTICE: *Cf.* Deut. 16.19–20, "Neither shalt thou take a gift; for a gift doth blind the eyes of the wise, and pervert the words of the righteous. Justice, justice shalt thou follow." *Cf.* also Prov. 29.4. But again, Greek ethics was also insistent on incorruptibility.
210. WORKING IN: *Energei* is a familiar technical term in Aristotelian (and other) philosophy. NO MAN DOING INJUSTICE . . . CAN ESCAPE HIS NOTICE: God's close surveillance of human injustice is familiar in Greek thought as far back as Hesiod (*Works and Days* 252 ff.). BENEFACTOR: This attribute of God is of course much older in Hebrew than in Greek thought, but *euergetes* as an epithet of divinity is common enough in the Hellenistic period; *cf.* its frequent application to deified rulers. IMITATING HIM: *Cf.* on 190.

him how he might be humane. And that man said, "By observing that the race of man comes to maturity and even to birth at the cost of much time and suffering; one must therefore not punish men on slight provocation nor inflict injuries upon them, realizing that human life is comprised of pains and penalties. Taking all things into consideration, then, you will turn to mercy, for God too is merciful."

[209]He gave this man his approval, and inquired of the one next in order, "What is the most essential quality of kingship?" "To keep oneself incorruptible," he replied, "to be sober the greater part of life, to honor justice, and to make friends of men of this character; for God too is a lover of righteousness."

[210]He applauded this man, and said to the next, "Wherein does piety consist?" That man declared, "In the realization that God is working in and has knowledge of all things at all times, and that no man doing injustice or working evil can escape His notice; for as God is the benefactor of the whole world, so would you, imitating him, be void of offense."

[211]He approved of this man, and said to the next, "What is the essence of kingship?" He declared, "To rule oneself well, and not to be carried away by wealth and fame into unseemly and extravagant desires—if you would reckon well. For to you all things needful are possible; God, to whom nothing is needful, is also gentle. Do you think such thoughts as become a man, and do not reach after many things, but only such as are sufficient for kingship."

[212]He complimented this man, and asked the next how his deliberations might be for the best. That man responded, "If in everything he constantly set justice before him and

---

211. TO RULE ONESELF WELL: *Cf.* Prov. 16.32, "And he that ruleth his spirit than he that taketh a city"; but the Delphic *gnōthe sauton* was interpreted in the same sense. Similarly THINK SUCH THOUGHTS AS BECOME A MAN can be parallelled in both traditions (the rabbinic "king of flesh and blood," and numerous tags in Sophocles); there is no need to follow Tramontano's suggestion *ad loc.* that this is a covert admonition against Ptolemaic deifications.

212. JUSTICE: A recurrent theme in the questions; *cf.* 188, 209.

ἀδικίαν τοῦ ζῆν στέρησιν εἶναι· καὶ γὰρ ὁ θεὸς διὰ παντὸς τοῖς δικαίοις ἀγαθὰ προσημαίνει μέγιστα. ²¹³Τοῦτον δὲ ἐπαινέσας εἶπε πρὸς τὸν ἑξῆς Πῶς ἂν ἐν τοῖς ὕπνοις ἀτάραχος εἴη; ὁ δὲ ἔφη Δυσαπολόγητον ἠρώτηκας πρᾶγμα. συναναφέρειν γὰρ οὐ δυνάμεθα ἐν τούτοις τοῖς κατὰ τὸν ὕπνον ἑαυτούς, ἀλλὰ περιεχόμεθα ἀλογίστῳ κατὰ <τάδε> αἰσθήσει. ²¹⁴πάσχομεν γὰρ κατὰ τὴν ψυχὴν ἐπὶ τοῖς ὑποπίπτουσιν ὡς θεωρουμένοις· ἀλογιστοῦμεν δέ, καθόσον ὑπολαμβάνομεν καὶ ἐπὶ πέλαγος καὶ ἐν πλοίοις ἢ πολεῖν, ἢ πέτασθαι φερομένους καὶ διαίρειν εἰς ἑτέρους τόπους, καὶ τοιαῦτα ἕτερα, †καὶ ὁ ταῦθ᾽ ὑπολαμβάνων μὴ καθεστάναι†. ²¹⁵πλὴν ὅσον ἔμοιγε ἐφικτόν, οὕτω διείληφα· κατὰ πάντα τρόπον σέ, βασιλεῦ, καὶ τὰ λεγόμενα καὶ τὰ πραττόμενα πρὸς εὐσέβειαν ἐπανάγειν, ὅπως <ἑαυτῷ> συνιστορῇς, ὅτι τὸ κατ᾽ ἀρετὴν συντηρῶν οὔτε χαρίζεσθαι προαιρῇ παρὰ λόγον, οὐδὲ ἐξουσίᾳ χρώμενος τὸ δίκαιον αἴρεις. ²¹⁶ἐπὶ πλεῖον γάρ, ἐν οἷς ἕκαστος πράγμασιν ἐγρηγορὼς τὴν διαγωγὴν ποιεῖται, καὶ καθ᾽ ὕπνον ἐν τοῖς αὐτοῖς ἡ διάνοια τὴν ἀναστροφὴν ἔχει, †ὡς δὲ† πάντα διαλογισμὸν καὶ πρᾶξιν ἐπὶ τὰ κάλλιστα τρεπομένην κατευθύνει καὶ ἐγρηγορὼς καὶ ἐν ὕπνῳ. διὸ καὶ περὶ σὲ διὰ παντός ἐστιν εὐστάθεια. ²¹⁷Κατευφημήσας δὲ καὶ τοῦτον εἶπε πρὸς ἕτερον Ἐπεὶ σὺ δέκατος τὴν ἀπόκρισιν ἔχεις, ὡς ἂν ἀποφήνῃ, πρὸς τὸ δεῖπνον τραπησόμεθα. ²¹⁸ἠρώτα δέ Πῶς ἂν μηδὲν ἀνάξιον ἑαυτῶν πράσσοιμεν; ὁ δὲ εἶπεν Ἐπίβλεπε διὰ παντὸς εἰς τὴν σεαυτοῦ δόξαν καὶ τὴν ὑπεροχήν, ἵνα τούτοις ἀκόλουθα καὶ λέγῃς καὶ διανοῇ, γινώσκων ὅτι πάντες ὧν

---

213 ταδε T-Mend., τηδε MSS, W conjectures ταδε τη
214 και ο ταυθ᾽ υπολαμβανων μη καθεσταναι 'locus perobscurus' — T, Schmidt suggests και τοιαυθ᾽ ετερα υπολαμβανομεν καθεσταναι, W καιτοι ταυθ᾽ υπολαμβανομεν κ., T α κατα ταυθ᾽ υπολαμβανομεν κ.
215 εαυτω edd., εαυτου MSS
216 ως δε MSS, ος δε Schard, θεος δε T's trans., altering εγρηγορως to εγρηγοροτος, W prints ος δε and suggests εχει after τρεπομενην

213–216. The psychology of dreams and their validity as presages of the future were very common themes of investigation among the Hellenistic philosophers of all schools, and especially the Peripatetic and Stoic; Demetrius of Phalerum himself also wrote one such treatise. Philo too

regarded injustice as deprivation of life; for God also always promises the greatest blessings to the just."

²¹³He commended this man, and asked the man next in order how he might be undisturbed in his sleep. He declared, "You have asked a question hard to answer, for in sleep we are not able to bring our true selves into play, but are held fast by sensations in which reason has no part. ²¹⁴In our minds we have the experience of actually seeing the things which pass before us, but we are unreasonable if we suppose that we are indeed on shipboard traversing the sea or borne aloft on wings and passing to other climes and doing other such things which we then suppose to be taking place. ²¹⁵Nevertheless, insofar as I for my part have been able to arrive at a solution, this is my understanding of the matter. In every way, Your Majesty, you must make piety the objective of whatever you say and do, so that you may be certain in your own mind that, adhering to virtue, you do not choose to grant favors contrary to reason nor, abusing your power, set justice aside. ²¹⁶For as a rule, the same business to which a man gives his attention while awake, his mind occupies itself with in sleep also, and he who has his every thought and action set towards the best ends is well directed both awake and asleep. And therefore with you there is always tranquillity."

²¹⁷This man too he extolled, and said to the next, "Since yours is the tenth turn to answer, when you have made your response we shall turn to the meal." Then he asked, "How can we avoid doing anything unworthy of ourselves?" ²¹⁸And he said, "Always look to your own fame and eminence, so that what you say and think may be in keeping with them, knowing that all men over whom you rule think and talk

---

devotes two treatises to the subject, but it is clear that the source here is secular and not Jewish philosophy.

216. THE SAME BUSINESS TO WHICH A MAN GIVES HIS ATTENTION WHILE AWAKE: An echo of Artabanus' advice to Xerxes in Herodotus 7.16.   AND HE WHO: An emendation suggested by Thackeray would yield the translation "but God directs"; the alteration is plausible, for the concluding words of other responses mention the name of God.

ἄρχεις περὶ σοῦ καὶ διανοοῦνται καὶ λαλοῦσιν. ²¹⁹οὐ γὰρ ἐλάχιστόν σε δεῖ τῶν ὑποκριτῶν φαίνεσθαι· τὸ γὰρ πρόσωπον, <ὃ δέον αὐτοῖς> ἐστιν ὑποκρίνεσθαι, τοῦτο συνθεωροῦντες ἀκόλουθα πάντα πράσσουσι· σὺ δὲ οὐχ ὑπόκρισιν ἔχεις, ἀλλ' ἀληθῶς βασιλεύεις, θεοῦ δόντος σοι καταξίως τῶν τρόπων τὴν ἡγεμονίαν. ²²⁰Τοῦ δὲ βασιλέως εὖ μάλα συγκροτήσαντος μετὰ φιλοφροσύνης ἐπὶ πλείονα χρόνον, τοὺς ἀνθρώπους καθυπνοῦν παρεκάλουν. καὶ τὰ μὲν πρὸς τούτους ὡς ἔληξεν ἐπὶ τὴν ἑξῆς ἐτράπησαν τῆς συμποσίας διάταξιν.

²²¹Τῇ δὲ ἐχομένῃ, τῆς αὐτῆς διατάξεως γενηθείσης, ὅτε καιρὸν ὑπελάμβανεν ὁ βασιλεὺς εἶναι τοῦ πυνθάνεσθαί τι τῶν ἀνδρῶν, ἠρώτα τὸν πρῶτον τῶν ἀπολιπόντων πρὸς τὴν ἑξῆς ἐρώτησιν Τίς ἐστιν ἀρχὴ κρατίστη; ²²²ἐκεῖνος δὲ ἔφη Τὸ κρατεῖν ἑαυτοῦ καὶ μὴ συγκαταφέρεσθαι ταῖς ὁρμαῖς. πᾶσι γὰρ ἀνθρώποις φυσικὸν εἶναι τὸ πρός τι τὴν διάνοιαν ῥέπειν· ²²³τοῖς μὲν οὖν πολλοῖς ἐπὶ τὰ βρωτὰ καὶ ποτὰ καὶ τὰς ἡδονὰς εἰκός ἐστι κεκλίσθαι, τοῖς δὲ βασιλεῦσιν ἐπὶ χώρας κατάκτησιν, κατὰ τὸ τῆς δόξης μέγεθος· πλὴν ἐν πᾶσι μετριότης καλόν. ἃ δὲ ὁ θεὸς δίδωσι, ταῦτα λαμβάνων σύνεχε· τῶν δ' ἀνεφίκτων μὴ ἐπιθύμει. ²²⁴Τοῖς δὲ ῥηθεῖσιν ἀρεσθεὶς πρὸς τὸν ἐχόμενον εἶπε Πῶς ἂν ἐκτὸς εἴη φθόνου; διαλιπὼν δὲ ἐκεῖνος ἔφη Πρῶτον εἰ νοῆσαι, ὅτι ὁ θεὸς πᾶσι μερίζει δόξαν τε καὶ πλούτου μέγεθος τοῖς βασιλεῦσι, καὶ οὐδεὶς περὶ ἑαυτόν ἐστι βασιλεύς· πάντες γὰρ θέλουσι μετασχεῖν ταύτης τῆς δόξης, ἀλλ' οὐ δύνανται·

---

219 ο δεον αυτοις T, ο δεον αυτους W, (see exeg. note)
    ουδε αυτο MSS
220 καθυπνουν W suggests καταπαυειν
224 περι εαυτον MSS-T, παρ' εαυτον MSS-W

---

219. ACTORS: The figure is commonplace, especially among Stoics; cf. Epictetus, *Encheiridion* 17, "Thou art an actor in a drama ... It is thy part to act well the character given thee." But it is rather a strange figure for the Palestinian "priests" to use.

220. TO TAKE SOME REST: The Greek has *kathupnoun*, "to go to sleep"— which makes the sentence following strange. Either the sentences should be transposed, or we should read *katapauein*, with Wendland. The translation offered is a straddle.

222. TO RULE ONESELF: Cf. 211. For parallels in Philo see Wolfson 2.236, and cf. *Abot* 4.1, "Who is mighty? He that subdues his *yezer*. Who is rich? He

about you. ²¹⁹You ought not to show yourself inferior to the actors, for they look to the role they must play and suit their actions to it. You, however, are not playing a part, but are truly king, God having granted you the leadership which your character merits."

220 ²²⁰When the king had graciously applauded loud and long, the guests were urged to take some rest. And when the discourse with these men was ended, they addressed themselves to the next order of the banquet.

²²¹On the succeeding day the same order was followed, and when the king judged the time was come for making inquiries of the men he asked the first in turn of those left for questioning, "What is the highest rule?" ²²²That man declared, "To rule oneself and not to be carried away by passions. In the temper of all men there is some innate proclivity. ²²³In the majority it is likely that the cant is towards food and drink and pleasure, while for kings it is acquisition of territory and extent of fame. Yet in all things moderation is a good principle. What God gives take and hold; do not long for what is out of reach."

²²⁴The king was pleased with what he had said, and asked his neighbor how he might be beyond envy. After a pause he declared, "If you reflect, first of all, that it is God who apportions fame and great wealth to all kings, and that no one is king by his own power. All men wish to partake of this glory, but they cannot, for it is a gift of God."

---

that is contented with his portion." On the other hand, control of passions was similarly stressed by the Stoics and others. *Cf.* 108 and note on 273.

223. FOR KINGS IT IS ACQUISITION OF TERRITORY: A reflection of the study of "characters," as practised by the Peripatetics and illustrated by Theophrastus' *Characters;* these are the traits of the *anēr basilikos: cf.* Aristotle, *Politics* 1285b.

224. ENVY: One of the "perturbations of the soul" which the Stoics sought to remove; *Test. XII Patriarchs, Simeon* makes the story of Joseph the text for a treatise on envy.   NO ONE IS KING BY HIS OWN POWER: In biblical history kings are of course divinely elected; *cf.* also Ben Sirah 10.4 and Wisd. 6.3. But Hellenistic theory also arrived at the notion of the divine right of kings, culminating in the principle that the king is *nomos empsychos*, "law incarnate."

225 θεοῦ γάρ ἐστι δόμα. ²²⁵Ἐπαινέσας δὲ τὸν ἄνδρα διὰ πλειόνων ἐπηρώτα τὸν ἕτερον Πῶς ἂν καταφρονοίη τῶν ἐχθρῶν; ὁ δὲ εἶπεν Ἠσκηκὼς πρὸς πάντας ἀνθρώπους εὔνοιαν καὶ κατεργασάμενος φιλίας, λόγον οὐθενὸς ἂν ἔχοις· τὸ δὲ κεχαριτῶσθαι πρὸς πάντας ἀνθρώπους καὶ καλὸν δῶρον εἰληφέναι παρὰ θεοῦ τοῦτ' ἔστι κράτιστον. ²²⁶Συναινέσας δὲ τούτοις τὸν ἑξῆς ἐκέλευσεν ἀποκριθῆναι, πρὸς αὐτὸν εἰπών Πῶς ἂν δοξαζόμενος διαμένοι; εἶπε δέ Τῇ προθυμίᾳ καὶ ταῖς χάρισι πρὸς τοὺς ἄλλους μεταδοτικὸς ὢν καὶ μεγαλομερὴς οὐδέποτ' ἂν ἀπολίποι δόξης· ἵνα δὲ τὰ προειρημένα σοι διαμένῃ, τὸν θεὸν ἐπικαλοῦ διὰ παντός. ²²⁷Εὐφημήσας δὲ τοῦτον ἕτερον ἠρώτα Πῶς τινα δεῖ φιλότιμον εἶναι; ἐκεῖνος δὲ ἔφη Πρὸς τοὺς φιλικῶς ἔχοντας ἡμῖν οἴονται πάντες ὅτι πρὸς τούτους δέον· ἐγὼ δ' ὑπολαμβάνω, πρὸς τοὺς ἀντιδοξοῦντας φιλοτιμίαν δεῖν χαριστικὴν ἔχειν, ἵνα τούτῳ τῷ τρόπῳ μετάγωμεν αὐτοὺς ἐπὶ τὸ καθῆκον καὶ συμφέρον ἑαυτοῖς. δεῖ δὲ τὸν θεὸν λιτανεύειν, ἵνα ταῦτ' ἐπιτελῆται· τὰς γὰρ ἁπάντων διανοίας κρατεῖ. ²²⁸Συνομολογήσας δὲ τούτοις τὸν ἕκτον ἐκέλευσεν ἀποφήνασθαι πυνθανόμενος Τίσι δεῖ χαρίζεσθαι; ἐκεῖνος δ' ἀπεκρίθη Γονεῦσι διὰ παντός, καὶ γὰρ ὁ θεὸς πεποίηται ἐντολὴν μεγίστην περὶ τῆς τῶν γονέων τιμῆς. ἑπομένως δὲ τὴν τῶν φίλων ἐγκρίνει διάθεσιν, προσονομάσας ICON TH ΨΥΧΗ ΤΟΝ ΦΙΛΟΝ. σὺ δὲ καλῶς ποιεῖς ἅπαντας ἀνθρώπους εἰς φιλίαν πρὸς ἑαυτὸν καθιστῶν. ²²⁹Παρακαλέσας δὲ καὶ τοῦτον

---

225 και καλον ... κρατιστον MSS, W
suggests και καλην δοξαν ειληφεναι
δωρον παρα, T (tr.) emends to και
καλων δωρων
227 Πως τινα MSS-T, προς τινα W

---

225. BENEVOLENCE: Note similarity to 194.
226. RENOWN: *Doxa* was a far more important goal, and motivation for conduct in Greek than in Hebrew thought, yet we have such passages as Sirah 41.13: "A good life hath its number of days; and a good name continueth forever." *Cf.* 279, 292.
226. LIBERAL AND MUNIFICENT . . . KIND ATTENTIVENESS AND ACTS OF GRACE: These and similar qualities become prominent in Hellenistic philosophic writing, and were probably stressed in "mirrors of princes."
227. LIBERALITY TO THOSE OF AN OPPOSITE OPINION: A reflection of another Hellenistic mitigation of Oriental despotism, as reflected also in the Hecataeus passage: see Introd. 44. Respect for the opinions of others is mentioned as a laudable trait of the translators at 122.

225 ²²⁵He commended the man in many words, and asked the next how he might despise his enemies. And he said, "If you have practised benevolence towards all men and have achieved friendships, you need reckon with no man. But to stand in all men's favor and to receive a good gift from God, that is of all things the best."

²²⁶He commended these sentiments, and bade the next man reply to the question how he might retain his renown. He said, "If you are liberal and munificent to all, with kind attentiveness and acts of grace, you will never lack renown; but that these qualities abide with you, call always upon God."

²²⁷He congratulated him, and asked the next with whom one should vie in liberality. That man declared, "That we must be liberal to those who are friendly disposed towards us is the opinion of all men; but I hold that we should show a bounteous liberality to those of an opposite opinion, so that by this means we might win them over to what is right and advantageous to themselves. But one must entreat God that these things be brought to pass, for He rules the minds of all men."

²²⁸He agreed with these words, and bade the sixth man answer the query, "To whom should favor be shown?" That man responded, "To parents always, for God has given the greatest commandment concerning honor to parents. Next He reckons the state of friendship, for He calls 'a friend the equal of a man's soul.' But you do well in turning all men to friendship to yourself."

²²⁹He spoke kindly to this man also, and asked the man

---

228. TO PARENTS ALWAYS: It is not necessary to assume that this is a direct echo of the fifth commandment, for Greek ethics also demanded that parents be honored; cf., e.g. Plato, Laws 4.717B.   FRIEND THE EQUAL: LXX Deut. 13.6, where, however, "equal" is descriptive and not a predicate. Aristotle defined "friend" as "a single soul dwelling in two bodies" (Diogenes Laertius, 5.20).

229. PIETY: In 210 piety is defined as realization of God's omniscience and providence, and at 2 it is called the greatest good of all, and an unerring gauge for guidance. Hence it can be spoken of as THE DEGREE OF BEAUTY, which is naturally associated with LOVE (for fellow men). But the response seems epigrammatic, and somewhat enigmatic by intention.

ἐπυνθάνετο καὶ τοῦ μετέπειτα Τί καλλονῆς ἄξιόν ἐστιν; ὁ δὲ εἶπεν Εὐσέβεια. καὶ γὰρ αὕτη καλλονή τίς ἐστι πρωτεύουσα. τὸ δὲ δυνατὸν αὐτῆς ἐστιν ἀγάπη· αὕτη γὰρ θεοῦ δόσις ἐστίν· ἣν καὶ σὺ κέκτησαι πάντα περιέχων ἐν
230 αὐτῇ τὰ ἀγαθά. 230Λίαν δὲ φιλοφρόνως ἐπικροτήσας εἶπε πρὸς τὸν ἕτερον Πῶς ἂν πταίσας πάλιν τῆς αὐτῆς κρατῆσαι δόξης; ὁ δὲ ἔφη, Σὲ μὲν οὐ δυνατόν ἐστι πταῖσαι, πᾶσι γὰρ χάριτας ἔσπαρκας, αἳ βλαστάνουσιν εὔνοιαν, ἣ τὰ μέγιστα τῶν ὅπλων κατισχύουσα περιλαμβάνει τὴν μεγίστην ἀσφάλειαν· 231εἰ δέ τινες πταίουσιν, ἐφ' οἷς πταίουσιν, οὐκέτι χρὴ ταῦτα πράσσειν, ἀλλὰ φιλίαν κατακτησαμένους δικαιοπραγεῖν. θεοῦ δὲ δῶρον ἀγαθῶν ἐργάτην εἶναι καὶ μὴ τῶν ἐναντίων. 232Συναρεσθεὶς δὲ τούτοις πρὸς τὸν ἕτερον εἶπε Πῶς ἂν ἐκτὸς γένοιτο λύπης; ὁ δὲ ἔφησεν Εἰ μηδένα βλάπτοι, πάντας δὲ ὠφελοῖ, τῇ δικαιοσύνῃ κατακολουθῶν· τοὺς γὰρ ἀπ' αὐτῆς καρποὺς ἀλυπίαν κατασκευάζειν. 233ἱκετεύειν δὲ τὸν θεόν, ἵνα μὴ τὰ παρὰ τὴν προαίρεσιν ἡμῶν ἀνακύπτοντα βλάπτῃ, λέγω δὴ οἷον θάνατοί τε καὶ νόσοι καὶ λῦπαι καὶ τὰ τοιαῦτα. <αὐτῷ> δὲ σοὶ εὐσεβεῖ καθεστῶτι τούτων οὐδὲν ἂν προσέλθοι. 234Καλῶς δὲ καὶ τοῦτον ἐπαινέσας τὸν δέκατον ἠρώτα Τί μέγιστόν ἐστι

---

233 αυτω T, MSS omit, W reads
ευσεβει δε σοι

230. FOR YOU IT IS NOT POSSIBLE TO FAIL: An extremely courtierlike retort, but the question is in any case answered in the FOR . . . YOU HAVE clause.
231. BUT IF ANY DO: Continues the tone of courtesy, attributing the possibility of failure only to the generalized third person, and then prescribing the remedy.   GIFT OF GOD: In Wisd. man is said to be unable to obtain wisdom without the help of God, and one of the conditions for obtaining the help of God is knowledge that wisdom is a gift of God for which one must pray (8.21), and that if one prays for it it will be given him (7.7); see Wolfson, *Philo* 1.449. Besides this passage, divine grace is referred to also in 236, 237, 238; on the doctrine of grace in Hellenistic Judaism, see A. D. Nock, *St. Paul* (Home Univ. Library, 1938), 75.
232. GRIEF: The chief "perturbation" against which Hellenistic philosophies sought to arm their adherents—as here, BY INJURING NO MAN etc.
233. BUT ONE MUST SUPPLICATE: A particularly characteristic example of our author's treatments of his original *Questions;* in logic prayers to avert grief have nothing to do with encountering grief philosophically; rendering *blaptē* by "stun" helps the logic.   BUT YOU: A graceful compliment to

following, "What is of like value with beauty?" And he said, "Piety, for piety is the first degree of beauty; its power is love, love is the gift of God. This you possess, embracing in it all that is good."

230 ²³⁰He applauded his reply very warmly, and asked the next how, after a failure, he might regain possession of the esteem he had had before. That man declared, "For you it is not possible to fail, for in all men you have inseminated favor, which burgeons into good will, which is the best of armor and when retained affords the greatest security. ²³¹But if any do fail, they must no longer do the things in which they fail, but beget friendships and act justly. But to be a worker of good deeds and not of the opposite sort is a gift of God."

²³²He was well satisfied with these remarks, and asked the next man how he might be beyond grief. He declared, "By injuring no man and helping all men and following righteousness, for the fruits of righteousness procure freedom from grief. ²³³But one must supplicate God that unforeseen blows may not stun us, I mean such things as deaths and diseases and griefs and the like. But you, who are firm in piety, none of these tribulations may approach."

²³⁴He commended him handsomely also, and asked the tenth man, "What is the highest form of glory?" And he

---

the king is combined with an assertion of the doctrine of retribution.
234. TO HONOR GOD: This does not seem, without rather involved exegesis, relevant to a question on "glory" (*doxa*); furthermore, making *to honor God* so directly the answer, and then specifying a spiritual approach for such honor, is out of keeping with our author's regular practice, where the devout additions are added on after a secular response. Perhaps Aristeas was awkward in altering something which struck him as unsuitable in his model; textual corruption would hardly explain the difficulty. NOT BY OFFERINGS AND SACRIFICES: At 170 sacrifices are not eliminated, but explained symbolically; at 172 the High Priest himself offers sacrifice, apparently to secure a safe journey for the translators. For the spiritualization of the notion of sacrifice, *cf.* II Enoch 45.3: "When the Lord demands bread or candles or flesh or any other sacrifice, then that is nothing; but God demands pure hearts . . . " and especially Philo, *On the Plantation*, 30: "It is impossible to show gratitude to God in a genuine manner by those means which people in general think the only ones, namely, offerings and sacrifices; for the whole world could not be a temple worthy to be raised to

δόξης; ὁ δὲ εἶπε Τὸ τιμᾶν τὸν θεόν· τοῦτο δ' ἐστὶν οὐ δώροις οὐδὲ θυσίαις, ἀλλὰ ψυχῆς καθαρότητι καὶ διαλήψεως ὁσίας, καθὼς ὑπὸ τοῦ θεοῦ πάντα κατασκευάζεται καὶ διοικεῖται κατὰ τὴν αὐτοῦ βούλησιν· ἣν καὶ σὺ διατελεῖς ἔχων γνώμην, ᾗ πάρεστι σημειοῦσθαι πᾶσιν ἐκ τῶν ὑπὸ σοῦ συντετελεσ-
235 μένων καὶ συντελουμένων. ²³⁵Μετὰ μείζονος δὲ φωνῆς πάντας αὐτοὺς ὁ βασιλεὺς ἠσπάζετο καὶ παρεκάλει, συνεπιφωνούντων τῶν παρόντων, μάλιστα δὲ τῶν φιλοσόφων. καὶ γὰρ ταῖς ἀγωγαῖς καὶ τῷ λόγῳ πολὺ προέχοντες αὐτῶν ἦσαν, ὡς ἂν ἀπὸ θεοῦ τὴν καταρχὴν ποιούμενοι. μετὰ δὲ ταῦτα ὁ βασιλεὺς εἰς τὸ φιλοφρονεῖσθαι προῆλθε διὰ τῶν προπόσεων.

²³⁶Τῇ δὲ ἐπιούσῃ κατὰ τὰ αὐτὰ τῆς διατάξεως τοῦ συμποσίου γενομένης, καθὼς εὔκαιρον ἐγένετο τῷ βασιλεῖ, τοὺς ἑξῆς ἠρώτα τῶν προαποκεκριμένων, εἶπε δὲ τῷ πρώτῳ Τὸ φρονεῖν εἰ διδακτόν ἐστιν; ὃς δ' εἶπε Ψυχῆς ἐστι κατασκευὴ διὰ θείας δυνάμεως ἐπιδέχεσθαι πᾶν τὸ καλόν, ἀποστρέφεσθαι δὲ τἀναντία. ²³⁷Συνομολογήσας δὲ τὸν ἐχόμενον ἠρώτα Τί πρὸς ὑγείαν μάλιστα συντείνει; ἐκεῖνος δὲ ἔφη Σωφροσύνη· ταύτης δὲ οὐκ ἔστι τυχεῖν, ἐὰν μὴ θεὸς κατασκευάσῃ τὴν διάνοιαν εἰς τοῦτο. ²³⁸Παρακαλέσας δὲ τοῦτον πρὸς τὸν ἕτερον ἔφη Πῶς ἂν γονεῦσι τὰς ἀξίας ἀποδώῃ χάριτας; ὃς δὲ εἶπε Μηδὲν αὐτοὺς λυπήσας· τοῦτο δ' οὐκ ἔστιν, εἰ μὴ θεὸς τῆς διανοίας ἡγεμὼν γένοιτο πρὸς τὰ κάλλιστα. ²³⁹Προσεπινεύσας δὲ τούτῳ τὸν ἑξῆς ἠρώτα

239 ανθυποτιθεις MSS-T, –τιθης W / αν αντιπρασσηται MSS-T αν α. W

His honor, except by means of praises and hymns, and those too must be such as are sung not by loud voices but by the invisible and pure mind, which shall raise the shout and song to Him."

235. FAR IN ADVANCE OF THE PHILOSOPHERS: *Cf.* Dan. 1.20 (probably not far removed in date from Aristeas), "And in all matters of wisdom and understanding that the king inquired of them, he found them ten times better than all the magicians and enchanters that were in all his realm." This passage shows why Aristeas added the devout tags to the responses. The attitude to the philosophers is by no means contemptuous, and their approval is particularly cherished; but they realize the peculiar (and sole) distinction of the Jewish view.

236. THE SOUL'S CONSTITUTION IS SUCH, even according to the philosophic schools, THAT IT CAN ACCEPT . . . AND REJECT; what appears to be added here, in keeping with the additions to other responses, is BY DIVINE POWER.

said, "To honor God, and that not by offerings and sacrifices but by purity of spirit and of the devout conviction that all things are fashioned and administered by God according to His will. And this is your abiding belief, as all men may discern from your actions in the past and in the present."

235 ²³⁵Then with a fuller voice the king greeted them all and spoke kindly to them, with the others present, especially the philosophers, joining in the commendation. For in their conduct and discourse these men were far in advance of the philosophers, for they made their starting-point from God. And after this the king proceeded to show his kindly feelings by drinking healths.

²³⁶On the following day, as the order of the banquet took the same course, when the king's opportunity came he began to question those next in order to the ones who had already given responses, and said to the first, "Can wisdom be taught?" And he replied, "The soul's constitution is such, by divine power, that it can accept all that is good and reject what is the contrary."

²³⁷He expressed his assent, and asked of his neighbor,"What contributes most to health?" That man declared, "Temperance; but this cannot be attained unless God dispose the mind to it."

²³⁸He spoke kindly to this man, and asked the next how one might render due thanks to parents. And he said, "By not distressing them; but this is not possible unless God becomes the mind's guide towards all that is best."

²³⁹He agreed fully with this man, and asked the next how

Cf. Prov. 8.14 and Wisd. 7.16.
237. TEMPERANCE: Again the common secular prescription for health, and UNLESS GOD DISPOSE THE MIND the pious addition.
238. PARENTS: See on 228.   BY NOT DISTRESSING THEM: Ben Sirah 3.12 has the identical verb in a similar context. Philadelphus' own parents were surely dead at the time imagined, and this shows the theoretical character of the entire catechism.
239. WHATEVER BEFALL YOU MAY CHOOSE SOMETHING YOU HAVE HEARD AND APPLY IT: This is a commonplace justification for education, as *e.g.* in Plutarch's *How the Young Man Should Study Poetry;* the pious addition is WITH GOD'S GUIDING HAND, etc.

Πῶς ἂν φιλήκοος εἴη; ἐκεῖνος δὲ εἶπε Διαλαμβάνων ὅτι πάντα συμφέρει γινώσκειν, ὅπως ἂν πρὸς τὰ συμβαίνοντα ἐκλεγόμενός τι τῶν ἠκροαμένων ἀνθυποτιθεὶς πρὸς τὰ τῶν καιρῶν †ἂν ἀντιπράσσηται†, σὺν χειραγωγίᾳ θεοῦ· τοῦτο 240 δ' ἐστίν, αἱ τῶν πράξεων τελειώσεις ὑπ' αὐτοῦ. ²⁴⁰Τοῦτον δὲ ἐπαινέσας πρὸς τὸν ἕτερον εἶπε Πῶς ἂν μηθὲν παράνομον πράσσοι; πρὸς τοῦτο ἔφησε Γινώσκων ὅτι τὰς ἐπινοίας ὁ θεὸς ἔδωκε τοῖς νομοθετήσασι πρὸς τὸ σώζεσθαι τοὺς βίους τῶν ἀνθρώπων, ἀκόλουθος εἴης ἂν αὐτοῖς. ²⁴¹Ἀποδεξάμενος δὲ αὐτὸν πρὸς ἕτερον εἶπε Τίς ὠφέλεια συγγενείας ἐστίν; ὁ δὲ ἀπεφήνατο Ἐὰν τοῖς συμβαίνουσι νομίζωμεν ἀτυχοῦσι μὲν ἐλαττοῦσθαι, καὶ κακοπαθῶμεν ὡς αὐτοί, φαίνεται τὸ συγγενὲς ὅσον ἰσχυόν ἐστι— ²⁴²τελουμένων δὲ τούτων καὶ δόξα καὶ προκοπὴ παρὰ τοῖς τοιούτοις ὑπάρξει· τὸ γὰρ συνεργὲς εὐνόως γινόμενον ὡς ἐξ ἑαυτοῦ ἀδιάλυτον πρὸς ἅπαντα—μετὰ δὲ εὐημερίας, μηδὲν προσδεῖσθαι τῶν ἐκείνων· ἀλλὰ δέον <θεὸν> ἱκετεύειν, πάντα ἀγαθοποιεῖν. ²⁴³Ὡσαύτως δὲ ἐκείνοις ἀποδεξάμενος αὐτὸν ἄλλον ἠρώτα Πῶς ἀφοβία γίνεται; εἶπε δέ Συνιστορούσης τῆς διανοίας μηδὲν κακὸν πεπραχέναι, θεοῦ κατευθύνοντος εἰς τὸ καλῶς ἅπαντα βουλεύεσθαι. ²⁴⁴Τούτῳ δὲ ἐπιφωνήσας πρὸς ἄλλον εἶπε Πῶς ἂν προχείρως ἔχοι τὸν ὀρθὸν λόγον; ὁ δὲ εἶπεν Εἰ τὰ τῶν ἀνθρώπων ἀτυχήματα διὰ παντὸς ἐπιβλέποι· γι-

---

242 το γαρ συνεργες κ. τ. λ. probably corrupt, W conjectures something like το γαρ συμπαθες ευνοως γινομενον δεσμον εξαπτεται αδιαλυτον προς αυτους απαντωντων δε απαντων μετα ευημεριας / <θεον> edd.

243 After Συνιστορουσης W suggests εαυτη

---

240. GOD PUT THE THOUGHTS IN THE MIND OF THE LAWGIVERS: The divine inspiration of the traditional nomothetes such as Lycurgus, Solon, and others was accepted in pagan thought even before the Stoics taught their doctrines of divine providence; the direct and specific use of *God* here may be an adaptation. Apparently the author conceives that the principle here stated would apply to Moses also, with the interesting implication that his legislation was not dictated in detail but that he devised it under a general mandate and inspiration: see Introd. 63.   FOR THE SAKE OF PRESERVING THE LIVES OF MEN: Fits with this concept and with the notion that the ritual prescriptions are intended mainly as a symbol and support for ethical conduct.

241. KINSHIP: It is probable that the reference here is not to relationship by blood but by office, "kin" like "friend" being used in the Persian and

he might become a ready listener. That man answered, "By understanding that knowledge is all profitable, so that whatever befall you may choose something you have heard and apply it to the crisis, with God's guiding hand; for it remains that the consummations of all deeds are His."

240 ²⁴⁰He commended this man, and asked the next how he might avoid doing anything contrary to law. To this he declared, "If you know that God put the thoughts in the mind of the lawgivers for the sake of preserving the lives of men you will become a follower of them."

²⁴¹He approved of this man, and said to the next, "What is the advantage of kinship?" And he explained, "If we consider that we ourselves lose by the misfortunes that befall them and share in our kin's suffering, the strength of kinship is evident. ²⁴²If we react in this way, our esteem and attainments will rise in their regard, for an active and kindly sympathy is in itself an indissoluble bond in all circumstances. But in their day of prosperity we should crave nothing of them, but supplicate God to give them every boon."

²⁴³He approved of this man as he had done the rest, and asked another, "How is fearlessness attained?" And he said, "When the mind is conscious that it has done no evil, God directing it so that all its counsels are good."

²⁴⁴He assented to this man, and of another asked how he might have right reason always at hand. He answered, "If he looked always at the misfortunes of men, understanding that

---

Ptolemaic courts as a title of preferment.
242. RISE IN THEIR REGARD: Naming this advantage corroborates the suggestion that the "kin" are here court officials. SUPPLICATE GOD seems to be the usual pious addition.
243. FEARLESSNESS (and the "virtues" in the sections following) are the regular objects of Hellenistic ethical teaching, especially Stoic, and WHEN THE MIND IS CONSCIOUS THAT IT HAS DONE NO EVIL is an application of the Stoic prescription that externals are to be classed as "things indifferent." GOD DIRECTING: The pious addition.
244. RIGHT REASON (*orthos logos*): A technical expression in Stoicism, and the response is in keeping with the Stoic doctrine of "things indifferent." Alternations in fortune is a Greek as well as Hebrew commonplace, but making GOD the agent is the Jewish touch.

νώσκων ὅτι ὁ θεὸς ἀφαιρεῖται τὰς εὐημερίας, ἑτέρους δὲ δοξάζων εἰς τὸ τιμᾶσθαι προάγει. ²⁴⁵Καλῶς δὲ καὶ τοῦτον ἀποδεξάμενος τὸν ἑξῆς ἀποκριθῆναι παρεκάλει Πῶς ἂν μὴ εἰς ῥαθυμίαν, μηδὲ ἐπὶ τὰς ἡδονὰς τρέποιτο; ὁ δέ Προχείρως ἔχων, εἶπεν, ὅτι μεγάλης βασιλείας κατάρχει καὶ πολλῶν ὄχλων ἀφηγεῖται, καὶ οὐ δεῖ περὶ ἕτερόν τι τὴν διάνοιαν εἶναι, τῆς δὲ τούτων ἐπιμελείας φροντίζειν· θεὸν δὲ ἀξιοῦν, ὅπως μηθὲν ἐλλίπῃ τῶν καθηκόντων. ²⁴⁶Ἐπαινέσας δὲ καὶ τοῦτον τὸν δέκατον <ἠρώτα Πῶς ἂν ἐπιγινώσκοι> τοὺς δόλῳ τινὶ πρὸς αὐτὸν πράσσοντας; ὁ δὲ ἀπεφήνατο πρὸς τοῦτο Εἰ παρατηροῖτο τὴν ἀγωγὴν ἐλευθέριον οὖσαν, καὶ τὴν εὐταξίαν διαμένουσαν ἐν τοῖς ἀσπασμοῖς καὶ συμβουλίαις καὶ τῇ λοιπῇ συναναστροφῇ τῶν σὺν αὐτῷ, καὶ μηθὲν ὑπερτείνοντας τοῦ δέοντος ἐν ταῖς φιλοφρονήσεσι καὶ τοῖς λοιποῖς τοῖς κατὰ τὴν ἀγωγήν. ²⁴⁷Θεὸς δὲ τὴν διάνοιαν <ἄξει> σοι, βασιλεῦ, πρὸς τὰ κάλλιστα. Συγκροτήσας πάντας τ' ἐπαινέσας κατ' ὄνομα, καὶ τῶν παρόντων ταὐτὰ ποιούντων, ἐπὶ τὸ μέλπειν ἐτράπησαν.

²⁴⁸Τῇ δὲ ἐχομένῃ τὸν καιρὸν λαβὼν ἐπηρώτα τὸν ἑξῆς Τίς ἐστιν ἀμέλεια μεγίστη; πρὸς τοῦτ' ἔφη Εἰ τέκνων ἄφροντίς τις εἴη, καὶ μὴ κατὰ πάντα τρόπον ἀγαγεῖν <σπεύδοι>· εὐχόμεθα γὰρ ἀεὶ πρὸς τὸν θεόν, οὐχ οὕτως περὶ ἑαυτῶν ὡς περὶ τῶν ἐγγόνων, ἵνα παρῇ πάντα αὐτοῖς τὰ ἀγαθά. τὸ δὲ ἐπιδεῖσθαι παιδία σωφροσύνης μετασχεῖν, θεοῦ δυνάμει τοῦτο γίνεται. ²⁴⁹Φήσας δὲ εὐλογεῖν ἄλλον

---

246 ηρωτα most MSS have ερωτα / αν supplied by edd. / επιγινωσκοι most MSS have επιγινωσκει
247 αξει edd., εξει MSS
248 σπευδοι edd. for MSS lacuna / επιδεισθαι ('desire') T-MSS, επιδεσθαι ('see') W / παιδια edd.-MS, παιδιαν MSS

245. THINK ALWAYS OF THE CARE OF THESE CHARGES: This is a specific echo of the Stoic concept of king as minister, as against the oriental concept of king as master; cf. Seneca, Thyestes 204 ff. HE MUST PRAY GOD: A clear example of the pious tag.
246. GUILE: What appears to be intended, as the response suggests, is the assumption of undue authority by court officials in controlling deliberations and diplomatic relations; the reign most liable to such criticism was that of Ptolemy IV Philopator (222–205).
248. SUCCEEDING DAY: The questions of the fifth day appear to have no special relevance to kingship, except insofar as a king must provide a pattern for ethical conduct, and especially not regard himself as immune

God takes away prosperity and advances others to fame and honor."

245 ²⁴⁵He cordially approved this man also, and requested his neighbor to answer the question how he might avoid turning either to ease or pleasure. "By being always aware," he replied, "that he is ruler of a large kingdom and leader of great multitudes, and that his mind must not be occupied with anything else but think always of the care of these charges; and he must pray God that he neglect none of his duties."

²⁴⁶He commended this man also, and asked the tenth how he might detect those that used guile in their dealings with him. And he told him, "By observing closely whether the deportment of those about him was forthright and whether orderly conduct was maintained in receptions and councils and other social contacts, and by seeing that they did not exceed the limits of propriety in congratulations and other aspects of behavior. But God will lead Your Majesty's mind to what is best."

²⁴⁷He applauded them all and commended them by name, and the others present did likewise, and then they turned to merry-making.

²⁴⁸On the succeeding day he seized the opportune moment and asked the man next in order, "What is the grossest negligence?" To this he declared, "If a man is indifferent to his children and does not devote every effort to their education. For we always pray to God not so much for ourselves as for our offspring, that all blessings be theirs. But to desire that children be endued with temperance comes about by the power of God."

²⁴⁹He declared that he had spoken well, and asked another

---

to ordinary principles of ethics. EDUCATION: More prominent in Jewish than in Greek ethics (where it is of course not absent), but TEMPERANCE seems to point rather to a philosophical Greek than to a Jewish curriculum. 249. LOVER OF HIS COUNTRY: The schools approved patriotism, even as an acknowledgment of benefits received, but the argument RESIDENCE ABROAD BRINGS CONTEMPT is out of keeping with Cynic-Stoic "cosmopolitanism." BY BESTOWING BENEFITS makes the response applicable to Ptolemy and kingship. The word itself (*euergetōn*) became a royal appellative; the third Ptolemy, Philadelphus' son, was called Euergetes.

ἠρώτα Πῶς ἂν φιλόπατρις εἴη; Προτιθέμενος, εἶπεν, ὅτι καλὸν ἐν ἰδίᾳ καὶ ζῆν καὶ τελευτᾶν. ἡ δὲ ξενία τοῖς μὲν πένησι καταφρόνησιν ἐργάζεται, τοῖς δὲ πλουσίοις ὄνειδος, ὡς διὰ κακίαν ἐκπεπτωκόσιν. εὐεργετῶν οὖν ἅπαντας, καθὼς συνεχῶς τοῦτ' ἐπιτελεῖς, θεοῦ διδόντος σοὶ πρὸς 250 πάντας χάριν, φιλόπατρις φανήσῃ. 250Τούτου δὲ ἀκούσας τοῦ κατὰ τὸ ἑξῆς ἐπυνθάνετο Πῶς <ἂν> ἁρμόσαι γυναικί; <Γινώσκων> ὅτι μὲν θρασύ ἐστιν, ἔφη, τὸ θῆλυ γένος, καὶ δραστικὸν ἐφ' ὃ βούλεται πρᾶγμα, καὶ μεταπῖπτον εὐκόπως διὰ παραλογισμοῦ, καὶ τῇ φύσει κατεσκεύασται ἀσθενές· δέον δ' ἐστὶ κατὰ τὸ ὑγιὲς χρῆσθαι, καὶ μὴ πρὸς ἔριν ἀντιπράσσειν. 251κατορθοῦται γὰρ βίος, ὅταν ὁ κυβερνῶν εἰδῇ, πρὸς τίνα σκοπὸν δεῖ τὴν διέξοδον ποιεῖσθαι. θεοῦ δ' ἐπικλήσει καὶ βίος κυβερνᾶται κατὰ πάντα. 252Συνανθομολογησάμενος δὲ τούτῳ τὸν ἑξῆς ἠρώτα Πῶς <ἂν> ἀναμάρτητος εἴη; ὁ δὲ ἔφησεν Ὡς ἅπαντα πράσσων καὶ μετὰ διαλογισμοῦ καὶ μὴ πειθόμενος διαβολαῖς, ἀλλ' αὐτὸς ὢν δοκιμαστὴς τῶν λεγομένων καὶ κρίσει κατευθύνων τὰ τῶν ἐντεύξεων καὶ διὰ κρίσεως ἐπιτελῶν ταῦτα ἀναμάρτητος, ἔφησεν, ἂν εἴης, ὦ βασιλεῦ. τὸ δ' ἐπινοεῖν ταῦτα καὶ ἐν τούτοις ἀναστρέφεσθαι θείας δυνάμεώς ἐστιν ἔργον. 253Διαχυθεὶς δὲ τοῖς εἰρημένοις τὸν ἕτερον ἠρώτα Πῶς ἂν ἐκτὸς θυμοῦ γένοιτο; πρὸς τοῦτ' εἶπε Γινώσκων ὅτι πάντων ἐξουσίαν ἔχει, καί, εἰ χρήσαιτο θυμῷ, θάνατον ἐπιφέρει· ὅπερ ἀνωφελὲς καὶ ἀλγεινόν ἐστιν, εἰ τὸ ζῆν ἀφελεῖται

---

250 <αν> edd. / Γινωσκων edd. for lacuna
252 <αν> edd. / ο δε εφησεν ως MSS,

ο δε εφη· σεμνως Mend. approved by T and Tramontano

250. LIVE AMICABLY WITH HIS WIFE: Hardly applicable to Philadelphus himself (see on 41), and hence indicative of the general tone of the questions. THE FEMALE SEX: Its shortcomings are a commonplace from Semonides of Amorgos onwards, and its inferiority to the male part of Peripatetic doctrine. The rash or fickle women in Prov. and Ben Sirah belong to a special class, but excessive conversation with a woman, even one's own wife, is discouraged in Abot 1.5.
251. LIFE IS STEERED STRAIGHT: The image is common in Greek, and a favorite with Plato.
252. FREE OF ERROR: The general question, for which ACTING ALWAYS WITH ... DELIBERATION is the correct philosophic response, is made spe-

how he might be a lover of his country. "By keeping in mind," he answered, "that it is good to live and die in one's country. Residence abroad brings contempt upon poor men, and upon rich disgrace, as though they were in exile for some wickedness. By bestowing benefits upon all men, then, as you constantly do—God giving you favor with all—you will show yourself a lover of your country."

250 ²⁵⁰When he had listened to this man, he inquired of the one next in order how he might live amicably with his wife. "By realizing," he declared, "that the female sex are rash and energetic in pursuing their desires and fickle through fallacious reasoning and of naturally weak constitution. One must deal with them sanely, and not, by opposing them, provoke quarrel. ²⁵¹Life is steered straight when the pilot knows to what haven he must set his course; but by invoking God life has a pilot always."

²⁵²He expressed his agreement with this man, and asked the next how he might be free of error. He declared, "By acting always with gravity and deliberation and not being persuaded by slanders but oneself testing what is said, and by administering questions of petitions with judgment and through judgment granting them, you will be free of error, Your Majesty. But to hold such convictions and to behave accordingly requires divine power."

²⁵³He was delighted with these remarks, and asked the next man how he might be beyond outbursts of wrath. To this he replied, "By realizing that he had power over all things, even, if he indulged his wrath, of inflicting death. But

---

cially applicable to the judicial function of the king. ADMINISTERING ... PETITIONS: This points to a date before 100, for by the beginning of the second century special officials took care of petitions and none reached the king, whereas in the third century though petitions were directed to the strategos of the nome some did reach the king; see Introd. 41.

253. WRATH: There were many treatises on controlling anger (those of Seneca and Plutarch are extant), and in all the remedy prescribed is the rule of reason; that is the prescription here given, with special applicability to a king, and the implication that might does not make right even for a king, who must also follow the right. The king's wrath in Prov. (16.14, 20.2) is looked at from the point of view of its object, not of the king.

πολλών, διά το κύριον είναι. ²⁵⁴πάντων δ' υπηκόων όντων και μηδενός εναντιουμένου, τίνος χάριν θυμωθήσεται; γινώσκειν δε δει διότι θεός τον πάντα κόσμον διοικεί μετ' ευμενείας και χωρίς οργής απάσης· τούτω δε κατακολουθείν αναγκαίον εστί σε, έφησεν, ώ βασιλεύ. ²⁵⁵Καλώς δε αποκεκρίσθαι φήσας τούτον επυνθάνετο του μετέπειτα Τί εστιν ευβουλία; Το καλώς άπαντα πράσσειν, απεφήνατο, μετά διαλογισμού, κατά την βουλήν παρατιθέντα και <τα> βλαβερά των κατά το εναντίον του λόγου διάστημα, ίνα προς έκαστον επινοήσαντες ώμεν ευ βεβουλευμένοι, και το προτεθέν ημίν επιτελήται. το δ' αυ κράτιστον, θεού δυναστεία παν βούλευμα <τελείωσιν έξει> σοι την ευσέβειαν ασκούντι. ²⁵⁶Κατωρθωκέναι δε και τούτον ειπών άλλον ηρώτα Τί εστι φιλοσοφία; Το καλώς διαλογίζεσθαι προς έκαστον των συμβαινόντων, απεφήνατο, και μη εκφέρεσθαι ταις ορμαίς, αλλά τας βλάβας καταμελετάν τας εκ των επιθυμιών εκβαινούσας, και τα προς τον καιρόν πράσσειν δεόντως μετριοπαθή καθεστώτα. ίνα δ' επίστασιν τούτων λαμβάνωμεν, θεραπεύειν δει τον θεόν. ²⁵⁷Επισημήνας δε και τούτον έτερον ηρώτα Πώς αν αποδοχής <εν ξενιτεία> τυγχάνοι; Πάσιν ίσος γινόμενος, έφη, και μάλλον ήττων ή καθυπερέχων φαινόμενος προς ούς ξενιτεύει. κοινώς γαρ ο θεός το ταπεινούμενον προσδέχεται κατά φύσιν, και το των ανθρώπων γένος τους υποτασσομένους φιλανθρωπεί. ²⁵⁸Επιμαρτυρήσας δε τούτοις άλλον ηρώτα Πώς <α> αν

255 <τα> T, W suggests τα ωφελιμα και / διαστημα W conjectures καταστημα / τελειωσιν εξει σοι edd., τεως ιν' εξισοι MSS
257 εν ξενιτεια edd., η ξενιτεια MSS, W suggests ει ξενιτευοι
258 α (αν) edd., αν MSS

254. HIS EXAMPLE ... YOU MUST FOLLOW: This is specifically Jewish doctrine, in which the sanction for ethics is the requirement to follow the pattern set forth by God.
255. WITH DELIBERATION: This counsel is naturally to be found in rabbinic literatue (*cf.* Abot "Be deliberate in judgment," the first injunction of the men of the Great Synagogue), but it is here more probably a reflection of the philosophic admonition to give reason primacy over emotion—an admonition peculiarly appropriate to a philosophic concept of kingship.
BUT WHAT IS MOST IMPORTANT: So patently a tag that we may assume that what precedes is a verbatim dictum of the philosophers.

it would be an unprofitable and grievous thing if he deprived many of life because his power was paramount. ²⁵⁴And when all men were his subjects and none opposed him, to what end should he fall into a rage? You must realize," he added, "that God governs the whole world with kindliness and without any passion; His example, Your Majesty, you must follow."

²⁵⁵He declared that this response was excellent, and inquired of the man who followed, "What is good counsel?" "Acting correctly in all things," he explained, "and with deliberation, comparing also the injurious effects of following the opposite course, so that after studying every point we may be well advised and our purpose be fulfilled. But what is most important, by God's sovereignty every counsel of yours shall have fulfillment, for you practise piety."

²⁵⁶He remarked that he too had spoken correctly, and asked another, "What is philosophy?" "It is to deliberate well over every contingency," he explained, "and not to be carried away by impulses, but to ponder the injuries which are the outcome of the passions, and to perform the duties of the moment properly, with emotions moderated. But to acquire a regard for these things we must pray to God."

²⁵⁷Him too he complimented, and asked another how he might obtain acceptance in a sojourn abroad. "By becoming everyone's equal," he declared, "and by behaving rather as an inferior than as a superior to those among whom you sojourn. For God accepts alike what is humble in nature, and the human race deals kindly with the lowly."

²⁵⁸He expressed assent to these words, and asked another man how he might so build that his works would abide in the

---

256 is virtually identical with 255, except that the question relates to *philosophia* instead of *euboulia* ("good counsel"). It is tempting to imagine that the model made an equation between the two: a king's *euboulia* is essentially *philosophia*, for both demand deliberation.

257. ACCEPTANCE IN A SOJOURN ABROAD: Seems hardly applicable to Philadelphus, though becoming everyone's equal is good Stoic doctrine for kings to follow. *Cf.* 249. On humility as a virtue *cf.* 263, 282.

258. WOULD SPARE THEM FOR THEIR BEAUTY: Involves no particular ethical content, but makes a nice transition to NEGLECTED NO ONE, and in turn to DID NOT COERCE. For principle of adequate wages, *cf. Tobit* 4.12, 12.1 ff.

κατασκευάσῃ καὶ μετὰ τοῦτο διαμένῃ; πρὸς τοῦτ' εἶπεν Εἰ μεγάλα καὶ σεμνὰ ταῖς ποιήσεσιν ἐπιτελοῖ, πρὸς τὸ φείσασθαι τοὺς θεωροῦντας διὰ τὴν καλλονήν, καὶ μηθένα τῶν κατεργαζομένων τὰ τοιαῦτα παραπέμποι, μηδὲ τοὺς ἄλλους ἀμισθὶ συντελεῖν ἀναγκάζοι τὰ πρὸς τὴν χρείαν. [259]διανοούμενος γὰρ ὡς θεὸς πολυωρεῖ τὸ τῶν ἀνθρώπων γένος, χορηγῶν αὐτοῖς καὶ ὑγείαν καὶ εὐαισθησίαν καὶ τὰ λοιπά, καὶ αὐτὸς ἀκόλουθόν τι πράξει τῶν κακοπαθειῶν ἀποδιδοὺς τὴν ἀντάμειψιν. τὰ γὰρ ἐκ δικαιοσύνης τελούμενα, ταῦτα καὶ διαμένει. [260]Εὖ δὲ καὶ τοῦτον εἰρηκέναι φήσας τὸν δέκατον ἠρώτα Τί ἐστι σοφίας καρπός; ὁ δὲ εἶπε Τὸ μὴ συνιστορεῖν ἑαυτῷ κακὸν πεπραχότι, τὸν δὲ βίον ἐν ἀληθείᾳ διεξάγειν. [261]ἐκ τούτων γὰρ κρατίστη χαρὰ καὶ ψυχῆς εὐστάθειά σοι γίνεται, μέγιστε βασιλεῦ, καὶ ἐλπίδες ἐπὶ θεῷ καλαὶ κρατοῦντί σοι τῆς ἀρχῆς εὐσεβῶς. Ὡς δὲ συνήκουσαν πάντες ἐπεφώνησαν σὺν κρότῳ πλείονι. καὶ μετὰ ταῦτα πρὸς τὸ προπιεῖν ὁ βασιλεὺς [λαμβάνειν] ἐτράπη, χαρᾷ πεπληρωμένος.

[262]Τῇ δ' ἑξῆς καθὼς πρότερον ἡ διάταξις ἦν τῶν κατὰ τὸν πότον ἐπιτελουμένων, καιροῦ δὲ γενομένου τοὺς ἀπολιπόντας ὁ βασιλεὺς ἐπηρώτα. πρὸς τὸν πρῶτον δὲ ἔφη Πῶς ἂν μὴ τραπείη τις εἰς ὑπερηφανίαν; [263]ἀπεκρίθη δέ Εἰ τὴν ἰσότητα τηροῖ, καὶ παρ' ἕκαστον ἑαυτὸν ὑπομιμνήσκοι, καθὼς ἄνθρωπος ὢν ἀνθρώπων ἡγεῖται. καὶ ὁ θεὸς τοὺς ὑπερηφάνους καθαιρεῖ, τοὺς δὲ ἐπιεικεῖς καὶ ταπεινοὺς ὑψοῖ. [264]Παρακαλέσας δὲ αὐτὸν τὸν ἑξῆς ἐπηρώτα Τίσι δεῖ συμβούλοις χρῆσθαι; τοῖς διὰ πολλῶν, ἔφη, πεπειραμένοις πραγμάτων καὶ τὴν εὔνοιαν συντηροῦσιν ἀκέραιον πρὸς αὐτὸν καὶ τῶν τρόπων ὅσοι μετέχουσιν αὐτῷ. θεοῦ

---

261 λαμβανειν T brackets, Mend. conjectures προποσιν λαμβανειν ο

βασιλευς, Cohn ποτηριον ο βασιλευς λαμβανων

259. EMULATE: Cf. on 254.
260. FRUIT: There are examples of this use of the word in both Greek and Hebrew; cf. especially Ben Sirah 1.6, "the root of wisdom," and 1.16, "its fruits." TO BE CONSCIOUS: Cf. 243, 232, 207.
261. FAIR HOPES: A Greek as well as Hebrew locution.
262. THE NEXT DAY: The sixth. PRIDE: The word is classical, but more common in LXX.

future. To this he answered, "If he would make his structures great and majestic, so that those who viewed them would spare them for their beauty, and if he neglected no one who wrought such works, and did not coerce others to perform his requirements without pay. [259]For if he reflected that God treats the human race considerately, supplying them with health and perceptivity and other gifts, he would himself emulate this principle and render due reward for laborious toil. And works consummated in righteousness are also abiding."

[260]He declared that this man too had spoken well, and asked the tenth, "What is the fruit of wisdom?" And he said, "To be conscious of no wrong-doing, and to lead one's life in sincerity. [261]For from these things there will accrue to you the highest joy and tranquillity of soul, mighty king, and fair hopes in God, while you wield power over your realm in piety."

After hearing them, all expressed approval with loud applause, and then the king, filled with joy, turned to the drinking of healths.

[262]On the next day the program of the banquet was carried forward as before, and when the opportunity came the king put questions to those that were left. To the first man he said, "How may one avoid yielding to pride?" [263]His response was, "By preserving equality and reminding himself at each turn that he is a man as well as a leader of men. And God humbles the proud, and the gentle and humble He exalts."

[264]He spoke kindly to him, and asked the next man, "Who should be employed as counsellors?" "Those who have been proven in many affairs," he declared, "and preserved their good-will to him unblemished, and all who shared his principles. To further these ends a manifestation of God is vouchsafed to those who are worthy."

---

263. REMINDING HIMSELF . . . THAT HE IS A MAN: *Cf.* 211.   GOD HUMBLES THE PROUD: A close parallel to I Sam. 2.7, but the sentiment is so general that no specific allusion may be assumed. *Cf.* also Ben Sirah 3.18.
264. THOSE WHO HAVE BEEN PROVEN: Again purely practical advice, which makes the pious tag more patently an addition.

265 δὲ ἐπιφάνεια γίνεται πρὸς τὰ τοιαῦτα τοῖς ἀξίοις. ²⁶⁵'Επαινέσας δὲ αὐτὸν ἄλλον ἠρώτα Τίς ἐστι βασιλεῖ κτῆσις ἀναγκαιοτάτη; Τῶν ὑποτεταγμένων φιλανθρωπία καὶ ἀγάπησις, ἀπεκρίνατο. διὰ γὰρ τούτων ἄλυτος εὐνοίας δεσμὸς γίνεται. τὸ δὲ γίνεσθαι κατὰ προαίρεσιν ταῦτα ὁ θεὸς ἐπιτελεῖ. ²⁶⁶Κατεπαινέσας δὲ αὐτὸν ἑτέρου διεπυνθάνετο Τί πέρας ἐστὶ λόγου; κἀκεῖνος δὲ ἔφησε Τὸ πεῖσαι τὸν ἀντιλέγοντα, διὰ τῆς ὑποτεταγμένης τάξεως τὰς βλάβας ἐπιδεικνύντα· οὕτω γὰρ λήψῃ τὸν ἀκροατὴν οὐκ ἀντικείμενος, συγχρώμενος δὲ ἐπαίνῳ πρὸς τὸ πεῖσαι. θεοῦ δὲ ἐνεργείᾳ κατευθύνεται πειθώ. ²⁶⁷Εὖ δὲ λέγειν φήσας αὐτὸν ἕτερον ἠρώτα Πῶς ἄν, παμμιγῶν ὄχλων ὄντων ἐν τῇ βασιλείᾳ, τούτοις <ἁρμόσαι>; Τὸ πρέπον ἑκάστῳ συνυποκρινόμενος, εἶπε, καθηγεμόνα λαμβάνων δικαιοσύνην· ὡς καὶ ποιεῖς θεοῦ σοι διδόντος εὖ λογίζεσθαι. ²⁶⁸Φιλοφρονηθεὶς δὲ τούτῳ πρὸς τὸν ἕτερον εἶπεν 'Επὶ τίσι δεῖ λυπεῖσθαι; πρὸς ταῦτα ἀπεκρίθη Τὰ συμβαίνοντα τοῖς φίλοις ὅταν θεωρῶμεν πολυχρόνια καὶ ἀνέκφευκτα γινόμενα. τελευτήσασι μὲν γὰρ καὶ κακῶν ἀπολελυμένοις οὐχ ὑπογράφει λύπην ὁ λόγος· ἀλλὰ ἐφ' ἑαυτοὺς ἀναφέροντες καὶ τὸ πρὸς ἑαυτοὺς συμφέρον λυποῦνται πάντες ἄνθρωποι. τὸ δ' ἐκφυγεῖν πᾶν κακὸν θεοῦ δυνάμει γίνεται. ²⁶⁹Ὡς ἔδει δὲ φήσας αὐτὸν ἀποκρίνεσθαι πρὸς ἕτερον εἶπε Πῶς ἀδοξία γίνεται; ἐκεῖνος δὲ ἔφησεν Ὅταν ὑπερηφανία καθηγῆται καὶ θράσος ἄληκτον,

---

267 αρμοσαι edd., αρμοση MSS

---

265. INDULGENCE: Thackeray translates "The good wishes and love of his subjects," and Meecham, "The friendship and love of his subjects." But in the Ptolemaic period *philanthropia* frequently means "amnesty," "moratorium," and the genitive *hupotetagmenōn* may be construed as objective rather than subjective. This makes GOOD-WILL ARISES logical and practical, and BUT IT IS GOD a patent appendage.

266. TO CONVINCE: This is good rhetors' doctrine, with no applicability to Philadelphus, except for the implication that even a king must use reason rather than force. As always when the advice is purely secular, the pious tag seems forced.

267. BY ASSUMING THE PROPER ROLE: See on 219. TAKING JUSTICE AS A GUIDE: A proper corrective to what might appear a counsel to hypocrisy.

268. REASON PRESCRIBES NO GRIEF: The doctrine of all the numerous "Consolations" written by philosophers of all Hellenistic schools (there are

265 ²⁶⁵He commended him, and asked another, "What is the most essential possession for a king?" "Indulgence and love to his subjects," was the response, "for by these an indissoluble bond of good-will arises. But it is God who brings it about that these things should come to pass as you would choose."

²⁶⁶He complimented him, and inquired of another, "What is the goal of discourse?" And that one declared, "To convince one's opponent by pointing out his errors in an attitude of deference. For in this way you will win your hearer over, not by contradicting him, but by using praise in order to persuade. But it is by the working of God that persuasion succeeds."

²⁶⁷He declared that he had spoken well, and asked another how, the multitudes in his kingdom being of such diverse origins, he might live amicably with them. "By assuming the proper role for each," he replied, "taking justice as a guide; for so indeed you do, since God grants you right judgment."

²⁶⁸He felicitated this man cordially, and said to the next, "What are the proper objects of grief?" To this he responded, "The accidents which befall our friends, when we see that they are protracted and ineluctable. For those that are dead, on the other hand, and released from evil, reason prescribes no grief. Yet all men do grieve, thinking only of themselves and their own interests. But escape from every evil comes to pass only by the power of God."

²⁶⁹He declared that this response was as it should be, and asked the next man, "How does ill-repute arise?" That one declared, "When overweening pride and frowardness incessant lead the way, dishonor and ruin of reputation follow

---

extant treatises by Cicero, Seneca, Plutarch); all point out that men who DO GRIEVE are THINKING ONLY OF THEMSELVES. Again the appendage is forced.

269. ILL-REPUTE: Repute (*doxa*) is a much more powerful incentive in Greek than in Hebrew ethics, and of special concern to kings (*cf.* 258), so that philosophers could use it as a lever in their admonitions; *cf.* 272.

ἀτιμασμὸς ἐπιφύεται καὶ δόξης ἀναίρεσις. θεὸς δὲ δόξης πάσης κυριεύει, ῥέπων οὗ βούλεται. ²⁷⁰Καὶ τούτῳ δ' ἐπικυρώσας τὰ τῆς ἀποκρίσεως τὸν ἑξῆς ἠρώτα Τίσι δεῖ πιστεύειν ἑαυτόν; Τοῖς διὰ τὴν εὔνοιαν, εἶπε, συνοῦσί σοι, καὶ μὴ διὰ τὸν φόβον μηδὲ διὰ πολυωρίαν, ἐπανάγουσι πάντα πρὸς τὸ κερδαίνειν. τὸ μὲν γὰρ ἀγαπήσεως σημεῖον, τὸ δὲ δυσνοίας καὶ καιροτηρησίας· ὃς γὰρ ἐπὶ τὸ πλεονεκτεῖν <ὁρμᾶται> προδότης πέφυκε. σὺ δὲ πάντας εὐνόους ἔχεις θεοῦ σοι καλὴν βουλὴν διδόντος. ²⁷¹Σοφῶς δὲ αὐτὸν εἰπὼν ἀποκεκρίσθαι, ἑτέρῳ εἶπε Τί βασιλείαν διατηρεῖ; πρὸς τοῦτ' ἔφη Μέριμνα καὶ φροντίς, ὡς οὐδὲν κακουργηθήσεται διὰ τῶν ἀποτεταγμένων εἰς τοὺς ὄχλους ταῖς χρείαις· καθὼς σὺ τοῦτο πράσσεις θεοῦ σοι τὴν σεμνὴν ἐπίνοιαν διδόντος. ²⁷²Θαρσύνας δὲ τοῦτον ἕτερον ἐπηρώτα Τί διαφυλάσσει χάριτα καὶ τιμήν; ὁ δὲ εἶπεν Ἀρετή. καλῶν γὰρ ἔργων ἐστὶν ἐπιτέλεια, τὸ δὲ κακὸν ἀποτρίβεται· καθὼς σὺ διατηρεῖς τὴν πρὸς ἅπαντας καλοκἀγαθίαν παρὰ θεοῦ δῶρον τοῦτ' ἔχων. ²⁷³Κεχαρισμένως δὲ καὶ τοῦτον ἀποδεξάμενος τὸν ἑνδέκατον ἐπηρώτα (διὰ τὸ δύο πλεονάζειν τῶν ἑβδομήκοντα) Πῶς ἂν κατὰ ψυχὴν καὶ ἐν τοῖς πολέμοις εἰρηνικῶς ἔχοι; ὁ δὲ ἀπεφήνατο Διαλαμβάνων ὅτι κακὸν οὐδὲν εἴργασται τῶν ὑποτεταγμένων οὐθενί, πάντες δὲ ἀγωνιοῦνται περὶ τῶν εὐεργετημάτων, εἰδότες, κἂν ἐκ τοῦ ζῆν ἀποτρέχωσιν, ἐπιμελητήν σε τῶν βίων. ²⁷⁴οὐ γὰρ διαλείπεις ἐπανορθῶν ἅπαντας τοῦ θεοῦ σοι καλοφροσύνην δεδωκότος. Ἐπισημήνας δὲ κρότῳ πάντας αὐτοὺς ἀπεδέξατο φιλοφρονούμενος, καὶ προπίνων ἑκάστῳ πλεῖόν τι πρὸς τὸ τερφθῆναι <ἐτράπη>, μετ' εὐφροσύνης τοῖς ἀνδράσι συνὼν καὶ χαρᾶς πλείονος.

---

270 ορμαται edd., οραται MSS   274 ετραπη edd. for lacuna

270. GOOD-WILL . . . NOT . . . OPPORTUNISM: Again merely prudential advice, with the pious tag bestowing a graceful compliment on the king, as frequently, e.g., in the following paragraphs.
271. NO WRONG BE INFLICTED: Prudential too, but prudence dictates righteousness, the regular line of the philosophers.
272. VIRTUE: This too is expedient, for it promotes doxa; see on 269.
273. ELEVENTH: Questions were traditionally in groups of ten (see Introd. 41), hence the explanation FOR THERE WERE TWO MORE THAN SEVENTY.

close. But God is the Lord of all reputation, and inclines it whither He will."

²⁷⁰The substance of this man's answer too he confirmed, and asked the next, "To whom is it fitting to entrust oneself?" "To those who attend upon you because of good-will," he replied, "and not because of fear or opportunism, calculating everything from the motive of profit. For the one is a token of love, the other of ill-will and time-serving, and the man whose impulse is to advance his own interest is by nature a traitor. But you have the good-will of all men, since God gives you good counsel."

²⁷¹He said that this response was very sage, and asked the next man, "What preserves a kingdom?" In reply he declared, "Care and watchfulness that no wrong be inflicted by those who are set in positions of authority over the people. And such is your practice, for God has bestowed grave reflection upon you."

²⁷²He made a heartening remark to this man, and asked the next, "What protects favor and honor?" And he said, "Virtue, for virtue is the consummation of good works, but rejects the evil; just as you preserve your generous deportment towards all men, by the gift you have of God."

²⁷³He accepted this with gracious favor, and asked the eleventh (for there were two more than seventy) how he might be peaceable in soul even during war. And he explained, "By realizing that no wrong has been done to any of your subjects and that all will join in the struggle in return for benefits received, knowing that even if they lay down their lives their dependents are in your tutelage. ²⁷⁴For you never fail to make reparation to all, God having bestowed a noble temper upon you."

He applauded loudly and expressed his hearty approval, and then drank generous healths to each of them and turned to enjoyment, sharing the men's society with merriment and gladness.

PEACEABLE IN SOUL: Free of "perturbations," the goal of philosophy.
IN RETURN FOR BENEFITS: Just rule is again proven to be good policy.
THEIR DEPENDENTS: Literally "lives" (*biōn*).
274. A variation of the concluding sentences at 220, 235, 265.

275 ²⁷⁵Τῇ ἑβδόμῃ δὲ τῶν ἡμερῶν, πλείονος παρασκευῆς γενομένης, προσπαραγινομένων πλειόνων ἑτέρων ἀπὸ τῶν πόλεων (ἦσαν γὰρ ἱκανοὶ πρέσβεις), ἐπηρώτησεν ὁ βασιλεὺς καιροῦ γενομένου τὸν πρωτεύοντα τῶν ἀπολιπόντων τῆς ἐρωτήσεως Πῶς ἂν ἀπαραλόγιστος <εἴη>; ²⁷⁶ἐκεῖνος δὲ ἔφη Δοκιμάζων καὶ τὸν λέγοντα καὶ τὸ λεγόμενον καὶ περὶ τίνος λέγει, καὶ ἐν πλείονι χρόνῳ τὰ αὐτὰ δι' ἑτέρων τρόπων ἐπερωτῶν. τὸ δὲ νοῦν ἔχειν ὀξὺν καὶ δύνασθαι κρίνειν ἕκαστα θεοῦ δώρημα καλόν ἐστιν· ὡς σὺ τοῦτο κέκτησαι, βασιλεῦ. ²⁷⁷Κρότῳ δὲ ἐπισημηνάμενος ὁ βασιλεὺς ἕτερον ἐπηρώτα Διὰ τί τὴν ἀρετὴν οὐ παραδέχονται τῶν ἀνθρώπων οἱ πλείονες; Ὅτι φυσικῶς ἅπαντες, εἶπεν, ἀκρατεῖς καὶ ἐπὶ τὰς ἡδονὰς τρεπόμενοι γεγόνασιν· ὧν χάριν ἀδικία πέφυκε καὶ τὸ τῆς πλεονεξίας χύμα. ²⁷⁸τὸ δὲ τῆς ἀρετῆς κατάστημα κωλύει τοὺς ἐπιφερομένους ἐπὶ τὴν ἡδονοκρασίαν, ἐγκράτειαν δὲ κελεύει καὶ δικαιοσύνην προτιμᾶν. ὁ δὲ θεὸς πάντων ἡγεῖται τούτων. ²⁷⁹Εὖ δὲ ἀποκεκρίσθαι τοῦτον εἰπὼν ὁ βασιλεὺς ἠρώτα Τίσι δεῖ κατακολουθεῖν τοὺς βασιλεῖς; ὁ δὲ ἔφη Τοῖς νόμοις, ἵνα δικαιοπραγοῦντες ἀνακτῶνται τοὺς βίους τῶν ἀνθρώπων· καθὼς σὺ τοῦτο πράσσων ἀέναον μνήμην καταβέβλησαι
280 σεαυτοῦ, θείῳ προστάγματι κατακολουθῶν. ²⁸⁰Εἰπὼν δὲ καὶ τοῦτον καλῶς λέγειν τὸν ἐχόμενον ἠρώτα Τίνας δεῖ

---

275 ειη edd., η MSS   vening lacuna with τον μετ' αυτον
279 βασιλευς ηρωτα] W-MS fills inter-

---

275. MANY OTHERS ... WERE ADMITTED: It is the technique of the rhetorical romance to provide a good audience for the denouement; see Introd. 52.
276. BY SCRUTINIZING: A simple bit of shrewd advice, to which the pious tag, including a compliment to the king, is attached.
277. INNATE PROPENSITY: Cf. 108, "All men being constitutionally prone to pleasure," and 222, "In the temper of all men there is some innate proclivity." There is an interesting parallel in Philo, who draws upon rabbinic doctrine. On Gen. 2.7, "Then the Lord God formed man of the dust of the ground, and breathed into his nostrils the breath of life; and man became a living soul," Genesis Rabbah 14.4 declares that man is comprised of two yezarim ("proclivities"), towards good and towards evil. With reference to the same verse Philo, Special Laws 4.24.123, says that man's twofold nature consists of an earthly soul which is the seat of desire and other irrational emotions, and a spiritual soul which is the seat of reason, acting

275 ²⁷⁵On the seventh of the days more bountiful preparation was made, for many others from the cities were admitted (there were many ambassadors present), and when the opportune moment came the king put a question to the first man of those left, asking how he could avoid being deceived. ²⁷⁶That man said, "By scrutinizing the speaker and the speech and the subject, and by asking, over a period of time, the same questions in different forms. But the possession of an acute intellect and the capacity to judge each detail is a fair gift of God; and this gift Your Majesty possesses."

²⁷⁷The king applauded loudly, and asked the next man, "Why do the majority of men not embrace virtue?" "Because all men are by nature intemperate and have an innate propensity to pleasure. It is for this reason that injustice burgeons and the mass of covetousness. ²⁷⁸But the virtuous state restrains those that are drifting to a state of self-indulgence, and bids them give preference to self-control and justice. But God is the guide of all these things."

²⁷⁹The king said that this man had made a good response, and asked, "Whose guidance ought kings follow?" And he declared, "The guidance of the laws, so that by just dealing they may repair the lives of men; just as you, by such conduct, have laid the foundations for an eternal memorial of yourself, through following the divine commandment."

280 ²⁸⁰He said that this man too had spoken well, and asked

as a restraint upon the emotions; see Wolfson 2.290.
278. STATE: *katastema* is a technical expression in the philosophers for "state of the soul."
279. WHOSE GUIDANCE: The Greek has simply "Whom," which has the effect of personifying the laws, as is done in Plato's *Crito*, to which the reader was doubtless expected to recognize the allusion. It was the heart of the treatises *On Kingship* that the king too was subject to and served the laws. DIVINE COMMANDMENT: For all his virtues (*cf.* Philo's eulogy, 22 above), Philadelphus cannot have followed what a Jewish sage would call the divine commandment; hence this passage demonstrates our author's universalist and spiritual concept of Judaism: see Introd. 63.
280. CROWN OF RIGHTEOUSNESS: Possibly deriving from the custom at the panhellenic games, "crown" (*stephanos*) came to be used of any honorary award, and in Ptolemaic Egypt of royal donatives and even bribes. In *P. Societa Italiana* 405 (III BCE) a business agent is complimented as

καθιστάνειν στρατηγούς; ὃς δὲ εἶπεν "Ὅσοι μισοπονηρίαν ἔχουσι, καὶ τὴν ἀγωγὴν αὐτοῦ μιμούμενοι, πρὸς τὸ διὰ παντὸς εὐδοξίαν ἔχειν αὐτούς, τὰ δίκαια πράσσουσι· καθὼς σὺ τοῦτο ἐπιτελεῖς, εἶπε, μέγιστε βασιλεῦ, θεοῦ σοι στέφανον δικαιοσύνης δεδωκότος. ²⁸¹'Ἀποδεξάμενος δὲ αὐτὸν μετὰ φωνῆς ἐπὶ τὸν ἐχόμενον ἐπιβλέψας εἶπε Τίνας δεῖ καθιστάνειν ἐπὶ τῶν δυνάμεων ἄρχοντας; ὁ δὲ ἀπεφήνατο Τοὺς ἀνδρείᾳ διαφέροντας καὶ δικαιοσύνῃ, καὶ περὶ πολλοῦ ποιουμένους τὸ σώζειν τοὺς ἄνδρας ἢ τὸ νικᾶν, τῷ θράσει <παραβάλλοντας> τὸ ζῆν. ὡς γὰρ ὁ θεὸς εὖ ἐργάζεται πᾶσι, καὶ σὺ τοῦτον μιμούμενος εὐεργετεῖς τοὺς ὑπὸ σεαυτόν. ²⁸²Ὁ δὲ ἀποκεκρίσθαι φήσας αὐτὸν εὖ, ἄλλον ἠρώτα Τίνα θαυμάζειν ἄξιόν ἐστιν ἄνθρωπον; ὁ δὲ ἔφη Τὸν κεχορηγημένον δόξῃ καὶ πλούτῳ καὶ δυνάμει, καὶ ψυχὴν ἴσον πᾶσιν ὄντα· καθὼς σὺ τοῦτο ποιῶν ἀξιοθαύμαστος εἶ τοῦ θεοῦ σοι διδόντος εἰς ταῦτα τὴν ἐπιμέλειαν. ²⁸³Ἐπιφωνήσας δὲ καὶ τούτῳ πρὸς τὸν ἕτερον εἶπεν Ἐν τίσι δεῖ πράγμασι τοὺς βασιλεῖς τὸν πλείω χρόνον διάγειν; ὁ δὲ εἶπεν Ἐν ταῖς ἀναγνώσεσι καὶ ἐν ταῖς τῶν πορειῶν ἀπογραφαῖς διατρίβειν, ὅσαι πρὸς τὰς βασιλείας ἀναγεγραμμέναι τυγχάνουσι πρὸς ἐπανόρθωσιν καὶ διαμονὴν ἀνθρώπων. ὃ σὺ πράσσων ἀνέφικτον ἄλλοις δόξαν κέκτησαι θεοῦ σοι τὰ βουλήματα συντελοῦντος. ²⁸⁴Ἐνεργῶς δὲ καὶ τοῦτον προσει-

---

281 παραβαλλοντας edd., περιβ. MSS
282 επιμελειαν MSS, επιτελειαν W
283 τας βασιλειας MSS, τους βασιλεις Mend. / ανεφικτον edd., εφικτον MSS

284 Ενεργως MSS, W conjectures ευνοως / παιζεται edd., πλιζεται MSS / βιω συμφερον (or συμφορον) και καθηκον edd., βιοι σωφρονων και κατεχων MSS

having acquired "a crown of good repute." But the expression occurs in LXX and other Jewish writings, e.g. Test. XII Patriarchs, Levi 8.2 (cf. II Tim. 4.8) in the same form as here.

281. DISREGARD FOR LIFE: Not simply pacifist, as RECKLESS shows, but a reflection of the higher value set on human life, especially by the Stoics.
282. EQUALITY: Cf. 257 and note.
283. RECORDS OF OFFICIAL JOURNEYS: We know that such records (as of all official proceedings: cf. 298) were kept, and Bickermann, "Zur Datierung" 283, suggests that Aristeas is itself in form such a record. It is interesting to note that Demetrius of Phalerum (according to Plutarch, *Sayings of Kings and Commanders* 189D) is said to have offered "Ptolemy" similar

his neighbor, "Whom should we appoint chief magistrates?" And he replied, "Those who have a hatred of evil and emulate the conduct of their ruler and do what is just, so that they might possess good repute always; just as you, mighty king, fulfill justice, God having bestowed upon you a crown of righteousness."

281After voicing his approval of this man, he looked to his neighbor and said, "Whom should we appoint commanders over our forces?" And he replied, "Men outstanding in courage and justice, and more concerned to save their men than to win a victory by reckless disregard for life. For just as God benefits all men, so do you, in emulation of Him, benefit those subject to you."

282He affirmed that he had made a good response, and asked another, "What man is worthy of admiration?" And he declared, "He that is furnished with renown and wealth and power, and yet is in spirit on an equality with all men; just as you are justly admired for so acting, since God grants you the capacity for attaining these things."

283He assented to this man also, and said to the next, "Upon what matters ought kings spend most of their time?" And he said, "In reading and in studying the records of official journeys such as are drawn up for the use of kings, for the people's amelioration and preservation. By so doing you have acquired renown unattainable to others, since God consummates your desires."

284He was emphatic in his address to him, and asked the next man what he should make his pastimes in hours of re-

---

advice: "Demetrius of Phalerum recommended to Ptolemy the king to buy and read the books dealing with the office of king and ruler. 'For,' as he said, 'those things which the king's friends are not bold enough to recommend to them are written in the books.'"

284. TO WATCH PLAYS: Strange advice from a Jewish teacher, for the later rabbis interpreted "sat in the seat of the scornful" (Ps. 1.1) to mean attendance at theaters; perhaps the emphasis is on PERFORMED WITH PROPRIETY, which may be a veiled reproof for the dissolute performances of the Egyptian court. SCENES FROM LIFE: In Hellenistic usage a "biologist" is a mimic artist who presents lifelike characters, in which there might be SOME EDIFICATION.

πῶν ἕτερον ἠρώτα Τίνας δεῖ ποιεῖσθαι τὰς διαγωγὰς ἐν ταῖς
ἀνέσεσι καὶ ῥαθυμίαις; ὁ δὲ ἔφη Θεωρεῖν ὅσα <παίζεται>
μετὰ περιστολῆς καὶ πρὸ ὀφθαλμῶν τιθέναι τὰ τοῦ βίου
μετ' εὐσχημοσύνης καὶ καταστολῆς γινόμενα <βίῳ συμφέρον καὶ καθῆκον>· ἔνεστι γὰρ καὶ ἐν τούτοις ἐπισκευή
285 τις. ²⁸⁵πολλάκις γὰρ καὶ ἐκ τῶν ἐλαχίστων αἱρετόν τι
δείκνυται. σὺ δὲ πᾶσαν ἠσκηκὼς καταστολὴν διὰ τῶν ἐνερ-
γειῶν φιλοσοφεῖς διὰ καλοκἀγαθίαν ὑπὸ θεοῦ τιμώμενος.
²⁸⁶Εὐαρεστήσας δὲ τοῖς προειρημένοις πρὸς τὸν ἔνατον
εἶπε Πῶς δεῖ διὰ τῶν συμποσίων διεξάγειν; ὁ δὲ ἔφησε
Παραλαμβάνοντα τοὺς φιλομαθεῖς καὶ δυναμένους ὑπομιμ-
νήσκειν τὰ <χρήσιμα τῇ βασιλείᾳ> καὶ τοῖς τῶν ἀρχο-
μένων βίοις—ἐμμελέστερον ἢ μουσικώτερον οὐκ ἂν εὕροις
τι τούτων· ²⁸⁷οὗτοι γὰρ θεοφιλεῖς εἰσι πρὸς τὰ κάλλιστα
πεπαιδευκότες τὰς διανοίας—καθὼς καὶ σὺ τοῦτο πράσσεις,
ὡς ἂν ὑπὸ θεοῦ σοι κατευθυνομένων ἁπάντων. ²⁸⁸Διαχυθεὶς
δὲ ἐπὶ τοῖς εἰρημένοις, ἐπυνθάνετο τοῦ μετέπειτα Τί κάλλιστόν ἐστι τοῖς ὄχλοις, ἐξ ἰδιώτου βασιλέα κατασταθῆναι
<ἐπ'> αὐτῶν, ἢ ἐκ βασιλέως βασιλέα; ἐκεῖνος δὲ ἔφη
Τὸ ἄριστον τῇ φύσει. ²⁸⁹καὶ γὰρ ἐκ βασιλέων βασιλεῖς
γινόμενοι πρὸς τοὺς ὑποτεταγμένους ἀνήμεροί τε καὶ σκληροὶ
καθίστανται· πολλῷ δὲ μᾶλλον καί τινες τῶν ἰδιωτῶν καὶ
κακῶν πεπειραμένοι καὶ πενίας μετεσχηκότες ἄρξαντες ὄχλων
290 χαλεπώτεροι τῶν ἀνοσίων τυράννων ἐξέβησαν. ²⁹⁰ἀλλὰ ὡς

286 χρησιμα τη βασιλεια edd., χρηματα   288 <επ'> edd., υπ' MSS / αριστον
της βασιλειας MSS   MS, αρεστον MSS

285. EXPRESS YOUR PHILOSOPHY IN YOUR ACTIONS: The substance of philosophic teaching *On Kingship*.
286. MORE HARMONIOUS AND SWEETER MUSIC: The classic instance of philosophic conversation being substituted for the more usual music as dinner entertainment is the *Symposium* of Plato, of which there are numerous echoes; in Rome, as the Elder Pliny's example shows, a philosophic book was sometimes read to the diners. The Alexandrians, and the Ptolemies in particular, were notoriously devoted to music.
287. SUCH MEN ARE BELOVED OF GOD: Another indication of Aristeas' universalist and spiritual concept of Judaism; see on 279 and Introd. 62.
288. NOBLEST BY NATURE: The Cynic-Stoic view, in which nature (*physis*) was paramount, and "convention" (*nomos*) a "thing indifferent."

laxation and ease. And he declared, "To watch plays performed with propriety and to set before one's eyes scenes from life presented with decency and restraint is profitable to one's life and appropriate; for even in such things there is some edification, ²⁸⁵since even out of the slightest matters frequently some desirable point finds demonstration. But you have practised every restraint, and express your philosophy in your actions, being honored by God through noble excellence."

²⁸⁶He was highly pleased with these sentiments, and said to the ninth, "How ought one conduct himself in banquets?" And he declared, "One ought invite lovers of learning and men capable of suggesting what may be useful to the realm and the lives of its subjects—more harmonious and sweeter music you could not find. ²⁸⁷For such men are beloved of God, since they have cultivated their minds for the fairest ends; and such, indeed, is your practice also, since all your doings are directed by God."

²⁸⁸He was delighted by these sentiments, and inquired of the man following, "Which is best for the people, that a commoner be set over them as king, or a king of royal descent?" That man declared, "The noblest by nature. ²⁸⁹For there are kings sprung of kings who prove cruel and harsh to their subjects; much more is this true of certain commoners, who have had experience of evils and have shared poverty, and who, when they came to rule over multitudes, turned out to be harder rulers than the unholy tyrants. ²⁹⁰But as I said

---

289. MUCH MORE . . . OF CERTAIN COMMONERS: Apparently a corrective to the extreme Cynic view, where suspicion of privilege would give automatic preference to those WHO HAVE HAD EXPERIENCE OF EVILS.   TURNED OUT TO BE HARDER RULERS: Willrich regarded this a plain allusion to Herod I, who was of course a commoner; Février (21) thought it might refer to Ptolemy Auletes (81–52 BCE) who was called "Bastard." But no definite allusion need be assumed, for the notion must have been commonplace to anyone concerned with *nomos* and *physis* and the theory of kingship, as all Hellenistic philosophers were.
290. GENTLENESS AND HUMANITY: *epieikeia* and *philanthropia*, favorite words with the Hellenistic teachers; see Introd. 41.

προεῖπον, ἦθος χρηστὸν καὶ παιδείας κεκοινωνηκὸς δυνατὸν ἄρχειν ἐστί· καθὼς σὺ βασιλεὺς μέγας ὑπάρχεις, οὐ τοσοῦτον τῇ δόξῃ τῆς ἀρχῆς καὶ πλούτῳ προσχών, ὅσον ἐπιεικείᾳ καὶ φιλανθρωπίᾳ πάντας ἀνθρώπους ὑπερῆρκας τοῦ θεοῦ σοι δεδωρημένου ταῦτα. 291Ἐπὶ πλείονα χρόνον καὶ τοῦτον ἐπαινέσας τὸν ἐπὶ πᾶσιν ἠρώτα Τί μέγιστόν ἐστι βασιλείας; πρὸς τοῦτο εἶπε Τὸ διὰ παντὸς ἐν εἰρήνῃ καθεστάναι τοὺς ὑποτεταγμένους, καὶ κομίζεσθαι τὸ δίκαιον ταχέως ἐν ταῖς διακρίσεσι. 292Ταῦτα δὲ γίνεται διὰ τὸν ἡγούμενον, ὅταν μισοπόνηρος ᾖ καὶ φιλάγαθος καὶ περὶ πολλοῦ ποιούμενος ψυχὴν ἀνθρώπου σώζειν· καθὼς καὶ σὺ μέγιστον κακὸν ἥγησαι τὴν ἀδικίαν, δικαίως δὲ πάντα κυβερνῶν ἀέναον τὴν περὶ σεαυτὸν δόξαν κατεσκεύασας, τοῦ θεοῦ σοι διδόντος ἔχειν ἁγνὴν καὶ ἀμιγῆ παντὸς κακοῦ τὴν διάνοιαν. 293Καταλήξαντος δὲ τούτου κατερράγη κρότος μετὰ φωνῆς καὶ χαρᾶς ἐπὶ πλείονα χρόνον. ὡς δὲ ἐπαύσατο, ὁ βασιλεὺς λαβὼν ποτήριον ἐπεχέατο καὶ τῶν παρόντων ἁπάντων καὶ τῶν εἰρημένων λόγων. ἐπὶ πᾶσι δὲ εἶπε Τὰ μέγιστά μοι γέγονεν ἀγαθὰ παραγενηθέντων ὑμῶν· 294πολλὰ γὰρ ὠφέλημαι, καταβεβλημένων ὑμῶν διδαχὴν ἐμοὶ πρὸς τὸ βασιλεύειν. ἑκάστῳ δὲ τρία τάλαντα προσέταξεν ἀργυρίου δοθῆναι καὶ τὸν ἀποκαταστήσοντα παῖδα. συνεπιφωνησάντων δὲ πάντων, χαρᾶς ἐπληρώθη τὸ συμπόσιον, ἀδιαλείπτως τοῦ βασιλέως εἰς εὐφροσύνην τραπέντος.

295 295Ἐγὼ δὲ <εἰ πεπλεόνακα,> τούτοις, ὦ Φιλόκρατες,

292 μεγιστον κακον T-MS, μεγιστον MSS   295 ει πεπλεονακα edd., ειπα πλειονα και MSS

291. THE GREATEST THING: This is in fact a summation of the king's whole duty—to maintain peace and administer justice; and these functions he performs when he

292. LOVES GOOD AND COUNTS IT IMPORTANT TO SAVE A MAN'S LIFE: The concluding "seal" is a more than usually handsome compliment.

293. BURST OF APPLAUSE: The demonstration at the beginning of the interrogation (186) is described in much the same words.

294. THE DOCTRINE WHICH YOU HAVE GROUNDED FOR ME WITH REFERENCE TO KINGSHIP: This would appear to be conclusive proof that the entire section constitutes an *On Kingship;* the absence of any reference to Judaism at this point is especially noticeable. Josephus, whose paraphrase resumes here, gives (102): "Then the king said that he had already ex-

before, a good disposition which has had a share in culture is capable of bearing rule; just as you show yourself a great king, not so much by attending to the renown of your rule and to wealth, as because you surpass all men in gentleness and humanity, God having bestowed these gifts upon you."

[291]He commended this man at considerable length, and then asked the man who was last of all, "What is the greatest thing in kingship?" To this he answered, "For the subjects to subsist always in a state of peace, and to procure justice quickly in their suits. [292]These things come to pass because of the ruler, when he is one who hates evil and loves good and counts it important to save a man's life. Just so do you regard injustice as the greatest evil, and by governing justly in all respects have built yourself an imperishable fame, since God grants you possession of a mind pure and untainted by any evil."

[293]When this man was finished there was a burst of applause, with ejaculations and jubilations, for a considerable space. And when it stopped the king took a goblet and poured a toast in honor of all present and of the words that had been spoken. In conclusion he said, "The greatest blessings have accrued to me by your coming here, [294]for I have profited greatly by the doctrine which you have grounded for me with reference to kingship."

He then enjoined that three talents of silver be given to each one, and also the slave who should hand it to him. All shouted their approval, and the banquet was filled with joy, while the king addressed himself to festivity unalloyed.

[295]If I have been tedious in this account, my dear Philoc-

---

perienced the greatest of blessings through their being there, for he had profited by learning from them how he ought to reign." AND ALSO THE SLAVE: Apparently presented by the king along with the money; Josephus seems to support this version. Andrews supposes the ellipsis of a verb and translates: "and appointed one of his slaves to deliver the money."
295. IF I HAVE BEEN TEDIOUS: The exculpation for the inclusion of the disproportionate *Questions* admits they were drawn from a written source, and the justification on the basis of the readiness of the respondents and the approval of the philosophers is as ingenious as it is lame.

συγγνώμην ἔχειν. τεθαυμακὼς γὰρ τοὺς ἄνδρας ὑπὲρ τὸ δέον, ὡς ἐκ τοῦ καιροῦ τὰς ἀποκρίσεις ἐποιοῦντο πολλοῦ χρόνου δεομένας, ²⁹⁶καὶ τοῦ μὲν ἐρωτῶντος μεμεριμνηκότος ἕκαστα, τῶν δὲ ἀποκρινομένων καταλλήλως ἐχόντων τὰ πρὸς τὰς ἐρωτήσεις, ἄξιοι θαυμασμοῦ κατεφαίνοντό μοι καὶ τοῖς παροῦσι, μάλιστα δὲ τοῖς φιλοσόφοις. οἴομαι δὲ καὶ πᾶσι τοῖς παραληψομένοις τὴν ἀναγραφὴν ἄπιστον φανεῖται. ²⁹⁷ψεύσασθαι μὲν οὖν οὐ καθῆκόν ἐστι περὶ τῶν ἀναγραφομένων· εἰ δὲ καί τι παραβαίην, οὐχ ὅσιον ἐν τούτοις· ἀλλ', ὡς γέγονεν, οὕτως διασαφοῦμεν ἀφοσιούμενοι πᾶν ἁμάρτημα. διόπερ ἐπειράθην ἀποδεξάμενος αὐτῶν τὴν τοῦ λόγου δύναμιν παρὰ τῶν ἀναγραφομένων ἕκαστα τῶν γινομένων ἔν τε τοῖς χρηματισμοῖς τοῦ βασιλέως καὶ ταῖς συμποσίαις μεταλαβεῖν. ²⁹⁸ἔθος γάρ ἐστι, καθὼς καὶ σὺ γινώσκεις, ἀφ' ἧς ἂν [ἡμέρας] ὁ βασιλεὺς ἄρξηται χρηματίζειν, μέχρις οὗ κατακοιμηθῇ, πάντα ἀναγράφεσθαι τὰ λεγόμενα καὶ πρασσόμενα, καλῶς γινομένου καὶ συμφερόντως. ²⁹⁹τῇ γὰρ ἐπιούσῃ τὰ τῇ πρότερον πεπραγμένα καὶ λελαλημένα πρὸ τοῦ χρηματισμοῦ παραναγινώσκεται, καί, εἴ τι μὴ δεόντως γέγονε, διορθώσεως τυγχάνει τὸ πεπραγμένον. ³⁰⁰πάντ' οὖν ἀκριβῶς <παρὰ τῶν> ἀναγεγραμμένων, ὡς ἐλέχθη, μεταλαβόντες κατακεχωρίκαμεν, εἰδότες ἣν ἔχεις φιλομάθειαν εἰς τὰ χρήσιμα.
³⁰¹Μετὰ δὲ τρεῖς ἡμέρας ὁ Δημήτριος παραλαβὼν αὐτούς,

298 ημερας T brackets, Mend. substitutes ωρας, ημερας <ωρας> W-   Gomperz
300 παρα των edd., παντων MSS

296. WILL FIND IT INCREDIBLE: This together with the insistence on credibility in the sentences following is virtually an admission of the fictional character of the episode. The romance writers regularly assert their veracity, and in tones as solemn as this, when their statements are most dubious.
297. FROM THOSE PERSONS WHO TRANSCRIBE: But the writer had himself been present throughout! Such careful "documentation" is a mark of fiction.
298. CUSTOM... TO RECORD IN WRITING: A correct allusion to the official *hypomnēmata;* cf. 283, and for another allusion to Ptolemaic court procedure, 182. For the public records generally see on 300.
299. AUDIENCES: *khrēmatismos*, "the transaction of business," but with special reference to the king's activity.
300. ARCHIVES: U. Wilcken, "Hypomnematismoi," *Philologus* 53 (1894),

rates, forgive me. I admired beyond measure the way in which the men on the spur of the moment framed responses which required long meditation; [296]since their interrogator had carefully pondered each question while the respondents replied to the queries one after the other, they seemed admirable to me, and also to the others present, but especially to the philosophers. I suppose that everyone likely to get hold of this account will find it incredible. [297]But to falsify concerning matters extant in writing is churlish. Indeed, if I were to pass over any point, it would be an impiety in a subject of this sort. But I describe the event exactly as it happened, solemnly acquitting myself of all error. Accordingly I endeavored to procure particulars of what transpired from those persons who transcribe the proceedings at the king's audiences and in his banquets, so impressed was I with the power of their discourse. [298]For it is the custom, as you surely are aware, to record in writing everything said and done from the moment the king begins to give audience until he retires to bed—a good and useful practice. [299]On the day following, before audiences commence, the actions taken and the remarks uttered on the previous day are read through, and if any procedure is found incorrect it receives rectification. [300]As I have said, then, I obtained accurate information on all particulars from the archives, and have recorded it in writing because I know how you cherish useful learning.
[301]After three days Demetrius took the men with him and

80–126, proved that careful and complete archives were kept in Egypt in the *Roman* period, and some older scholars have maintained that they were not so kept in the Ptolemaic period, whence we would infer a Roman dating ɔr our passage. But probability, supported by various items of evidence, ιakes it virtually certain that complete archives were kept by the Ptolemies lso, and hence no inference for dating can be drawn.
ɔ1–316. THE TRANSLATION AND ITS RECEPTION.
ɔ1. THREE DAYS: After the last banquet.   DEMETRIUS: The central gure in procuring the translation is not mentioned after the citation of his ιemorandum (29 ff.), though he may be imagined as present at the banuets among the philosophers.   BREAKWATER: Connecting Alexandria ιιh the ISLAND of Pharos. Wendland pointed out that Pharos was uninabited after 47 BCE, the year of Julius Caesar's Alexandrine War, and

καὶ διελθὼν τὸ τῶν ἑπτὰ σταδίων ἀνάχωμα τῆς θαλάσσης πρὸς τὴν νῆσον, καὶ διαβὰς τὴν γέφυραν, καὶ προσελθὼν ὡς ἐπὶ τὰ βόρεια μέρη, συνέδριον ποιησάμενος εἰς κατεσκευασμένον οἶκον παρὰ τὴν ἠϊόνα, διαπρεπῶς ἔχοντα καὶ πολλῆς ἡσυχίας ἔφεδρον, παρεκάλει τοὺς ἄνδρας τὰ τῆς ἑρμηνείας ἐπιτελεῖν, παρόντων ὅσα πρὸς τὴν χρείαν ἔδει καλῶς. ³⁰²οἱ δὲ ἐπετέλουν ἕκαστα σύμφωνα ποιοῦντες πρὸς ἑαυτοὺς ταῖς ἀντιβολαῖς· τὸ δὲ ἐκ τῆς συμφωνίας γινόμενον πρεπόντως ἀναγραφῆς οὕτως ἐτύγχανε παρὰ τοῦ Δημητρίου. ³⁰³καὶ μέχρι μὲν ὥρας ἐνάτης τὰ τῆς συνεδρείας ἐγίνετο· μετὰ δὲ ταῦτα περὶ τὴν τοῦ σώματος θεραπείαν ἀπελύοντο γίνεσθαι, χορηγουμένων αὐτοῖς δαψιλῶς ὧν προηροῦντο πάντων. ³⁰⁴ἐκτὸς δὲ καὶ καθ' ἡμέραν, ὅσα βασιλεῖ παρεσκευάζετο, καὶ τούτοις ὁ Δωρόθεος ἐπετέλει· προστεταγμένον γὰρ ἦν αὐτῷ διὰ τοῦ βασιλέως. ἅμα δὲ τῇ πρωΐᾳ παρεγίνοντο εἰς τὴν αὐλὴν καθ' ἡμέραν, καὶ ποιησάμενοι τὸν ἀσπασμὸν τοῦ βασιλέως, ἀπελύοντο πρὸς τὸν ἑαυτῶν τόπον. ³⁰⁵ὡς δὲ ἔθος ἐστὶ πᾶσι τοῖς Ἰουδαίοις, <ἀπονιψάμενοι> τῇ θαλάσσῃ τὰς χεῖρας, ὡς ἂν εὔξωνται πρὸς τὸν θεόν, ἐτρέποντο πρὸς τὴν ἀνάγνωσιν καὶ τὴν ἑκάστου διασάφησιν.

---

304 εκτος MSS, Cohn suggests νυκτος   305 απονιψαμενοι edd., απονιψαμενοις MSS

argued that the translation must therefore be earlier. The argument is not conclusive, for our passage does not necessarily imply that Pharos was inhabited, and indeed solitude might be a good reason for the choice, as the Philo passage (see Introd. 24) implies. The festival celebrated on the island in Philo's own time proves its traditional association with the translation. Josephus (103) says, "Because it was so quiet there."
302. MAKING ALL DETAILS HARMONIZE BY MUTUAL COMPARISONS: A clear statement that the translation was the product of scholarly labor, not of inspiration, as Philo and succeeding versions make it. Josephus says nothing of comparisons, but states (104) that they worked "painstaking as possible to make the translation accurate." UNDER THE DIRECTION OF DEMETRIUS: In keeping with Aristeas' insistence that the version was made for the Library, but see on 308.
303. NINTH HOUR: 3 P.M. The account of the daily program of the translators in this and the following section seems oddly disjointed, the start of their day being mentioned only after their closing hour and a parenthesis on the king's lavishness. H. Willrich, *Urkundenfälschung in der hellenistisch-*

crossed the breakwater, seven stades long, to the island; then he crossed over the bridge and proceeded to the northerly parts. There he called a meeting in a mansion built by the seashore, magnificently appointed and in a secluded situation, and called upon the men to carry out the business of translation, all necessary appliances having been well provided. [302]And so they proceeded to carry it out, making all details harmonize by mutual comparisons. The appropriate result of the harmonization was reduced to writing under the direction of Demetrius. [303]The sessions would last until the ninth hour, and afterwards they would break up to take care of their bodily needs, all their requirements being lavishly supplied. [304]In addition, everything that was prepared for the king Dorotheus arranged for them also, for he had been so instructed by the king. Every day they would come to the court early in the morning, and when they had made their salutation to the king they departed to their own place. [305]When they had washed their hands in the sea, as is the custom of all Jews, and had offered prayer to God, they addressed themselves to the interpretation and clarification

jüdischen Literatur (Göttingen, 1924), 88, interprets the passage to mean that the translators resided near the king's palace, whither they returned after each day's work. This he takes to indicate that Pharos was in fact uninhabited, and hence that Aristeas was written after 47 BCE. Tramontano *ad loc.* refuses to press the verb *apeluonto* and interprets the passage more reasonably to mean that the translators resided on the island and came to the mainland only for relaxation and to pay their respects to the king.

304. IN THE MORNING . . . MADE THEIR SALUTATION: Graetz took this to refer to the *salutatio matutina*, and hence to imply a Roman date. But there is no evidence (nor probability) that the Ptolemies did not hold a morning levée.

305. WASHED THEIR HANDS IN THE SEA . . . OFFERED PRAYER: L. Sukenik, *Ancient Synagogues in Palestine and Greece* (1934), 49 f., offers archaeological and literary (*Ant.* 14.258, Acts 16.13) evidence to show that Jews in Hellenistic countries built their synagogues by preference in the proximity of water. He sees a motive in "the ritual uncleanness of the land of the Gentiles," and cites an illustrative passage from *Mekilta* on Ex. 12.1.

CLARIFICATION: The Greek word (*diasaphēsin*) is rare; it occurs at LXX

³⁰⁶Ἐπηρώτησα δὲ καὶ τοῦτο Τίνος χάριν ἀπονιζόμενοι τὰς χεῖρας τὸ τηνικαῦτα εὔχονται; διεσάφουν δέ, ὅτι μαρτύριόν ἐστι τοῦ μηδὲν εἰργάσθαι κακόν· πᾶσα γὰρ ἐνέργεια διὰ τῶν χειρῶν γίνεται· καλῶς καὶ ὁσίως μεταφέροντες ἐπὶ τὴν δικαιοσύνην καὶ τὴν ἀλήθειαν πάντα. ³⁰⁷καθὼς δὲ προειρήκαμεν, οὕτως καθ᾽ ἑκάστην εἰς τὸν τόπον, ἔχοντα τερπνότητα διὰ τὴν ἡσυχίαν καὶ καταύγειαν, συναγόμενοι τὸ προκείμενον ἐπετέλουν. συνέτυχε δὲ οὕτως, ὥστε ἐν ἡμέραις ἑβδομήκοντα δυσὶ τελειωθῆναι τὰ τῆς μεταγραφῆς, οἱονεὶ κατὰ πρόθεσίν τινα τοῦ τοιούτου γεγενημένου. ³⁰⁸Τελείωσιν δὲ ὅτε ἔλαβε, συναγαγὼν ὁ Δημήτριος τὸ πλῆθος τῶν Ἰουδαίων εἰς τὸν τόπον, οὗ καὶ τὰ τῆς ἑρμηνείας ἐτελέσθη, παρανέγνω πᾶσι, παρόντων καὶ τῶν διερμηνευσάντων, οἵτινες μεγάλης ἀποδοχῆς καὶ παρὰ τοῦ πλήθους ἔτυχον, ὡς ἂν μεγάλων ἀγαθῶν παραίτιοι γεγονότες. ³⁰⁹ὡσαύτως δὲ καὶ τὸν Δημήτριον ἀποδεξάμενοι παρεκάλεσαν μεταδοῦναι τοῖς ἡγουμένοις αὐτῶν, μεταγράψαντα τὸν πάντα νόμον. ³¹⁰καθὼς δὲ ἀνεγνώσθη τὰ τεύχη, στάντες οἱ ἱερεῖς καὶ τῶν ἑρμηνέων οἱ πρεσβύτεροι καὶ τῶν ἀπὸ τοῦ πολιτεύματος οἵ τε ἡγούμενοι τοῦ πλήθους εἶπον Ἐπεὶ καλῶς καὶ ὁσίως διηρμήνευται καὶ κατὰ πᾶν ἠκριβωμένως, καλῶς ἔχον ἐστίν, ἵνα διαμείνῃ ταῦθ᾽ οὕτως ἔχοντα, καὶ μὴ γένηται μηδεμία διασκευή. ³¹¹πάντων δ᾽ ἐπιφωνησάντων τοῖς εἰρη-

---

307 τερπνοτητα edd., τερπνω τινα MSS   311 εκελευσαν edd.-Jos.-Euseb., εκελευσεν MSS

---

306. THEY EXPLAINED: This allegorical interpretation is not in Josephus, and Février holds that it is an interpolation from the same source as 83–171. HANDS ARE THE ORGANS OF ALL ACTIVITY: The same thought, in virtually the same language, is cited from Aristobulus in Eusebius, *Praep. Ev.* 8.10.8.

307. AS WE HAVE SAID BEFORE: Resumptive, after the interruption of 305–6; see on 3. SEVENTY-TWO DAYS . . . THE RESULT OF SOME DESIGN: This is as far as Aristeas goes in endowing the translation with the miraculous, perhaps in keeping with his pose of objective scholarship; the hint is elaborated in Philo and his followers.

308. ASSEMBLED THE COMMUNITY OF THE JEWS: This is the first mention of any interest in the enterprise on the part of the Egyptian community, and the fact that the translation was first presented to them would seem sufficient indication that it was made to satisfy their needs and not by royal

of each passage. ³⁰⁶I questioned them on this point too, why it was that they washed their hands before praying. And they explained that it was in witness that they had done no wrong, since the hands are the organs of all activity; in such beautiful and holy spirit do they make all things symbols of righteousness and truth. ³⁰⁷Thus, as we have said before, they forgathered every day to this spot, so delightful for its seclusion and its clear light, and carried out their appointed task. And so it came about that the work of transcription was completed in seventy-two days, as if this coincidence had been the result of some design.

³⁰⁸When the work was concluded Demetrius assembled the community of the Jews at the place where the translation was executed, and read it out to the entire gathering, the translators too being present; these received a great ovation from the community also, in recognition of the great service for which they were responsible. ³⁰⁹And they accorded Demetrius a similar reception, and requested him to have a transcription of the entire Law made and to present it to their rulers. ³¹⁰When the rolls had been read the priests and the elders of the translators and some of the corporate body and the leaders of the people rose up and said, "Inasmuch as the translation has been well and piously made and is in every respect accurate, it is right that it should remain in its present form and that no revision of any sort take place." ³¹¹When

order for the Library.   AT THE PLACE: Surely somehow connected with the festival on Pharos of which Philo speaks.   OVATION: Such a public manifestation is a virtual fixture in the Greek romances; see Introd. 52.
309. REQUESTED HIM: On the assumption that the work was in fact done for the king, it becomes necessary for a special request to be made that a copy be made for THEIR RULERS, *i.e.*, the heads of the Jewish community.
310. PRIESTS: Of the Alexandrian community.   ELDERS OF THE TRANSLATORS: In point of age.   CORPORATE BODY: *Politeuma* is a technical word for the political organization of the Jews within *polis* of Alexandria. The action of representative officials is calculated to give the version public and binding authority; ROSE UP contributes to the solemnity.
311. THEY BADE: MSS read "he bade," which must make the reference to Demetrius, but edd. all read the plural, and are supported by Josephus 109.
ACCORDING TO THEIR CUSTOM: The allusion may be to Deut. 4.2 (*cf.* 13.1), though no imprecation is given: "Ye shall not add unto the word which

μένοις, ἐκέλευσαν διαράσασθαι, καθὼς ἔθος αὐτοῖς ἐστιν, εἴ τις διασκευάσει προστιθεὶς ἢ μεταφέρων τι τὸ σύνολον τῶν γεγραμμένων ἢ ποιούμενος ἀφαίρεσιν, καλῶς τοῦτο πράσσοντες, ἵνα διὰ παντὸς ἀέννaa καὶ μένοντα φυλάσσηται.

312 Προσφωνηθέντων δὲ καὶ τούτων τῷ βασιλεῖ μεγάλως ἐχάρη· τὴν γὰρ πρόθεσιν, ἣν εἶχεν, ἀσφαλῶς ἔδοξε τετελειῶσθαι. παρανεγνώσθη δὲ αὐτῷ καὶ πάντα, καὶ λίαν ἐξεθαύμασε τὴν τοῦ νομοθέτου διάνοιαν. καὶ πρὸς τὸν Δημήτριον εἶπε Πῶς τηλικούτων συντετελεσμένων οὐδεὶς ἐπεβάλετο τῶν ἱστορικῶν ἢ ποιητῶν ἐπιμνησθῆναι; 313 ἐκεῖνος δὲ ἔφη Διὰ τὸ σεμνὴν εἶναι τὴν νομοθεσίαν καὶ διὰ θεοῦ γεγονέναι· καὶ τῶν ἐπιβαλλομένων τινὲς ὑπὸ τοῦ θεοῦ πληγέντες τῆς ἐπιβολῆς ἀπέστησαν. 314 καὶ γὰρ ἔφησεν ἀκηκοέναι Θεοπόμπου, διότι μέλλων τινὰ τῶν προηρμηνευμένων ἐπισφαλέστερον ἐκ τοῦ νόμου προσιστορεῖν ταραχὴν λάβοι τῆς διανοίας πλεῖον ἡμερῶν τριάκοντα· κατὰ δὲ τὴν ἄνεσιν ἐξιλάσκεσθαι τὸν θεόν, σαφὲς αὐτῷ γενέσθαι, τίνος χάριν τὸ συμβαῖνόν ἐστι. 315 δι' ὀνείρου δὲ σημανθέντος, ὅτι τὰ θεῖα

314 Θεοπόμπου edd., Θεοπέμπτου MSS /
λάβοι edd.-Euseb., λαβεῖν MSS

I command you, neither shall ye diminish from it...." Kahle and others have argued (see Introd. 69) that it is unlikely that such an imprecation should accompany the first promulgation of the LXX, and similarly unlikely that such intensity be shown regarding a document which had been in circulation a century or more, and hence that what is here dealt with is a *revision* of the original translation, to which official sanction is here given. In this view the present passage is central to the whole book. Josephus oddly omits the rigorous mandate fixing the text; he says (109): "They ordered that, if anyone saw any further addition made to the text of the Law or anything omitted from it, he should examine it and make it known and correct it; in this they acted wisely, that what had once been judged good might remain forever."

312. MARVELLED EXCEEDINGLY: The approval of the king is consistent with the general "apologetic" note of Aristeas, and the king's question, HOW HAS IT NOT OCCURRED . . .? is precisely the question an interlocutor might be imagined to address to such an apologist.

313. THROUGH GOD: The insistence on the divine origin of the Law is an interesting foreshadowing of Philo; see on 177. In 31 Hecataeus is cited as authority for the statement that secular writers have abstained from men-

all had assented to what had been said, they bade that an imprecation be pronounced, according to their custom, upon any who should revise the text by adding or transposing anything whatever in what had been written down, or by making any excision; and in this they did well, so that the work might be preserved imperishable and unchanged always.

312When these proceedings were reported to the king he rejoiced greatly, for he thought that the purpose he cherished had been securely carried out. The whole work was read out to him also, and he marvelled exceedingly at the intellect of the lawgiver. To Demetrius he said, "How has it not occurred to any of the historians or poets to make mention of such enormous achievements?" 313And he said, "Because the Law is holy and has come into being through God; some of those to whom the thought did occur were smitten by God and desisted from the attempt." 314Indeed, he said, he had heard Theopompus say that when he was on the point of introducing into his history certain matter which had previously been translated from the Law, too rashly, he suffered a derangement of the mind for more than thirty days; upon the abatement of the disorder he implored God that the cause of what had befallen be made plain to him, 315and when it was

tioning the Law because of its sacred character, and it is likely that the statement is in fact the genuine Hecataeus' (see on 31). It is quite possible that 313-316 similarly derive from Hecataeus. THE THOUGHT DID OCCUR: A highly significant admission that a translation had existed long before the version here authorized (see on 311), even though it may not have existed in the fourth century, to which Theopompus and Theodectes belong. No one would assume that the Greek writers knew the Hebrew.

314. THEOPOMPUS: Of Chios, *ca.* 376–300, esteemed as a historian next after Herodotus and Thucydides. He was at the court of Ptolemy I in 305, but not of Ptolemy Philadelphus. Knowledge of exotic literatures might appropriately be attributed to Theopompus, for he apparently knew the *Avesta*: F.H.G. No. 71.   SAY: The Greek may bear the meaning "I have heard *of* Theopompus," *i.e.*, not directly. In any case, it is apparently assumed that a translation of the Law existed in Theopompus' time.

315. MEDDLESOME: Photius, *Cod.* 176, describes Theopompus as *polupragmon*, which has the same connotation.   COMMON: Frequently in the sense of "unclean," "profane."

βούλεται περιεργασάμενος εἰς κοινοὺς ἀνθρώπους ἐκφέρειν, ἀποσχόμενον δὲ οὕτως ἀποκαταστῆναι. ³¹⁶καὶ παρὰ Θεοδέκτου δὲ τοῦ τῶν τραγῳδιῶν ποιητοῦ μετέλαβον ἐγώ, διότι παραφέρειν μέλλοντός τι τῶν ἀναγεγραμμένων ἐν τῇ βίβλῳ πρός τι δρᾶμα τὰς ὄψεις ἀπεγλαυκώθη· καὶ λαβὼν ὑπόνοιαν, ὅτι διὰ τοῦτ' αὐτῷ τὸ σύμπτωμα γέγονεν, ἐξιλασάμενος τὸν θεὸν ἐν πολλαῖς ἡμέραις ἀποκατέστη. ³¹⁷Μεταλαβὼν δὲ ὁ βασιλεύς, καθὼς προεῖπον, περὶ τούτων τὰ παρὰ τοῦ Δημητρίου, προσκυνήσας ἐκέλευσε μεγάλην ἐπιμέλειαν ποιεῖσθαι τῶν βιβλίων καὶ συντηρεῖν ἁγνῶς. ³¹⁸παρακαλέσας δὲ καὶ τοὺς ἑρμηνεῖς, ἵνα παραγίνωνται πυκνότερον πρὸς αὐτόν, ἐὰν ἀποκατασταθῶσιν εἰς τὴν Ἰουδαίαν,—δίκαιον γὰρ εἶπε τὴν ἐκπομπὴν αὐτῶν γενέσθαι· παραγενηθέντας δέ, ὡς θέμις, ἕξειν αὐτοὺς φίλους, καὶ <πολυωρίας> τῆς μεγίστης τεύξεσθαι παρ' αὐτοῦ. ³¹⁹τὰ δὲ πρὸς τὴν ἐκπομπὴν αὐτῶν ἐκέλευσεν ἑτοιμάζειν, μεγαλομερῶς τοῖς ἀνδράσι χρησάμενος. ἑκάστῳ γὰρ στολὰς ἔδωκε τῶν κρατίστων τρεῖς καὶ χρυσίου τάλαντα δύο καὶ κυλίκιον ταλάντου καὶ τρικλίνου πᾶσαν κατάστρωσιν. ³²⁰ἔπεμψε δὲ καὶ τῷ Ἐλεαζάρῳ μετὰ τῆς ἐκπομπῆς αὐτῶν ἀργυρόποδας κλίνας δέκα καὶ τὰ ἀκόλουθα πάντα καὶ κυλίκιον ταλάντων τριάκοντα καὶ στολὰς δέκα καὶ πορφύραν καὶ στέφανον διαπρεπῆ καὶ βυσσίνων ὀθονίων ἱστοὺς ἑκατὸν καὶ φιάλας

317 περι τουτων τα παρα του Δημητριου edd., περι των του Δημητριου MSS
318 πολυωριας edd.-Mahaffy, πολυδωριας MSS
319 χρησαμενος T-MSS, χαρισαμενος

W-MSS / κυλικιον T-MSS, κυλιδιον MSS, κυλικειον W-Wilwilcken
320 κυλικιον MSS-Jos. / ιστους edd.-Jos., εις τους MSS

316. THEODECTES: *Ca.* 380–334, a friend of Aristotle, who refers (*Nicomachean Ethics* 1150b) to one of his plays, and a pupil of Isocrates. He was defeated by Theopompus in oratory in Artemisia's contest, but won in tragedy. It is unlikely that Demetrius, who was only ten years old at Theodectes' death, should have heard him, and indeed I HAVE HEARD need not necessarily refer to Demetrius but *may* refer to Aristeas, though it is easier to take it with Demetrius, and the ragged chronology of the whole passage permits us to do so. It was a tradition in Hellenistic Jewish writings that great secular writers drew from Jewish wisdom; Aristobulus, Philo, and Josephus say that Pythagoras, Socrates, and Plato learned from the Jews. THE BOOK: This is the first recorded use of *Bible* for the sacred

signified to him in a dream that it was his meddlesome desire to disclose divine matters to common men, he desisted, and was thereupon restored to health. ³¹⁶"And of Theodectes also, the tragic poet, I have heard," he added, "that when he was on the point of introducing into one of his plays something recorded in the Book, his vision was afflicted with a cataract. Conceiving the suspicion that this was the reason for his calamity, he implored God and after many days recovered."

³¹⁷When the king heard the account of these things from Demetrius, as I have said before, he bowed deeply and gave orders that great care be taken of the books and that they be watched over reverently. ³¹⁸He also urged the translators to make visits to him, after they had been restored to Judaea. It was but just he said, for them to be sent home; but if they visited him he would treat them as friends, as it was his solemn obligation to do, and they would receive rich marks of his consideration. ³¹⁹He ordered that preparations for their sending off be seen to, treating the men munificently. To each he gave three costumes of the highest quality, and two talents of gold, and a sideboard of a talent's weight, and complete furnishings for the dining-room. ³²⁰To Eleazar he sent, with their escort, ten couches with legs of silver, and all their appurtenances, and a sideboard of thirty talents, and ten costumes, and a purple robe, and a magnificent crown, and a hundred webs of fine woven linen, and shallow bowls, and

---

Scriptures; elsewhere Aristeas uses *hē graphē*, "the Scripture" (155, 168) and *ta logia*, "the oracles, sayings" (158, 167). The only play we know of whose theme was drawn from the Bible is Ezekielos' *Exagogē*, on the Exodus. HE IMPLORED GOD: Another indication of Aristeas' universalism; God not only protects His books, but answers the prayers of non-Jews.
317–321. THE DEPARTURE OF THE TRANSLATORS.
317. BOWED DEEPLY: More likely to the books than to their bearers.
318. RICH ... CONSIDERATION: MSS *poludorias* means "rich gifts"; *poluorias* is appropriately delicate, and was suggested by Mahaffy.
319. SIDEBOARD: Reading *kulikeion* (instead of *kulikion*, "cup"), for a talent seems excessive for the value ("weight" might be so rendered) of a cup.
320. TO ELEAZAR: The presents are the conventional ones for royalty; *cf.* King Alexander's gifts to Jonathan on his appointment as High Priest (I Mac. 10.20) and see on 41, 46.

καὶ τρυβλία καὶ κρατῆρας χρυσοῦς δύο πρὸς ἀνάθεσιν. ³²¹ἔγραψε δὲ καὶ παρακαλῶν, ἵνα, ἐάν τινες τῶν ἀνδρῶν προαιρῶνται πρὸς αὐτὸν ἀνακομισθῆναι, μὴ κωλύσῃ, περὶ πολλοῦ ποιούμενος τοῖς πεπαιδευμένοις συνεῖναι, καὶ εἰς τοιούτους τὸν πλοῦτον κατατίθεσθαι δαψιλῶς, καὶ οὐκ εἰς μάταια. ³²²Σὺ δέ, καθὼς ἐπηγγειλάμην, ἀπέχεις τὴν διήγησιν, ὦ Φιλόκρατες. τέρπειν γὰρ οἴομαί σε ταῦτα ἢ τὰ τῶν μυθολόγων βιβλία. νένευκας γὰρ πρὸς περιεργίαν τῶν δυναμένων ὠφελεῖν διάνοιαν, καὶ ἐν τούτοις τὸν πλείονα χρόνον διατελεῖς. πειράσομαι δὲ καὶ τὰ λοιπὰ τῶν ἀξιολόγων ἀναγράφειν, ἵνα διαπορευόμενος αὐτὰ κομίζῃ τοῦ βουλήματος τὸ κάλλιστον ἔπαθλον.

---

321. URGING THAT IF ANY OF THE MEN CHOSE TO RETURN . . . HE ACCOUNTED IT A PRIVILEGE: An appropriate pendant to 124 and 126.
322. CONCLUSION.
322. THE STORY: *Diēgesis*, as in 1. In keeping with regular literary usage the epilogue echoes actual words as well as sentiments of the proem.
ROMANCERS: The very comparison suggests that the difference is of degree rather than kind; Aristeas is not claiming to write history.   WHAT-

plates, and two mixing bowls of gold as a dedicatory offering. ³²¹He also wrote a letter urging that if any of the men chose to return to him Eleazar might not prevent, for he accounted it a privilege to associate with cultured men, and would rather lavish his wealth upon such men than on vanities.

³²²You have the story, my dear Philocrates, just as I promised. I believe such an account will afford you greater pleasure than the books of the romancers. For you are devoted to the study of things capable of profiting the mind, and you occupy most of your time with such things. I shall try to write down whatever else is worth telling, so that their perusal may win you your wish's highest prize.

EVER ELSE: In 6 Aristeas refers to a previous communication, "on the race of the Jews," next came the present work, and the other things "worth telling" which is here promised, might presumably deal with political matters, especially as referring to the diaspora. There is no evidence to show the other two works were actually written, though some scholars hold that the first named is intended to suggest an actual work of a real Aristeas; see Introd. 41.

INDEX

Abot, 93, 156, 174, 186, 198, 200
Abrahams, I., 84, 176
Acco, 146
acting and actors, 186, 212
Acts, 219
Adad Nirari IV, 148
"adjudged," 10, 98
Agatharchides, 98
Alexander, 48, 101, 170
Alexander Jannaeus, 10, 115, 146
Alexander Romance, 52
Alexandria, 94, 143 f.
allegorical interpretation, 15, 152, 220
altar, 134
Amasis, 43
Anacharsis, 51
Andreas, 98
Andrews, 158, 167, 215
anger, 199
animals, allegorized, 163 f.
Antigonus Gonatas, 169, 178
Antiochus Epiphanes, 121, 133
Antiphanes of Berge, 49
antisemitism, 63, 114, 158
Antonia, the, 12, 140
Antonius Diogenes, 49
aparkhai, 115
Apollonius, 46
apologetics, 20, 60
Arabs, 147
archaizing, 6
archives, 216
archisomatophulax, 98
Aristaeus, 94
Aristarchus, 27
Aristeas, personality of, 3 f., 115, 222
Aristeas, as Greek book, 54
Aristobulus, 26, 73, 102, 220

Aristotle, 58, 143 f., 149, 153, 164, 182, 187, 224
Arrian, 180
Arsinoe, 5, 116, 170
Ascalon, 10, 115, 146
Asclepiades of Myrlea, 57
Athenaeus, 42, 48, 122
Augustine, 78, 84
Azariah de Rossi, 83, 168

Babylon, 100
bankers, 108
Barnabas, 164
Baron, S., 84
benevolence, 188
Bentley, R., 5
Bevan, E., 7
"Bible," first use of, 224
Bickermann, E., 8, 10, 17, 35, 112, 170, 210
bowls, 128
Braun, M., 63
Breccia, A., 46

Caesar, Julius, 11, 94
Cahana, A., 9, 86, 133, 159
Callistratus, 48
Callixinus of Rhodes, 47, 122
Cambyses, 100
Cedrenus, 145
Chelkias, 119
chreia, 50, 154 f.
Christ-Schmid-Stählin, 51
Chronicles I, 133
Cicero, 57, 154, 205
citadel, in Jerusalem, 12, 139
Clement of Alexandria, 27, 76
Cleopatra, 119
Clermont-Ganneau, 14, 46
Coele-Syria, 30, 98

229

Cohen, J., 33
Cohn, L., 26
Colson, F. H., 22
commoners as kings, 11, 213
Corinthians I, 153
Cowley, 100
"crown of righteousness," 209
cud chewing, 161
curtain in Temple, 14, 133
Cynic homilies, 50
Cyprus, 94

Daniel, 192
Davids, R., 41
decree of Ptolemy Philadelphus, 105
Demetrius (historian), 97
Demetrius of Phalerum, 7, 25, 51, 96, 110, 184, 210, 217, 219
Demetrius Poliorcetes, 96
Deuteronomy, 148, 160 ff., 182, 189, 221
diaphonein, 71, 79
diaspora, 114
diegesis, 56, 226
dietary usages, 152, 170
Dio Chrysostom, 42, 51 f.
Diodorus Siculus, 43, 49, 111, 159, 173, 180
Diogenes, 51
Diogenes Laertius, 49, 179, 189
Diomede, 78
Dionysus, cult of, 35
discrepant numbers, 104
Dositheus, 115, 120
Dorotheus, 171
dreams, 184
Dziatzko, 56

Egypt, country and mores of, 9, 155, 160, 171
Egypt, Jewish community in, 99, 220
ekphrasis, 47, 56, 133
Elder Philo, 60
Eleazar, 92 f., 112, 116, 118, 139, 151, 153, 167, 225
Elisha, 172
Enoch II, 191

envy, 187
Epictetus, 186
epieikeia, 41, 213
Epiphanius, 56, 76, 118
erroso, 111, 118
Esther, 120, 157
euergetes, 182, 197
Euhemerus, 49, 154
Eusebius, 4, 26 f., 56, 76, 92, 94, 102, 135, 159, 180, 220
eutukhei, 111
Exodus, 121, 133 f.
Ezechias, 98
Ezekielos, 60, 225
Ezra, 38, 121

Fairbanks, A., 48
Février, J. G., 11, 16, 18, 38 f., 135 f., 140, 213, 220
Finckh, C. E., 57
flagons, 130
Frankel, Z., 72, 81
Freudenthal, M., 95
Friends (as title), 118
Fuchs, L., 99

Gaster, M., 67, 83
Gaza, 10, 98, 115, 146
Genesis, 172
Genesis Rabbah, 208
gentiles, 61, 149
gifts, 120, 225
Ginzberg, L., 16, 82
Glueck, N., 148
gnothe sauton, 183
God, name of, 139
gold, writing in, 168
Golden Rule, 181
Goodenough, E. R., 41
Graetz, H., 165, 219
graphe, 161, 225
Greek form of Aristeas, 54 ff.

Habakkuk, 132
Hadas, M., 33, 49, 52, 63
Hecataeus, 43, 98, 110, 130, 132, 134, 142, 145, 147, 188, 222 f.

INDEX 231

Heliodorus, 15
Herod, 74, 141
Herodotus, 53, 95, 99, 138, 185
Hesiod, 182
high priest, 9, 92 f., 137, 141
Hillel, 93
Hody, H., 5, 78, 84
Homer, 17, 47 f., 79
hoshen, 138

Idumaea, 10, 143
informers, 15, 107, 164 f.
inspiration of lawgivers, 194
Ipsus, 98
Irenaeus, 75
Isaiah, 156
Isocrates, 95, 181, 224

Jerome, 78
Jerusalem, 12 f., 130, 132, 139, 142, 144
Jews and gentiles, 149
Job, 156
John Chrysostom, 76
Joppa, 10, 115, 146
Jordan, 147
Josephus, 12, 18, 56, 97, 112, 114, 119 f., 130, 132 f., 140, 142, 167, 169, 171 ff., 178, 222
Joshua, 147
Josippon, 120
Judaea, 132
Judah Maccabee, 141
Judaism and Jews, Aristeas on, 59
Judges, 145
justice, 183
Justin Martyr, 74 f.

Kahle, P., 18, 69, 110, 222
Kings I, 121
kingship, treatises on, 40
kingship in Egypt, 43
kinship, 95, 194

letters, 56, 97, 112
Leviticus, 142, 152, 158, 160
Libanius, 42

Library, Alexandrian, 96f.
Lieberman, S., 68, 149
Liebesny, H., 30, 105
linguistic usage, 17
Lochias, 170
logia, 138, 169
Lucian, 49
Lumbroso, G., 85
Lycurgus, 194

Maccabees, books of, 93; I, 114, 121, 133, 149, 175, 225; II, 149, 171; III, 31 ff., 98, 105, 134, 156 f., 170 f., 172; IV, 110
Macurdy, G. H., 116
Mahaffy, J. P., 130, 225
Manetho, 71
manuscripts of Aristeas, 84
Marcus, R., 13, 46, 89 f., 92, 99, 140
Meecham, H. G., 17, 38, 56, 86, 111, 145, 181, 204
Megillah, 80
Mekilta, 219
"men of God," 156
Menander, 153
Mendelssohn, L., 85
Menedemus of Eretria, 7, 178
mezuzah, 163
Milindapanha, 40
mines, 148
misanthropy, 159
Molière, 165
Momigliano, R., 114
Moses, 63, 153, 158, 194
Motzo, B., 26, 69
Mueller, B. A., 57
Mühl, M., 41, 181
music, 212

names, 118; Hasmonaean, 11
narratio, 57
nationalism, 63, 156
naval victory, 7, 169
Nehemiah, 38, 141
Nicanor, 98, 171
Nock, A. D., 190
nomos empsychos, 187

Numbers, 158
numbers, discrepant, 104

Oldfather, C. H., 43
Olmstead, A. T., 99, 131
Onias, 115, 119
oracle, 138
Orlinsky, H. M., 83
Orphics, 102

paganism, condemnation of, 19, 51
Palestine, 64, 94, 154
Palmerius, 84
pantokrator, 172
papyri, 99 f., 104 f., 145, 165, 171, 209
parents, honor of, 189, 193
pathemata mathemata, 181
Pausanias, 14, 133
Peisistratus, 79, 144
Peripatetic, 184
Persians, 113
Petrie, F., 99
Pharos, 11, 94, 217, 221
philanthropia, 41, 204, 213
Philo, 11, 21 ff., 95, 112, 144, 149, 153, 157, 160 f., 174 f., 177, 180, 184, 186, 191, 208, 218
Philocrates, 92
philosophy, 110, 157
Philostratus, 47, 49
Phocylides, 165
Photius, 223
pilgrims, 19, 137, 141
Plato, 42, 189, 198, 209, 212
Plutarch, 42, 50, 96, 193, 199, 205, 210
Pöhlmann, R., 49
Polybius, 57, 98
Pompey, 10, 146
prayer, 102
priests, 121, 136, 172
progymnasmata, 50, 57
Proverbs, 102, 153, 156, 174, 180, 182 f., 193, 198 f.
Psalms, 172, 175 f., 212
Psalms of Solomon, 181
Psammetichus, 99

Ptolemais, 10, 115, 146
Ptolemy I, 6, 94, 96, 101, 106; II, 96, 112, 198; III, 197; IV, 27, 98, 196; VI, 115; Auletes, 11, 109, 213
Pytheas of Marseilles, 49

questions on kingship, 41, 173
Quintilian, 57

Rabelais, 165
rabbinic texts on Aristeas legend, 80
Reichel, G., 57
Reitzenstein, R., 58
religion, 15, 37, 59 ff., 103, 174
repute, 188, 205
Riessler, G., 11
Ritschl, F., 79
Rohde, E., 49, 52
romances and romancers, 51, 216, 226
Rostovtzeff, M., 46, 108, 113
royal pages, 172

sacrifices, 166, 191
Samaria, Samaritans, 67, 143
Samuel I, 203
Sandys, J. E., 53
Sayce, A., 100
Scaliger, 78
Schard, S., 84
Schmidt, M., 85
scholarship, Alexandrian, 52
Schürer, E., 9, 13
script, Hebrew, 168
seating order, 171
Semonides, 198
Seneca, 196, 199, 205
Septuagint, 66, 93, 123, 137, 219; legend of, 73; as revision, 69, 222
seventy-two, as number of translators, 39, 42, 71, 111
Sextus Empiricus, 57
Sibylline Oracles, 165
Simon, 10, 146
Sirah, 27, 65, 69, 133, 135, 154, 174, 178, 181, 187 f., 193, 198, 202 f.
Soferim, 80, 168
Solon, 194

INDEX 233

Sophocles, 93, 183
Sosibius, 98
Sphaerus of Borysthenes, 49
Stählin, G., 20
Stein, M., 65
Stoics, 17, 49 f., 102, 177 f., 184, 186 f., 194 ff., 210, 212, 257
Strabo, 11, 49
Strack-Billerbeck, 181
style, 17, 93, 95 f., 98, 103, 109, 111, 115
Sukenik, L., 219
symposia, 42, 212
synkrisis, 50, 143

table of shewbread, 121
Tacitus, 14 f., 131, 135, 159, 165
Targumim, 69
Tarn, W. W., 7, 18, 41, 178
Tcherikover, V., 38, 46, 60, 64 f., 99
tefillin, 163
teleology in human body, 161
Temple, 13 f., 132
Tertullian, 76, 179
Testament of XII Patriarchs, 187, 210
Thackeray, H. St. J., 12, 26, 56, 85, 113, 123, 127, 143, 167, 185, 204
Theagenes of Rhegium, 17
Themistius, 42
Theocritus scholium, 117
Theodectes, 8, 67, 110, 223 f.
theology, 36, 62, 153, 177
Theon, 57
Theophrastus, 41, 96, 187
Theopompus, 8, 49, 67, 110, 223 f.
Thucydides, 176
Tiberius, 15
Timon, 57
Timothy II, 210
title of book, 56, 92
Tobias, 46

Tobit, 257
topography of Jerusalem, 14
Tracy, S., 36
Tramontano, R., 9, 13, 26, 47, 56, 86, 99, 115, 133, 158, 183
translation, motive of, 114; prior to LXX, 8, 28, 66, 121
truth, 180
Tychsen, O. G., 83
Tzetzes, 79

Ullman, B. L., 58
universalism, 65, 156, 209, 212, 225
utopias, 48, 148

vestments, 137
Vincent, P., 6, 13, 131 ff.
Vives, Ludovicus de, 78, 84

washing of hands, 219
water supply, 134
Wendland, P., 52, 85, 94, 143, 146, 166, 186, 217
Westermann, W. L., 30, 104, 107 f.
Wilcken, U., 30, 105, 216
Willrich, H., 10, 139, 213, 218
Wisdom of Solomon, 154, 156, 177, 181, 187, 190, 193
Wolff, F. A., 78
Wolfson, H. A., 16, 102, 151, 153, 155, 174, 186, 190, 209
women, 198
Wutz, F. X., 83

Xenophon, 42

Zedekiah, 100
Zeitlin, S., 93, 139, 168
Zeno, 154
Zenon Papyri, 45, 92
Zeus, 65, 101
zizit, 162

Made in United States
North Haven, CT
18 February 2022